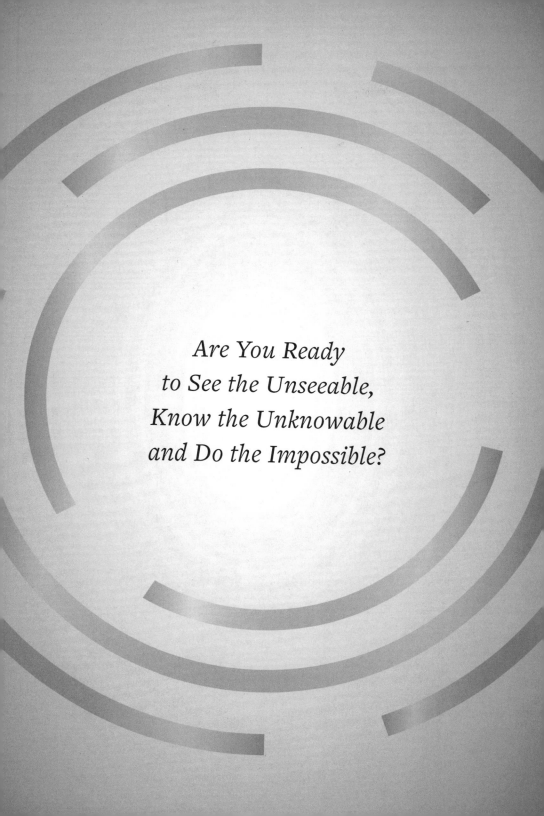

*Are You Ready
to See the Unseeable,
Know the Unknowable
and Do the Impossible?*

The Courage to Change Everything

Other Books from Ken D Foster

Ask and You will Succeed

Ask and You will Succeed Revised

Release Renew Evolve

The Time Factor

The EZ of Business Success

Programs from Ken D Foster

Soul N Money

The Greatest Year Ever

Release Renew Evolve

Joint Ventures to Wealth

How to Be a Powerful Authentic Speaker

Ken D Foster on Voices of Courage
Radio / Podcast / TV

voicesofcourage.us

Contact Ken D Foster

KenDFoster.com

contactken@kendfoster.com

The Courage to
CHANGE
EVERYTHING

Daily Strategies & Essential Wisdom
To Awaken Your Inner Genius

CLASSIC EDITION

KEN D FOSTER

©Copyright 2019 by Ken D Foster
1345 Encinitas Blvd. Suite 115
Encinitas, CA 92024

Cover Design: Autumn Lew
Book Layout: Katy Brown
Editors: Peter Littlejohn Cook, Nancy Fredericks,
Julie Paun, Denise Romero, and DeAnna LoCoco
Photographers: Yelena Yahontova, Ann Landstrom
Web Design: Deb Auger

ISBN: 978-0-578-52886-1
Printed in China
Shared Vision Publishing

Library of Congress Control Number: 2019907554
Kenneth Donald Foster
Published October 2019

Dedication

This book is dedicated to my best friend and amazing
wife Judy, who has walked this courageous journey
with me as we have evolved and grown in love.

And to those who are choosing to live a life
of excellence, filled with courage and self-realization.
It is my hope that you will apply the principals set
forth, evolve your thinking, increase your energetic
frequency and accomplish your greatest dreams.

Contributors

A special thanks to:

Senator Steven Thayne, Idaho State Senator, Author of seven books

Stephen M.R. Covey, *New York Times* Best-Selling Author of The Speed of Trust

Bryan Geoffrey Business Owner

Chris S Richie, Colonel US Marine Corps

Deb Auger, Web Designer, Graphic Artist

Christopher Van Buren, Marketing Strategist

Autumn Lew, Founder of Graphic Minion Studios, Graphic Designer

Jackie Lapin, Amazon Best Selling Author, Publicist

Mark Robert Waldman, Executive MBA Faculty, College of Business Loyola Marymount

Nancy Fredericks, Founder of Nancy Fredericks International, Leadership Coach, Editor

Alex Rennie, Video Production

Bob Steinberger, Attorney

Janet Switzer, Best Selling Author, Business Strategist

Bill Gladstone, Book Agent and Publisher

Rob Spence, Entrepreneur, Friend and Partner in many projects that matter

Chris Jaeb, Business Strategist, Friend and Founder of Broadcast.com

Swami Sri Yukteswar Giri, a Kriya Yogi, Author of *The Holy Science*

Marci Shimoff, *New York Times* Best-Selling Author of *Happy for No Reason*

John Assaraf, *New York Times* Best-Selling Author, Chairman & CEO NeuroGym

Lisa Nichols, *New York Times* Best-Selling Author, Founder of Motivating the Masses, Inc.

Bill Bartmann, Best-Selling Author, Nobel Peace Prize Nominee

Bobbi DePorter, Author, President, Quantum Learning Network

Robert Allen, Multiple *New York Times* Best-Selling Author

Helice "Sparky" Bridges, Author, Founder of Ignite What is Right

Peter Little John Cook, Transformation Leader, Editor

Sharon Lindenberg, Editor

David Riklan, Founder of SelfGrowth.com

Christy Whitman, *New York Times* Best-Selling Author of *The Art of Having It All*

Marcia Wieder, Best-Selling Author of Dream

Peggy McColl, *New York Times* Best Selling Author

Camille Hughs, Business Owner, Internet Marketer

Christopher Dilts, Right Source Digital Marketing

Julie Paun, Graphic Designer

Kristi Rhoem, Sports and Entertainment Media Relations

Adrian Rose, Executive Assistant

Sandra D Robinson, Speaking Coach

Buck VanSickle Business Owner

Robin Jillian, Business Owner

Angela Bussio, Business Owner

Steven Sexton, Financial Advisor

Deva Jones, Business Owner

Lauren Jay, Entrepreneur

Rachael McKinney, Entrepreneur

Susy Lopez, Marketing Manager

Todd Pierik, Production Manager

Cameron Branda, Media Engineering

Tom Gay, Founder Refer.com

Paul Freidman, Entrepreneur

Peggy Lebo, Award winning singer, songwriter

Contents

Endorsement From Idaho Senator Steven Thayn

The Courage to Change Everything is aimed at helping people transform their thinking and lives through using the power of courage. It has universal applicability. It can help entrepreneurs, someone in poverty, a housewife, a worker, a youth, a senior and, yes, even politicians. In fact, anyone who is sincere about becoming the best version of themselves.

Ken D Foster artfully charts the path to discovering this courage. He shows how to listen to "the voice of the Wisdom-Self," connect with your intuition and use reason, compassion and feeling to create amazing relationships and solve intractable problems.

Ken teaches that our suffering is often a call back to the path of our destiny from which we have strayed. This is an amazing thought. I have read scores of books trying to find clues to what makes the fabric of an ideal society. One of the keys is that each person has a unique role and contribution which must be cultivated and encouraged. Ken points out that sometimes we have to feel the pain to make the change needed to understand our gifts, talents and roles we must play for lifelong success.

This book is a must-read for anyone who desires to reach their full potential, improve themselves, improve their relationships and eventually improve the world. Have the courage to listen to the voice within you. Ken shows you how.

Steven Thayn
State Senator Idaho

Reviews & Endorsements

"The Courage to Change Everything is an inspired piece of work. It will guide you on what may be the most important journey of your life. The inner journey to connect with your courage and design your destiny. It will awaken your spirit and inspire you to overcome the challenges facing you. If you are looking to advance your thinking and evolve your life, get this book."

Lisa Nichols
Founder and CEO of Motivating the Masses, Inc.
New York Times Best-Selling Author

"The Courage to Change Everything is not just for business leaders and entrepreneurs but for every individual who is choosing to grow their life. This book will help anyone stay highly motivated, living their dreams and generating wealth in all areas of life." I encourage you to pick up this book and start living your potential."

John Assaraf
New York Times Best-Selling Author
Chairman & CEO NeuroGym

"The Courage to Change Everything is filled with time-honored wisdom along with easy to implement daily strategies for authentic success. This book offers a journey into excellence, showing you how to live in courageous and magical ways."

Marci Shimoff
New York Times Best-Selling Author
Happy for No Reason and *Chicken Soup for the Woman's Soul*

"Ken D Foster's book bridges the gap between fear and fearless living. He shows you how to tap into your inner wisdom, increase courage, build on it and bring it into every aspect of your business and life. He provides a roadmap for accelerating success by helping you tap into your Soulful-Self to find the courage to change what you thought was impossible to break.

Bill Bartmann
Best-Selling Author
Nobel Peace Prize Nominee
CEO of CFS2

"Ken gives courage a whole new meaning in this beautiful book as he sincerely shares thoughts about his life and learnings. His determination to be in a high state of consciousness every day inspires us, and his profound reflections give us insights and encouragement to apply his findings to our own lives. *The Courage to Change Everything* is a compelling read that will make a difference in your life.

Bobbie DePorter, Author
President - Quantum Learning Network / SuperCamp
Excellence in Teaching / The Quantum Learning System

"Every great accomplishment I have achieved, took courage, focused effort and reprogramming my mind to change what I perceived as impossible. If you want to achieve success which is uncommon for most, then I encourage you to read and apply the principles in this life altering book! It will help you to overcome your greatest challenges and redefine what is possible."

Denise Muller-Korenek
Paced Bicycle Land Speed Record Holder 183.9 MPH

"What life wouldn't be better by studying the daily courage reminders in Ken D Foster's excellent new book *The Courage to Change Everything*? Courage is a quality we ALL need in today's changing world and Ken reminds you every day how to achieve it."

Robert Allen
#1 *New York Times* Best-Selling Author
Creating Wealth
Nothing Down
Multiple Streams of Income
The One Minute Millionaire

"*The Courage to Change Everything* can be life-changing if you apply the principles daily. It will help you find out what you are made of, what you want your business and life to be about and what is possible when you live a life of courage. This book shows you how courage makes the invisible - visible, the unknown - known and the impossible - possible."

Helice "Sparky" Bridges, Author,
Founder of Ignite What is Right
Empowered 40 million people so far!

"Talk about a life changing read, Ken's book is rooted in wisdom, inspiration and powerful guidance that speaks to the heart of the problems facing most of us in our business and life. This really isn't a traditional book that you read cover to cover, it delivers bits size pieces that are easy to understand and implement daily. This book is a must-read."

John Howard
Olympic Cyclist, National World Cycling Champion
and Ironman Triathlon World Champion

"True success doesn't come at the expense of yourself or others. It's the result of aligning with your highest values and implementing strategies that are for the highest good of all. Ken D Foster has beautifully aligned head and heart with daily words of wisdom that we all can use. If you apply the principals in this book, true success is guaranteed."

Cynthia Kersey,
Best-Selling Author of *Unstoppable*,
CEO, Unstoppable Foundation

"Ken D Foster's new book, *The Courage to Change Everything*, will take you on a journey of awareness, action and change that will make you a better version of yourself. It's for anyone that wants more wealth, happiness and prosperity in their business and life. He will teach you how to achieve extraordinary feats by harnessing the power of courage. I recommend that you read his book and work your way through the many practical suggestions that he provides. You'll see incredible changes in your life."

David Riklan
Founder—SelfGrowth.com
Over 100 Million Visitors Since 1995

"The currency of courage is an essential tool for individuals and organizations who are looking to create quantum success in today's highly evolving and changing business environments. Ken D Foster has given readers a roadmap to increase courage in business and everyday life and therefore become more authentic, creative and prosperous. Anyone who reads and incorporates these principals in their organization will have major positive changes now and in the future."

Christy Whitman
New York Times Best-Selling Author of *The Art of Having It All*

"Ken D Foster shows us how unleashing courageous thinking is the way to have a highly successful business and life. This solution-oriented book is an enlightening read for anyone who is ready to create new patterns of behavior, increase performance and cement the benefits of courage, trust and creativity into their life. If you are prepared for a new paradigm, then read this book. It is brilliant!"

Mark Robert Waldman
Executive MBA Faculty, College of Business
Loyola Marymount University
Author of 14 Books

"Courage is a critical competency for all who are looking to stay competitive in these highly evolving and changing business environments. Ken D Foster provides a clear roadmap to access this along with the necessary confidence to live a more authentic, creative and fulfilling life. It's time. It's your time and here's how."

Marcia Wieder
CEO of Dream University
Best-Selling Author of DREAM

"This is the book whose time has come. It speaks to the heart of problems facing many and delivers the path to sustainable solutions. This isn't a book you have to read cover to cover. It delivers bits size pieces that are easy to understand and implement. I recommend this book."

Peggy McColl
New York Times Best-Selling Author

Foreword By
Stephen M.R. Covey

I'll never forget listening to my father consistently repeat an expression of courage that, over time, became extremely meaningful and inspired me.

Courage is the quality of every quality at its highest-testing point.

He also would quote Winston Churchill:

Courage is the first of the human qualities because it is the quality which guarantees all the others.

So, when my friend Ken D Foster asked me to write the forward to this book on courage, I asked myself, "Is this a book I can fully embrace?" Will it help those who read it detect, discover and develop their courage? Will it increase self-trust and build confidence in entrepreneurs? Can it genuinely impact positive change within the readers themselves and the organizations in which they work? The answers came back a resounding yes!

We live in a world that is increasingly over-managed and under-led. The kind of leadership needed today not only requires us to understand how to lead from the head; it also requires us to lead from the heart as our starting place. Such leadership requires great courage. Indeed, the root of the word courage comes from the Latin word cor, which means *heart*.

So, courage was initially used to mean; "To speak one's mind by telling all one's heart." And this is where Ken's book starts—he wonderfully creates the conditions for each of us to focus on personal and professional courage and, in so doing, we begin to tap into the bottomless well of power and wisdom that lies within us. When we combine this courage with sound leadership strategies, we're then better prepared to conquer the most significant challenges and seize enormous opportunities in both business and life.

My life's work has been focused on one of the collaborators of courage; trust. In my books, The Speed of Trust and Smart Trust, I illustrate how trust is the one thing that changes everything and how extending trust is the defining skill that transforms managers into leaders.

Why? Because high-trust relationships and cultures not only create greater economic prosperity, they also develop higher levels of energy and joy. When trust goes up in relationships, and within organizations, creativity flourishes, collaboration increases, communication flows easier, fulfillment grows, speed goes up, and costs go down. And someone needs to go first. That's what leaders do, they go first. Indeed, the first job of a leader is to inspire trust; the second job is to extend trust.

As Ken points out, trust and courage go hand in hand. When there is high trust in a culture, people become more courageous. They become more open and authentic. They're not afraid to take appropriate risks—helping them become more creative and innovative. They exercise courage in talking straight, confronting reality, and making and keeping commitments—all of which, in turn, reinforces the trust.

Similarly, it takes courage to trust another person. Indeed, to trust is to take a risk. But not to trust is also to take a risk. I find that in today's collaborative, interdependent world, not trusting is more often the greater risk.

Courage is required not only to extend trust to others but also to learn to trust ourselves. Self-trust is the foundation from which all other levels of trust emerge. For example, we'll have a hard time sustaining trust with others if we don't trust ourselves as that distrust of self will inevitably project out into our relationships. As Emerson put it, "Self-trust is the first secret of success...the essence of heroism self-trust, all the virtues are comprehended."

Ken makes a strong argument that through courage and trust we can better tap into our creative genius, which opens the doors to innovation. Innovation occurs when there is a collision of differences in an environment of trust.

When leaders create a culture of courage, trust, and creativity starting with themselves and extending to their teams, they can achieve breakthrough results, higher productivity, and increased prosperity.

This kind of creativity is a catalyst for getting sustained results. Indeed, today's challenges can be far better solved through creative collaboration than through unhealthy conflict. But for real collaboration to occur, we need courage and trust. It's just hard to collaborate with people you don't trust.

For Ken, there is no shortage of solutions—there is only a shortage of courage, trust, and creativity. Organizations and leaders who establish a high-trust culture of courage and innovation can create a space for authentic entrepreneurial thinking, efficiently leveraging new ideas, and developing an unprecedented level of collaboration. The net result is sustained superior performance.

Too many organizations have unwittingly separated people from their creative selves by inadvertently (or sometimes deliberately) fostering environments characterized by unhealthy competition, infighting, turf wars, politics and misaligned priorities.

These actions ultimately lead to low morale, turnover, disengagement, bureaucracy, and toxic micromanagement. Such low-trust organizations fall short of their achieving targeted objectives time after time. But it doesn't have to be that way.

Nowhere is the need for courage more apparent than for entrepreneurs. Entrepreneurs at all levels have unique responsibilities, challenges, and daily demands. The fast and agile companies of the future will be a direct reflection of how much trust and courage entrepreneurs have developed in their organizational cultures—and in their leadership.

In a low-courage, low-trust environment, most individuals are struggling and hurting inside because they instinctively know the benefits of high-courage, high-trust cultures—and they know what they're missing.

They intuitively understand that having the courage to live their highest values and being congruent with who they are, will increase their self-trust which, in turn, will help them build relationship, team and organizational trust. They can sense how their lives and relationships would be far more fulfilling if they could bridge the gap between low courage and low trust.

Finally, I also find that the best kind of courage has an exciting and often paradoxical companion—humility. The combination of humility and courage enables us to be open, and openness is vital to trust. Indeed, to be open inspires credibility and trust; to be closed fosters suspicion and mistrust.

Humility enables us to acknowledge that there are principles out there we may not currently be aware of, and courage allows us to follow them once we discover them. Throughout history, most paradigm shifts in science and life have been shifts from conventional thinking—shifts that require this simultaneous blend of humility and courage.

But none of this can happen if there is a lack of courage to explore greater trust. It takes courage to pave new ground and approach leaders with ideas that may be foreign to them. It takes courage to step out and speak up when old systems are not working.

It takes courage to look within yourself and notice what you are tolerating or where you have been playing small and not living your values or purpose. It takes trust to confront issues during turbulent times. Without courage, there will always be a diminishment of trust, but with it, you can get real and see what is working—and what is not—and you can increase your influence and accelerate your success.

Gandhi gave us all a beautiful challenge: "Let us become the change we seek in this world." To that, I add, "Let us model the courage we seek in our world." I hope that this book will help us recognize, develop and exercise far greater courage and creativity in growing prosperity, energy and joy in all dimensions of life to the end that this world may be a better place for all of us.

Introduction

There is most likely no one reading this book for the first time that has maximized their full potential. However, I know at this very moment you can achieve extraordinary feats by harnessing the unlimited power of courage. I know this because I have used my courage to transform every part of my life and the lives of my clients.

The results of applying daily courage have been nothing short of extraordinary. Why? Because your history does not have to be your destiny. You can tap into higher states of consciousness, and with courage, rewrite the scripts you are running in your mind with truth and faith unleashing the hidden power of your Wisdom-Self. Then you will watch in awe the unfoldment of your Self-actualization.

The word courage derives from the French word "Coeur" and the Latin word "cor," meaning, "Heart." Therefore, the deeper meaning implies heartfulness, and so when I am speaking of courage, I'm talking of our heart's hunger and longing to be real and on purpose, and connected to your true nature. I want to impress upon you that courage is not merely an act of will; it is a robust presence that dwells within everyone. It is a powerful force, and when released it fosters a radical shift within your consciousness which supports you in attaining higher levels of self-knowledge and self-worth while transcending any limitations in your life.

Even though we haven't met, I am sure we have a lot in common. Most likely, just like me, you have undergone trying times or tragedies and have overcome many difficult situations. Just like me, sometimes you forget just how far you've come, for you are a work in progress, still growing and evolving. Like me, you forget from time to time that you are a magnificent, brilliant being, who has the power to shape your destiny. You forget that you have courage within you and convince yourself that you're timid or not enough, but that's not true! Right?

You may have had more than your share of challenges during this lifetime. You may have grown up in an abusive home. You may not have had the opportunities that other families provided. You or your family members may have had to deal with mental, emotional or physical problems. You may have grown up in a country that restricted your freedoms. You may have had business failures or lost family and friends to addiction. Some of you may have chronic issues that repeat themselves again and again. I have had my share of all the above, but I know that all these challenges are not there to crush you but to empower and strengthen you. Each problem comes with a gift. When you find it, you will have more humility, compassion, wisdom, and strength.

So, let me ask you a few questions. Are you ready to increase your awareness, evolve yourself and do what it takes to bring out your courage? Will you commit to stepping outside of your comfort zone, even if just a little bit at first? Are you ready to allow yourself to live from your highest values, increasing your wisdom and bringing forth your unique gifts, talents, and brilliance in ever more significant ways? Will you do whatever it takes to become a master of your mind and heart and therefore of yourself?

If you said yes to these questions, then I know you are ready to become the driver of your destiny. How do I know that? Because, if you are willing to look at your inner environment more than at any outer condition, you can transform your life and have higher levels of peace, happiness, fulfillment, and abundance.

As so many wisdom-guided sages who have gone before us such as Jesus Christ, Krishna, Moses, Buddha, Laozi, Confucius, Muhammad, and Yogananda have inferred, we are infinite, conscious and blissful souls at our core. We have the power within us to move the mountains of challenges that face us. We can never be permanently confined to our failures, because our "Soul Consciousness" is ever calling us to expand ourselves, grow beyond our problems, and realize our full potential.

You may be wondering, "what is Soul Consciousness? I am speaking of deep wisdom which comes from the Superconscious states of mind or as I refer to it, The Wisdom-Self. The Wisdom-Self is beyond the physical experience of our traditional senses; taste, touch, smell, sight, and hearing. It is the observer behind our senses and thinking. The Wisdom-Self is our "intuition" or "gut feeling" or the "still small voice."

The Wisdom-Self encompasses every possible thought or combination of ideas in the universe. It is the source of all power and where all answers are revealed. It is the door to increasing your frequency or resonance and aligning yourself with higher states of consciousness where everything is possible.

I want to talk a little bit about frequency. It is defined as the rate at which a vibration occurs that constitutes a wave, either in a material (as in sound waves), or in an electromagnetic field (as in radio waves and light), usually measured per second. Therefore, frequency is a rate at which things vibrate. Thoughts also have a frequency, but scientists have not been able to measure speed or impact of the electromagnetic field generated, which is referred to as the frequency radiation of the human body. They also, don't know how far negative or positive thought travels outside the human body. But Neuroscience has revealed that certain thoughts will release chemicals into the brain which can change emotional states. I wish to emphasize that the scientific community has just begun to tap into the unlimited realms of consciousness, so please keep an open mind as you explore new concepts contained in the book. By doing so, you will be able to release many of your programmed limitations which will result in greater understanding and awareness.

If you have chronically tried and failed many times at having a successful business, relationship, losing weight, or any number of issues where you feel like failure has become chronic, one of the main reasons is that you have not been able to consistently align with higher thought frequency which you need to bring your dream into manifestation. When you are not able to hold a higher rate of frequency, you may distract yourself, give up or start something new. Sound familiar?

Think about it this way! Up to this point in time your health, lifestyle, habits, successes, and failures are mostly a result of your thinking. Right? Well, not really. It has been a function of how receptive you have been to your Wisdom-Self. When you are in resonance with your Wisdom-Self, which is the seat of your intuition, you will raise your frequency, make consistently good choices and carry them out. This will lay the foundation for ongoing success.

The opposite is true also. If you consistently resonate with lower frequencies or limited thought, you are bound to recreate your circumstances repeatedly. As Albert Einstein once said; "We cannot solve our problems with the thinking we used to create them." So, your greatest thinking will most likely, keep you stuck, and spinning around in circles.

So how do you tap into your Wisdom-Self, increase your frequency and make better choices? It is easy to talk about, but it takes practice to master. According to Spiritual Teacher Eckert Tolle; "The next step in human evolution is to transcend thought." Think about this. Whom would you be if you didn't think? The answer is, you would be "You." The "You" who is the observer of the thoughts.

We all have thoughts that pass by our mind, but we are not these thoughts. Thoughts exist separate from us. Thoughts are universal, not individual, we are all tapping into the same Universal thought field. The thought field wasn't created by us; nor is it a part of us. So, why let incessant thoughts flow past your mind and then identify with them as "Yours"?

Do you think you need more help to solve your problems? Do you think you need more information to be happier? Do you need to research more on your computer, tablet or phone to be smarter? Do you need more intellectual understanding to make better choices? Do you need more social connections to be wealthier? No, you don't need any of this; what you need is more wisdom!

So, how do you obtain wisdom? Primarily, there are three ways to gain Wisdom; "personal experience," "learning from others," or "tapping into your Wisdom-Self." All three methods work, but the last way supersedes the other two. So, let me give you a quick exercise to tap into the Wisdom-Self.

Stop what you are doing for a moment, close your eyes and slowly take in a deep breath. Hold your breath for a count of five as you lightly tense all of your muscles. Now, exhale slowly and release your breath. Do this several times! Now, forget the breath and notice the peace you feel. Allow the peace to expand into every particle of your being. Peace is the first sign that you have tapped into the Wisdom-Self and therefore raised your frequency. This exercise will also help you to lower your overall tension and stress levels, and help you relax when you are feeling anxious.

You will likely notice that as your thoughts subside, your breathing slows down. Breath and thinking are tied together. The slower your breath, the quieter your thoughts become. As you do this exercise, if a thought comes in, notice the thought, but don't become attached to it. Just notice you have a thought. Remember "You" are the observer of the thoughts, not the thoughts themselves. Just let the thoughts flow by your mind.

I once heard a Minister describe it this way. Birds are like thoughts, when they are flying overhead, there is nothing you can do, but if a bird nests on your head, you can shoo it away. The same applies to your thoughts. If one starts to roost in your mind, you can choose to shoo it away. This is an excellent exercise to practice daily. At first, it may seem challenging to observe your thoughts but don't give up. Eventually, you will master it and as you do, it will be easier to connect with your Wisdom-Self.

INFUSE YOUR MIND WITH WISDOM

Years ago, I started searching for teachers who had accomplished great things and seemed to be geniuses. The ones I studied had one thing in common; they had developed their intuition and were wise. As I read books or listened to audios from these teachers, I noticed that when I tuned into the wisdom they were teaching, my mind was transformed into a receptive state of consciousness. I felt higher and lighter. At different times I would experience states of love, peace joy, and bliss, I realized as I experienced these states, I would have insights into my problems. Many of these problems were not simple problems. Some I had been working on for years, but as I concentrated on even one facet of wisdom, there was a transforming effect on my thinking. As a result, everything started to improve in both my business and life. What I had discovered is that when I raised my consciousness and tuned into a higher frequency of thought everything started aligning for my highest and best self to emerge. As you will soon experience, infusing your consciousness with courage and high-frequency wisdom, will transform your life.

Think of it this way. Out of Spirit comes individual Souls. So, the Spirit is over the Soul or as I call it in the book, "Wisdom-Self." Out of the Wisdom-Self comes individual minds and personalities. So, the Wisdom-Self is·over the Mind. The Mind, (conscious and subconscious) is over the Emotions. In other words, what you focus on you feel. You will either feel empowered or disempowered. The Emotions are over Actions. If you feel inspired, you will take inspired actions. If you don't feel motivated, you won't take action, right!? The Actions you take are over your Results, and the Results are over your Destiny.

Therefore, if you want to change your destiny doesn't it make sense to generate your life from the consciousness of your Wisdom-Self? Of course, it does! Moreover, here is the secret! Training your mind for success starts with raising your frequency by dwelling on courageous and inspiring thoughts. You don't realize how powerful your thoughts work in the ether. Just one idea may change your destiny. However, you must get rid of all doubt if you are to succeed. Disbelief is your

SPIRIT

SOUL

MIND

FEELING

ACTION

RESULTS

DESTINY

greatest enemy. So, be determined that nothing will stand in your way of connecting with your Wisdom-Self and reprograming your mind for success.

TAP INTO YOUR GENIUS

In this book, I have decoded some of the most relevant and influential success philosophies, which offer daily actionable steps at extremely high levels of frequency, helping you to bridge the gap from where you are to where you want to be. As you read and apply the principles in these pages, you are lifted into higher states of consciousness and accordingly this knowledge is etched into your subconscious mind for lasting success. Just like upgrading your computer software, you will be upgrading your thinking, increasing your wisdom and quickening the speed of your progress.

The mind is the source of infinite power when aligned with high-frequency thoughts and noble intentions. "For as he thinketh in his heart, so is he." (Proverbs 23:7). This wisdom is speaking about the principal factor working in all of creation, the power of the Wisdom-Self. The Wisdom-Self is continually guiding us with truth and understanding. When you can consciously connect with this voice and focus on its wisdom, you will make good choices which impact what you become. It is this infinite life force that creates everything of value.

However, don't just take my word for it. Study the history of those who have tapped into the creative force. Learn from those who later in life led nations, like George Washington, Nelson Mandela, Thomas Jefferson, Abraham Lincoln, Mahatma Gandhi and a host of others. Study the lives of those who have lead industry such as Steve Jobs, Elon Musk, or Andrew Carnegie. Learn how to tap into the unlimited power of the Wisdom-Self from people like Dr. George Washington Carver, Luther Burbank, or Martin Luther King. Study saints and sages such as Paramahansa Yogananda, Saint John of the Cross, Saint Theresa of Avila or Pope John XXIII or Saint Germain. Research the lives of musicians such as George Harrison of the Beatles who wrote his most celebrated music after learning to meditate. Alternatively, study other meditators who tap into the infinite source such as Madonna, Oprah, Wayne Dyer, or Eckert Tolle. Find out where the source of Albert Einstein's and Leonardo da Vinci's genius originated.

I will give you a hint. These people all have one thing in common. They have raised their frequency by tapping into the infinite power of the Wisdom-Self. Albert Einstein once said: "I want to know God's thoughts; the rest are details." The results of his life speak loudly to the fact that he obtained and maintained the connection with the deific mind. You can too, this is your time to change everything for the better. You don't have to advance your bad habits and limiting thinking into your future. You can choose to drop them. At any moment you could leave this planet and drop your mortal body suit. Those limitations would fall away instantly because they are not yours in the first place. So, don't admit them. Choose to leave your limiting ways of thinking and acting behind. Then build your new consciousness daily by committing here and now to set aside a few minutes a day to read and apply the principles outlined in this book. You will be amazed at how much you can do when you cast off your limitations and tune into your Wisdom-Self.

MEET YOUR CHALLENGES HEAD ON

Let me emphasize an important point. As you read the book, many of your beliefs may be challenged. You may get upset and want to set the teaching down. You may find yourself rationalizing why you don't have time for this or need to change.

If this happens, this is the time to redouble your efforts because you are on the verge of a breakthrough. By working through disempowering beliefs and connecting deeply with your Wisdom-Self, you will gradually emerge from self-created slavery. The more you cast off obstructive thoughts and self-doubt, the quicker you will progress and succeed.

In the song "Christmas Cannon" by the Trans-Siberian Orchestra, the lyrics say; "We are waiting, we have not forgotten. This night we pray, our lives will show this dream he had; each child still knows." Never doubt that there is a place inside you where your most significant dreams and knowing reside. Your dreams are unique to you and will empower you if you dare to pursue them.

Also, I can pretty much guarantee as you pursue your dreams it won't be an easy road, but every challenge will build power. Moreover, the more strength you develop, the more wisdom, courage, and confidence you will have. Soon you will become unstoppable. Remember, you will always be supported by unseen forces so, don't stop until you realize your most fabulous dreams because if you don't give up, you will be amazed at how great life can be.

HOW TO GET THE MOST OUT OF THE BOOK

This book will help you raise your frequency, increase your wisdom, power, and passion daily. Each morning read the guidance for the day. Then find a quiet place to sit and meditate on the thoughts contained within it. Strive to attune your mind to the deep meanings in the messages. Contemplate how to apply the knowledge in your own life.

Then tune into the feeling of courage and ask; "If I were courageous what would I do?" This simple question will help keep your frequency high and focused on meaningful actions.

During the day recall the thoughts from the daily guidance as often as you can. Try to find one line that you can hold onto during the day to inspire courageous actions. Without a doubt, without hesitation but with full resolve be determined to make the ideals work for you during the day.

At the bottom of the daily guidance are questions. Ask the questions repeatedly, until you realize how to apply them practically. Some of the questions are difficult to answer but don't give up. If you keep asking, eventually you will receive the answers.

At night before retiring, mentally contemplate the thoughts that brought you courage and inspiration during the day. You may want to record these thoughts in a diary, so you will remember the beliefs that empower you.

Also, ask each evening: What worked for me today? What didn't work for me today? Where can I improve tomorrow? By doing this, you will be setting a foundation to notice what needs to change or improve daily.

By dwelling on the wisdom contained within these pages and by striving to put what you learned into consistent daily practice, you will find your awareness expanding and your consciousness transforming.

Right thinking is the fountain of success. When you think right, you make the right choices. The right decisions will lead to the right actions, and right actions lead to outstanding results. Follow this formula for ongoing success and the unfoldment of your Self-Realization.

CHAPTER 1

FOUNDATION

Day 1

*"The bravest thing you can do when you are not brave is
to profess courage and act accordingly."*

CORRA HARRIS

What is your life like? On a scale of one to ten, with one being dismal and ten
being outstanding, rate the following areas. Health and Fitness, Business or Career,
Finances, Relationship, Family, Spiritual Life, Fun Life. Are you living the life of
your dreams in all these areas? If so, then great! Keep doing what you are doing.
However, if you are not, then make a point to change course and take all these areas
to a ten.

It all starts with noticing what you are projecting onto the world and not only how
you show up in life physically but mentally, emotionally and spiritually. Stop right
now and think about how you consistently show up.

Assess whether you are consistently projecting success or mediocrity; peace or
chaos; health or illness; joy or sadness; love or anger; wealth or poverty? Remember all these states have a frequency to them. You are either attracting or repelling
success.

You have greatness within you! Do you believe that? If so, then tune in, turn on
your courage and bring it to the forefront of your mind. Start by tapping into all you
were created to be, acknowledging where you need to change and then be obsessed
with doing better. It is as simple and as hard as that.

Today ask

"What are three steps I can take to expand my influence?"

"What is a personality trait I will change or improve upon?"

"How can I remember to project my brilliance into the world?"

Actions

Let go of being hard on yourself. Bringing your greatness into the world takes
time, so be easy on yourself and enjoy the journey. As you do, decide on the attitude that will bring you the greatest results.

Day 2

"It takes courage to pick yourself up when you have fallen. But try again you must if you want to achieve your highest calling."

KEN D FOSTER

What will happen if you don't try to generate your most fabulous dreams? Most likely you will live a life with a nagging sense of regret and never reach your full potential.

Your dreams have been given to you as your own personal Northern Star to help you become mentally, emotionally, physically robust and spiritually aware. It starts when you make up your mind to take charge of your life.

So, do you want to be totally in charge of your life? If you do, then see yourself as the creative source in your own life. Permit yourself to tap into your dreams and open up your brilliance by asking compelling and possibility questions like the ones below. When you do this, your dreams will expand, and you will start to get the answers to your next steps.

Today ask

"What is the most remarkable thing I can do to open the doors of success?"

"What can I let go of thinking that will forever change the way I perceive success?"

"How can my mind be mentally charged with success thoughts?"

Actions

Make up your mind that nothing will stop you from succeeding.

Day 3

"Courage is not simply one of the virtues, but the form of every virtue at the testing point."

C.S. LEWIS

When you are aware and spiritually alive, you know the truth when you hear it, sense it or see it; just as you can perceive lies. Awareness can move us into action, stop us from making mistakes, show us new directions, enlighten us, empower us and guide us to the life of our sweetest dreams.

The most significant gift we can give our families and ourselves is to become aware of the truth of who we are. This isn't found in a book, a workshop or from some new teaching. Awareness is accessed in stillness and found by noticing your oneness with your soul. It is always available when you are open to being still.

When you tune into your senses, notice how you feel, then tune into the observer of how you feel. This is Awareness. This is where it is found. It is within you. When you tap into Awareness then use it to make important decisions and things will change for the better. In fact, if you make a spiritual effort now to increase your awareness by paying attention to it more often, things will get better in the future.

It takes courage to listen, to speak and to act on your inner truth. You may not become a superstar doing this, but you will become the best you can be and achieve success beyond your greatest imagination.

Today ask

"What can I become more aware of?"

"What am I pretending not to see?"

"What am I aware of that will move my goals forward at lightning speed?"

Actions

Take two different steps to accomplish one goal today.

Day 4

"Courage is about using your brain and your heart when every cell of your body is screaming at you to fight or flee—and then following through on what you believe is the right thing to do."

JIM BUTCHER

One of the leading causes of failure is thinking you have all the answers and generating your life merely from your logical mind. This is a trap because you are only using a small portion of what is available to you.

If you are choosing to increase your success, then you should use all your God-given faculties. In fact, it is essential to develop insight and intuition. Developing insight into yourself to realize who you are is just as important as improving your intuition; both connect you to your higher self.

In truth, until your insight and intuition are fully developed, you will need advice, wisdom and guidance from others, or you are bound to fail. So, if you would like to have a success that is enduring, then find the magic in learning from others who are realized.

I say realized because many people are like records, repeating quotes or wise thoughts they have learned from others without real inner wisdom. Stretch your limits and put yourself in front of people who are incredibly intuitive, confident and are living examples of what you choose to have in your life.

Today ask

"What am I committed to learning?"

"Who is a realized master at teaching intuition, that I can learn from?"

"What are three action steps I can take to deepen my intuition?"

Actions

Determine the highest qualities and skill sets of a person with whom you would like to mentor.

Day 5

*"Courage is not the absence of fear or despair; it
is the capacity to continue despite them, no matter
how great or overwhelming they become."*

ROBERT FANNEY

Are you living a destiny of greatness or mediocrity? Look at the direction of your life and you will know. Is your life getting better or not? Is it filled with unfulfilled dreams? If so, you can turn it around but first, you must simplify.

Chaos and clutter are the signs that you are heading down the wrong path. Most of the time when I see mess and clutter, it's a sign that the person is staying too busy and distracted from what is truly important to their success.

Order, simplicity and clarity are what's needed. The easiest way to achieve this is to start simplifying your life. Decide what you want. Prioritize what you will accomplish and let go of the distractors.

Today ask

"How will I simplify my life?"

"What will I stop doing that will create more ease in my life?"

"How can increase the love in my heart as I simplify my life?"

Actions

Pick one area that you would like to improve upon. It can be cleaning up your office, getting the dent repaired on your car, buying a new vehicle, building a better relationship or any other area that you want to make better. Then take three action steps that will help you complete it.

Day 6

"If you are not tapping into your courage, you are not utilizing your God-given power to master your life."

KEN D FOSTER

One of the areas that will stop your success is harmful habits. Where do harmful habits originate? As you are probably aware, at the most basic level, they are just unconstructive thoughts that have been ingrained in your mind and displayed as behaviors.

Since they are thoughts repeated time and time again, it is essential first to acknowledge the harmful habits that exist and second, recognize that you are committed to breaking the habit. You can control the harmful conveyor belt of thoughts crossing your mind. To do this, you must remember that you are an infinite being and you have the power to overcome anything you choose.

When harmful habits are knocking at your door, try getting some distance from them by taking a deep breath and quiet your mind. After all, the mind is what is creating them, so stop the mind chatter for a few minutes.

This will take practice but notice the thoughts that are upsetting you or encouraging you to follow through on a harmful habit and ask: "What has to happen for me to release these thoughts now?" This will help!

Today ask

"What has it cost me to keep my negative habits?

"Which negative habit will I overcome no matter what?"

"How can I remember to align with my highest self and stay empowered?"

Actions

Pick one harmful habit you would like to release. Then, take a few minutes to quiet your mind chatter and reflect on how much power you have within you to release this habit permanently. Then do what it takes to replace your negative habit with an empowering new one.

Day 7

"Intuition is the voice of the soul and the foundation of all courage. If you want a fulfilling life, follow your heart."

KEN D FOSTER

Awareness is the master key to success. Many people just plow through their days without paying attention to the signs of spirit, body, mind and environment.

They remain unaware of the ease, joy and glorious ways of living that exist around them. They are so focused on task-oriented living that the sublime subtleties of life just pass them by along with countless opportunities.

Believe it or not, there are always intuitive messages guiding us through life. But without developing awareness and becoming conscious of these messages, you will just miss out.

If you are just using your rational mind to get through life, you are only using a small number of your capabilities. There is so much more abundance awaiting you as you open yourself to receive it.

Today, take some time to connect with your breath, focus on listening intensely, looking for things you have not seen before, feel the sensations of the spaces you are in, really taste what you are eating and notice your inner voice.

Today ask

"How can I become more aware and realize when my Wise-Self is speaking?"

"How can I expand my awareness of the infinite possibilities of spirit?"

"How much more success will I have when I allow myself to connect deeply with my intuitive wisdom?"

Tap into your higher-self and increase your intuition with Ken D Foster's guided meditations on Business, Wealth, Expanding Possibility, Peace, and Health. Yours for free at couragetochange.us/meditation

Day 8

Many people are like butterflies flittering from one thing to the next and never landing on one goal or project that is large enough to bring out their greatness. They look for the easy things to do and when tough times come along, they go to a movie or find a diversion to keep them in their comfort zone. This is no way to live!

Life brings us challenges and opportunities to help us grow mentally, emotionally, physically and spiritually. If you are not taking advantage of what is coming your way—the good, bad and the ugly—you are missing the chance to live a life of excellence.

Look for every day to be a great day despite difficulties! Even though Spirit's ways are not the easiest ones, they will build character, strength, courage and ultimate success.

I am not telling you it will be easy. An easy life is not necessarily a great life, but I am telling you to look for the good in all difficulties. By doing so, you will eventually weed out the mindset that created the challenges in the first place.

Today ask

"What is the one challenge in my business or life that I am determined to overcome?

"As an infinite being, how can any person, place or thing block my success?"

"What am I choosing to accomplish today that will propel my confidence and success threefold?"

Actions

Hold in your mind one new belief which will increase your confidence and success.

Day 9

*"Courage can't see around corners, but
goes around them anyway."*

MIGNON MCLAUGHLIN

How much worry will it take for you to succeed? Will it take one year, ten years or twenty years of worry for you to be successful? It seems kind of silly even to ask these questions.

So many people believe that worry is a path to success, but it isn't, especially when we worry about things we have no control over. Instead, it's a formula guaranteed to create a life of misery.

When it comes to success, worry can paralyze your forward momentum. So, don't focus on it! Have you ever thought about giving up worry for good? To do this, you may have to figure out what you get out of worrying.

People worry for many reasons: Sometimes it feels good to worry or blame someone or something else for their challenges. But for most, it is just a habit that needs to be overcome.

Much suffering and failure come from worry, but it doesn't have to be that way. When you can cast aside your mental burden of worrying, you will be free at once to start creating your dreams with peace and happiness.

Today ask

"What are three steps I can take today to eliminate worry?"

"How can worry be a thing of the past in my life starting now?"

"What courageous thoughts can I focus on today?

Actions

Make an effort to watch your mind and be conscious of any worrying you may do. Remember, when worries enter your mind take your mind off them. Instead, focus on faith in your creator, faith in your abilities, faith in your intuition. Note: (As you do this you will have freedom from worries).

Day 10

"The highest courage is to dare to appear to be what one is."

JOHN LANCASTER SPAULDING

Follow-through is the great secret of success. It sounds easy. Commit and then follow through to completion. Many people have challenges with follow-through. Why is this? Primarily because they spend their time thinking the wrong thoughts and focusing on the wrong actions.

Think about a project you have not completed. Do you know why you haven't finished it? Is there a small voice inside of you saying: "I don't have what it takes, I am too busy, I will get to it tomorrow or it is just not a priority"?

If so, how do you feel day after day not completing what you set out to accomplish, if you are like most, not too good! Negation of your dreams and the willpower to achieve them will stop you dead in your tracks every single time. But you can turn this around quickly by taking charge of your mind, setting a completion date and remembering who you are.

If you have any of the above tendencies, you have probably forgotten that you, as an infinite being, have the power to overcome any poor habit of thinking. Remember, whatever point of view you have about yourself will be real for you.

So, take on a new point of view such as: "I can easily change poor thoughts into good ones and generate ongoing success."

Today ask

"What will my thoughts be focused on to awaken my greatness?"

"What is my plan to get rid of distractions so that I can complete my projects?"

"When would be a good time to make the changes that will lead me to my ultimate success?"

Actions

No matter how many times you have done this and not followed through, make a list of three changes you will make to be more successful. Then take three action steps to change.

Day 11

*"You can attain everything you want in life when you tap into your courage
and follow your inner knowing."*

KEN D FOSTER

What are the highest achievements possible for you between now and the time you leave this planet? Are you clear on your life's purpose or are you wandering aimlessly without a sense of direction or a real plan?

Underlying all successful people in the world is a common foundation. They value truth, know why they are here, and have a plan for their lives. Do not be satisfied with what you have accomplished, but strive to become the best version of yourself.

Start today and commit to awakening your inner genius by getting in touch with your life's' purpose. Then come up with a plan to attain it. This may sound daunting for some, but I guarantee if you spend the time, it will be well worth it.

Today ask

"What about life is important to you?"

"Who are you committed to becoming?"

"What brings you the greatest fulfillment?"

Actions

Meditate for a few minutes, then contemplate each of the three questions until the answers come. Then complete these two sentences: My life purpose is to.....
My plan is to.....

Actions

Take some time to still your mind and be open to receive some new wisdom which will propel your success.

Day 12

*"Courage is what shows up when you set your
intentions to do something no one else has done,
something that will leave a mark on the world"*

KEN D FOSTER

Why are business and personal plans so important for the success-minded? Because they will cause you to refine your thinking until you arrive at the essence of what is important and the understanding of what direction to take.

This is particularly if the plans are done with the intention of expanding your consciousness and growing your life. They also cause you to form questions that cannot be answered with the logical mind alone.

The flipside of planning is running your business or life by impulse, whims and reactions. You may have some early success but unless your intuition is fully developed, this kind of thinking inevitably leads to chaos, uncertainty and an over-whelming lack of direction.

Planning makes our lives so much easier and yet, so few make plans daily. The reason, I believe, is that the old way of planning involved a lot of time. Yet today's Question Planning Process™ is easy.

I will give you an example of some questions you can use to start your day. They will drive the superconscious mind to the answers while you choose the direction and take consistent actions.

Today ask

"What incredible memories will I create today which will move my life forward?"

"What are the three most important things I can accomplish today to increase my success?"

"Who can help me accomplish my greatest challenges and expand my success easily and quickly?"

Actions

Prioritize what you are choosing to accomplish: Then make a commitment to complete what you start.

Day 13

"The stories of past courage can teach, offer hope, and
provide inspiration, but they cannot supply courage itself.
For this each man must look into his own soul."

JOHN F. KENNEDY

You cannot have continued success without the ability to notice subtle differences and appreciate what is happening around you moment by moment. With your full attention centered in the present moment, you become aware and with that awareness you can expand your consciousness. It is with that awareness that the creative spirit within you opens you up to unlimited possibilities.

Successful men and women spend much of their time in the present moment. They understand that the future is always generated in the present moment. Let me explain. By being completely present in the moment you can create a compelling future by visualizing and contemplating what it will look like. You remain completely in the moment focused on your future.

By this means you can also decide on the direction and any challenges you may face along the way. Then you can take some immediate actions around your future dreams.

Through this process you will someday look back from the future and see what was created during the moments of your visualization, contemplation and actions.

Today ask

"What will it take for me to expand my awareness and be fully present?"

"How can I open to receive and feel the creative spirit flowing through me today?"

"What can I do to expand my connection to my soul and create a compelling future?"

Actions

Practice withdrawing your mind from all distractions and be fully present to the tasks at hand.

Day 14

> *"Courageous people are not necessarily mentally or emotionally stronger than the average person, rather they see their challenges as opportunities to grow and become more fruitful."*

KEN D FOSTER

Freedom is a sacred word in the United States. But most people are not free. They are slaves to chasing money, better relationships, sex, cars, houses etc. But true freedom ultimately brings with it unending happiness and abundance. Let me explain.

When you consistently apply proven business principles to your business, your business will thrive. When you meditate on a regular basis, your intuition will increase, and you will make better choices.

When you treat your body with proper diet and exercise, your body will be healthy. When your relationships are filled with compassion and respect, you will have harmony.

My point is this: When you stop chasing things and start focusing on developing inner wisdom, true success will come. It all starts with acknowledging areas that are not working and then transforming these areas one at a time. As Sri Yukteswar said: "Wisdom is the greatest cleanser." So, set your course to freedom from all limitations.

Today ask

"If freedom from all limitations was my goal, where would I start?"

"What is my plan to have freedom in all areas of my life?"

"What can I do today to change myself so that my challenging situations go away?"

Actions

Contemplate this statement and determine how you will incorporate it into your life: "It is important not to attempt to change your circumstances prior to changing yourself. If you do, most likely the circumstances will reappear in a different form. With a steady course of inner change, you will find true freedom."

Day 15

*"Adventure can be an end in itself. Self-discovery is the
secret ingredient that fuels daring."*

GRACE LICHTENSTEIN

There is something that is more potent than your willpower. It's your environment. Environment is stronger than most people's will. So, why not create an environment that will support your success?

Several times over the last decade, I have been fortunate to have my wife and her "energy-worker" friends go through my home and office environments to assist me to align these areas for success. Each time I did this, my energy increased, money flow grew, and I had more harmony in my relationships.

This didn't happen by accident. I had to take a risk and trust the process. It took much work, planning and moving things around until the energy flowed correctly. But I can tell you this: It was so worth it!

Let me ask you a few questions to inspire you. Have you set up a winning environment for you to thrive in? Do your surroundings reflect who you really are? In other words, does your environment reflect your highest purpose and values? Do you feel good when you walk into each room?

Decide how to take them to the next level. Maybe you need to paint or clean up some clutter, buy some drapes, add a new picture, or even move. You deserve to feel good and live and work in joyful, energizing environments.

Today ask

"What can I take out of my environments that are static?"

"What are the three steps I can take to energize my environments?"

"Whom do I know who's an expert in environmental management, or an energy worker, that can help me enliven my environments?"

Actions

Take three action steps on creating an empowering environment. Note: (By making your environment shine, you will become a brighter star filled with more energy and enthusiasm for success).

Day 16

"In times of great adversity, it is the courage to overcome that sets the course for greatness."

KEN D FOSTER

Today, we are checking in to see how gratitude is working in our lives. It is easy to be grateful when things are going well. But when things get tough, are you grateful for the gifts that your problems bring to you?

The basis for gratitude should not be material abundance. Sure, it is great to create or receive things, but things don't make a great life. Greatness is found within and demonstrated in the material world.

Wise men seek to build a foundation of moral and ethical values and live from them. They are grateful for realizing the truth—and the certainty of this truth sets them free to live the life of their greatest dreams.

They are on a soulful journey, ever seeking to know the thoughts and ways of their creator. It all starts with gratitude for everything that comes your way. Because in every challenge there is a gift waiting to be unwrapped with the hands of wisdom.

Today ask

"What am I truly grateful for?"

"How can I increase my gratitude?"

"What will it take to have so much gratitude in my life that my problems just disappear?"

Actions

Find the gifts that are helping you transform into a greater version of yourself in at least two challenges you are having. For those of you who need examples of empowering questions to ask, I encourage you to get my best-selling book; Ask and You Will Succeed, 1001 Extraordinary Questions to Create Life-Changing Results. It will expand your consciousness and show you how to tap into your genius. You can find it on KenDFoster.com or Amazon.

Day 17

*"The world is not perishing for the want of clever
or talented, or well-meaning men. It is perishing for
the want of men of courage and resolution."*

ROBERT J. MCCRACKEN

Magnificence is your birthright. But your birthright cannot come into fruition without the inner battle to overcome limited thinking. Most people are not born as virtuosos or masters of their lives. They must evolve their mind and spiritual powers to bring forth their greatest talents.

Many do this alone by trying to become enlightened by reading books or attending workshops by unenlightened fakers. But the wise seek master teachers who have realized knowledge and then become good students by immersing themselves in the teachings until they themselves become a master.

It is important to find realized masters, because otherwise you will one day wake up and find that you have been subject to "the blind leading the blind."

Today ask

"What three steps will I can take today to find the right teacher for me?"

"How can a realized master show up for me as soon as possible?"

"How can I learn what I must learn to evolve myself?"

Actions

Make a list of possible teachers who will truly empower you mentally, emotionally, physically and spiritually. Note: This may be hard for the ego to accept. But when you—the student—are ready and you set your intention to find the teacher, you will be guided by your intuition and soon the teacher will appear.

Day 18

*"Full responsibility for all that is showing up in your life
takes courage, humility, and wisdom."*

KEN D FOSTER

Are you ever tempted to blame the government, your family, the economy or others for your circumstances? A wise sage, Sister Gyanamata once prayed: "Lord, don't change my circumstances, change me." This is the way to overcome your challenges, although it takes courage to say that prayer and mean it.

Many times, we look outside ourselves, blaming others for the way we feel or what is happening to us. But, in truth, we are continually creating our own reality. There is cause and effect working in our lives constantly and since you are the cause, you reap the effects. You are the designer of your destiny—for better or worse.

Take another look at the direction of your life. Is it going the way you would like it to go? Are you attracting amazing people and circumstances into your life? If not, then make up your mind to change things for the better, right here and now.

Today ask

"What must happen for me to clear away of any past beliefs, choices, actions, judgments, or anything else that is or has been blocking my success?"

"If I could choose a new direction for my life, what would it be?"

"What could possibly stop me from changing directions?"

Actions

Make a list of three challenges you have right now that are blocking your success.

Tap into your higher-self and increase your intuition with Ken D Foster's guided meditations on Business, Wealth, Expanding Possibility, Peace, and Health. Yours for free at couragetochange.us/meditation

Day 19

*"Courage is the most important of all the virtues, because
without courage you can't practice any other virtue
consistently. You can practice any virtue erratically,
but nothing consistently without courage."*

MAYA ANGELOU[11]

One of the fastest ways to material success is finding a product or service that sings to your heart, and is of great service to others. Service is one of the chief aims for any truly successful person, and to the extent that you bring value to others, and meaning to your own life, you will reap the rewards of success.

Can it truly be that simple? The answer is yes. Think of any successful person or company; they all bring tremendous value to others. They always look for ways to contribute.

I have found that when you are contributing, the tendency is to forget what you "can't do" and to start doing what many would see as impossible. This happens because as you connect to your higher self, energy and creativity flow through you naturally.

It is amazing how many blessings show up along the path to success which are uncommon to most people's awareness.

Today ask

"What can I do today that will make someone's life better?"

"How can I accelerate the amount of contributions I give to the world?"

"Who am I evolving into as I increase my service to others?"

Actions

Decide how you will increase your service to your family and community.

Day 20

"Have you ever heard of courage and wisdom
getting in the way of success? Of course not, but
ignorance and self-defeating thoughts do."

KEN D FOSTER

Did you know that your thoughts permeate everything in your environment? They are in your walls, carpets, clothes, pictures, desk, and anywhere you spend time. And since thoughts have the power to attract what you do and do not want, it is important to spend time on creating a joyful environment to work and live in.

First, start with your mind and cleanse out all negations such as worry, anger, fear or harm by asking: "Truth, am I willing to let go of any negativity here and now?" and "Truth, when will I let go of this?"

Then fill your mind with thoughts of loving anticipation and certainty that you will create an amazing space where you will be able to receive abundance and prosperity. Next, cleanse any negative or useless thoughts, feelings, emotions or anything else from your environment that is not serving you at the highest level.

A popular and effective way of doing this is using white sage or incense to cleanse the environment while saying prayers to release any negativity as you go from room to room.

Today ask

"What will it take to create a powerful environment that supports my dreams?"

"How can I infuse my environment with the energy of abundance and prosperity?"

"How can I bring in more beauty and expansion into my environment?"

Actions

Focus your attention on creating an environment that supports your spirits vision of success.

Day 21

*"If you are lucky enough to find a way of life you love,
you have to find the courage to live it."*

JOHN IRVING[12]

One of the most important principles that will bring you long-lasting success is unconditional respect. You may ask: "What is unconditional respect?" Well, it is about having positive regard for yourself, your family, friends, community, nations, and humanity. It is about honoring your soulful path and the path of others. It's living from compassion and commitment to excellence.

Unconditional respect isn't about living your life from others' thoughts, feeling and points of view about what they see as right, wrong, good, bad or respectful. It's about being aware that you are an infinite spirit who is connected to everyone and living from personal integrity with positive regard toward all. It is realizing that what you do to others or your environment you also do to yourself.

Unconditional respect is a way of living and having respect for the gift of life that has been given to you and then doing your very best to bring forth your greatness into this world to be an example for others to follow.

It may not be common for most. But it is the way of those who are willing to be uncommon and step into their soulful calling by living joyfully and gracefully while here on earth.

Today ask

"What has to happen for me to increase respect in my life?"

"How can I align and enjoy bringing more respect into my life?"

"Who do I have in my circle of friends that I could give more respect to?"

Actions

Determine where you can increase your courage to embrace a deeper respect for everything. You can tap into courage by asking the right questions. For those of you who need examples of empowering questions to ask, I encourage you to get my best-selling book; Ask and You Will Succeed, 1001 Extraordinary Questions to Create Life-Changing Results. It will expand your consciousness and show you how to tap into your genius. You can find it on KenDFoster.com or Amazon.

Day 22

"It takes courage to grow up and become who you are."

E. E. CUMMINGS[13]

Since thinking will either empower you or disempower you, what thoughts will you choose to focus on today? Will you accept thoughts of success, happiness, and health, or feelings of lack, failure and of what is wrong?

It seems that answer is simple, but I would like to challenge you to become conscious of what you, so you raise your awareness. Notice when you lose your center and are unhappy, tired, overwhelmed, angry or upset.

What thoughts are you dwelling on during those moments? Whatever they are could you let them go and ask a new question like: *"What am I judging?"* or *"What am I afraid I am going to lose something?"* or *"What do I believe I won't get?"* or *"Where am I trying to be right?"*

By asking these questions, you can become quickly aware of areas you are judging instead of being aware, and shift your focus.

Awareness does not judge anything as good, bad, right or wrong. Awareness notices and adjusts. It feels light and is empowering, compassionate, caring and ready to respond appropriately. Wouldn't you rather create your life from consciousness than judgment?

Today ask

"Where can I let go of judgments and bring in awareness?"

"How can my business and life generate more contribution?"

"What am I now aware of that will change my life for the better?"

Actions

List five ways you judge yourself and then come up with a solution to stop it permanently. Note: (Remember: the more you focus on infinite, powerful, confident, possibility thinking the more success you will have).

Day 23

"Courage is the birthplace of wisdom, happiness, and success."

KEN D FOSTER

One of the keys to living a life filled with success is keeping a mental diary. It is essential to keep a close eye on your thoughts, choices, and actions during the day. Are they leading you to the feeling of empowerment or feeling disempowered? Are they helping you move forward in the direction of your dreams, or stopping you dead in your tracks?

What you predominantly think about will determine your successes or failures. Why? Because what you focus on you will feel. If you focus on what is not working in your life, you will feel disempowered. You will most likely have a lack of energy. Without energy, you will not take inspired actions that lead to success. Therefore, keep track of what you are putting into your mind.

Many thoughts cross your mind every day. In fact, the social scientists tell us we have about sixty-thousand thoughts per day. The type of thoughts that pass through your mind will depend solely on where your mind's eye is focused.

For example, if you are focusing your mind on creating a specific project, you will attract thoughts that help you solve the issues of the project. But if you let your mind wander, then you will start to draw views that will reflect your wandering. So, I recommend you only dwell on thoughts that are positive and moving you forward in the direction of your highest dreams.

Today ask

"What projects am I committed to completing no matter what?"

"What thoughts will empower me to complete these projects?"

"What thoughts will assure my success?"

Actions

Spend a few minutes focusing on your most important projects and understanding what your next steps will be. Note: (During the day notice how your body, mind, and spirit feel. Then make the necessary adjustments to your thinking to stay focused, powerful and feeling calm).

Day 24

*"Failure is only postponed success as long
as courage coaches ambition."*

HERBERT KAUFMAN

We are here for one reason and one reason only, which is to build a friendship and get closer to that force we call God, Spirit, Love, Universe, or Higher Power. If we don't dare to develop this relationship, then everything else in life will eventually be empty.

There are millions of "successful people" in the world of business that live an empty existence. They rationalize that everything is just how they want it, but deep inside they know this is a lie.

A superiority-complex born of self-pride or an inferiority-complex born of self-loathing will limit you. You were not created in the image of pride or pity; you were created in the image of God. The Creator and Savior of yourself is within yourself.

You are here to experience a deep connection with Spirit. You are here to obtain higher knowledge, and change yourself at all levels. You are here to be all you can be, but not in by driving yourself to the grave by trying to be better than most. The path to enlightenment is not a path of tearing others down so you can look better. It is a path of deep love with your creator, self, and others.

Today ask

"What is my highest purpose for being alive?"

"Who am I becoming because of pursuing my highest purpose?"

"What steps will I take to get closer to my soul in the next thirty days?"

Actions

What can you do that is bigger than yourself and will glorify your highest purpose?

CHAPTER 2

OVERCOMING CHALLENGES IN BUSINESS AND LIFE

Day 25

"Love is the most difficult and dangerous form of courage.
Courage is the most desperate, admirable and noble kind of love."

DELMORE SCHWARTZ

To be successful in life, you must build yourself up. Self-confidence is essential in almost every aspect of your life, yet so many people struggle to find it. Why? Because they are looking outside of themselves to find it, rather than doing the work, it takes to build it.

Self-confidence is built primarily by positive self-talk and keeping commitments with yourself. Think about it. When something goes wrong in a friend's life, do you criticize them and put them down, or do you have compassion and speak to them with warm words?

Most likely you talk to them kindly. However, what happens when something goes wrong in your life? Are you as kind to yourself as you are to your friends? When we are compassionate to others and ourselves, we build esteem.

It is also true that making and keeping commitments to yourself will build esteem quickly—mainly when they stretch you. The key is keeping the promises you make; so be aware of your obligations.

Today ask

"What can I achieve, if I keep the commitments I make no matter what?"

"What can I do, that I haven't accomplished before, that will build up my self-confidence?"

"How can I substantially build my self-confidence, starting today?"

Actions

Make a list of three commitments you will keep, no matter what.

Day 26

"Cast out of your mind disempowering thoughts and become unstoppable by replacing negativity with courageous actions to accomplish your dreams."

KEN D FOSTER

Everyone has challenges, but how you go about solving them, will determine if they are resolved permanently or not. Will making more money, having more time, advances in technology and medicine make your business or life better? Well, sometimes! But only if you get to the real causes of why your challenges are there in the first place. Taking full responsibility for what shows up in your life and looking for the answers within yourself is a good start.

Every challenge comes with a three-part solution for lasting change; Physical, Mental—Emotional, and Spiritual solutions. On the Physical plane you may need to assess what is working and what is not. You may need to hire a specialist who helps with healing your body or creating a system in your business.

On the Mental-Emotional level you will need to assess what beliefs, choices or actions are causing the challenge to show up in your life. These are the areas where introspection is most valuable. Ask yourself a question like, "What would someone have to believe for this challenge to be showing up in my life?"

With the Spiritual level, you can get insights into the purpose of the challenge and how the test is helping you grow, strengthen or evolve. Meditation and contemplation are valuable tools to help you understand why the challenge is showing up at the present time.

Today ask

"What is my most pressing and persistent challenge and what are three solutions to change it Physically, Mental-Emotionally, and Spiritually?"

"What will my life be like when my most pressing challenge is overcome?"

"How will I celebrate when my most pressing challenge is complete?"

Actions

Be aware of any procrastination coming up which would stop you from completing your most pressing challenge. Commit to setting up goals and a timeline of completion to put this challenge behind you permanently.

Day 27

*"Become aware of your magnificence and
find the courage to express it."*

KEN D FOSTER

Have you ever done something for the wrong reasons and ended up feeling lost or let down? This happens to everyone when they are not aligned with their highest values. Living life focused on priorities, aligned with what you truly value is an amazing way to create consistent, profitable results.

Think about what you value for a moment. Maybe it is family, freedom, health, ease and grace, loyalty, gentleness, self-restraint, free time, simplicity, spiritual living, straightforwardness, wealth, truth or compassion.

Whatever your highest values are, choose one and then live life from that value for a week and see how much more alive you feel, how much more energy you have and how much more aligned with yourself you are.

Today ask

"What value am I committed to actualizing?"

"How can I live my highest values each day?"

"How will my life get better and better by living my highest values?"

Actions

Determine which value you will lead your life from this week. Maybe you highly value love, friendship, trust, compassion, or service. Whatever you choose, allow this value to permeate everything you do.

Tap into your higher-self and increase your intuition with Ken D Foster's guided meditations on Business, Wealth, Expanding Possibility, Peace, and Health. Yours for free at couragetochange.us/meditation

Day 28

"Courage combined with faith is an unstoppable force."

KEN D FOSTER

Have you ever been in a situation where you tried to think of every possible way to get out of it and you seemingly exhausted your mind? Celebrate! It can be an amazingly good place to be in because you eventually realize that it will take more than your limited thinking to overcome the problem.

Can you relate? It is in the moments of utter frustration that you can choose to surrender your limiting beliefs and start looking for an alternative answer.

Most of the time when people are stuck, their thinking is polarized. They think concerning absolutes. It is either this way or that way. Seldom do they ask, "How many possible solutions are there to this problem?"

When this happens, many times the door will open where you least expect it. It is surrender that walks you through it because you have created a new path, yet unexplored by the mind.

Remember, there are always more solutions than problems. But you must surrender to your old ways of thinking, open up your creativity and change your point of view for solutions to flow.

Today ask

"If I knew I could overcome all stressors, what could I do right now to generate peace?"

"How will I increase my choices, so I will always succeed in overcoming my problems?"

"What must I remember to be a successful problem-solver?"

Actions

Think of one problem you are facing, and then challenge yourself to come up with ten solutions to that problem.

Day 29

You cannot grow without resistance, nor create success without growth. Weight training is an excellent example of this concept. If there were no weights to lift, the body-builder would not grow the muscle.

The same is valid for business or your personal life. If you are not experiencing struggles and growing past them, you are not putting the success of today, into the storehouse of tomorrow. This is a real bank account of progress. Save a little every day, and you will never have lack.

Therefore, each difficulty you have comes with a guarantee. It promises you the opportunity to become all you can be as you overcome it.

So where do you start? Most people think doing more and more is the answer. The wise ones bring in more awareness, information, and understanding, before beginning anything.

They, in fact, tap into their intuition. This leaves them open to receive new tactics and approaches for overcoming the challenge well before they proceed. By doing this first, they assure their success.

Today ask

"What is possible for me when I prevail against my biggest challenges?"

"What will change if I tap into my awareness before engaging problems?"

"How can it get better than this?"

Actions

Think about the challenges facing you and then, bring introspection into the equation to gain wisdom.

Day 30

*"What would life be if we had no courage
to attempt anything?"*

VINCENT VAN GOGH

When problems arise, most people get into the drama of the problem. Emotion clouds the issue and shuts down their solutions. Instead, find a space where you can quiet your mind before you contemplate the problem, addressing it with reason.

Think of a glass full of water and dirt. When you mix the water with the dirt, it turns to mud, clouding the water. However, if you set the glass down, the mud will sink to the bottom, and the water will become clear.

The same is true of your mind. There are infinitely more solutions than problems, but you must approach them with an empty mind.

Today ask

"What can I do to be at peace before I try to solve my problems?"

"What could instantly solve my problems permanently?"

"What beliefs will I let go of to solve my problems?"

Actions

Think of one problem that has evaded solutions for a while. Take time to meditate and quiet your mind and then come up with ten solutions that will solve this challenge, forever?" Note: (Make sure you use the word "forever" in your solutions, so the problem is permanently solved).

Day 31

*"Courage is an inside job. It is developed by knowing
yourself and befriending God."*

KEN D FOSTER

When challenges come, turn your attention toward the soul. Success is a natural outpouring of soulful thinking and actions. Take some time to quiet your mind and focus on remembering the times when you were "in the flow" of success in the past.

Don't dwell on problems or access past experiences that didn't work. These were temporary lessons for you to learn and strengthen yourself. The more significant your troubles, the greater your opportunity to maximize your talents, gifts and soulful power to overcome them. Today is a new day and success can be yours.

At' this moment, you can decide to overcome any obstacle blocking your success.

Tell yourself: "I am filled with the courage of a hero and the happiness of a conqueror." "I am a powerful infinite being. Every day in every way life is flowing toward me with ease, grace, and abundance."

By avowing your real power, you will strengthen your mental capabilities and remain unshakable no matter how difficult the challenge.

Today ask

"What five affirmative statements I can make that will empower me to remember who I am and keep me generating success?"

"How can I tap into my soulful power to overcome any challenges?"

"What am I choosing to focus on that will bring me unending success?"

Actions

"Pick a challenge you would like to overcome and take three steps toward overcoming it.

Day 32

"With courage you can see what you have never seen before."

KEN D FOSTER

Most people are prisoners of their mind, erroneously thinking they are powerless to do anything different. They are stuck in the limitations of the world, thinking how life is showing up for them is "just the way it is".

But truly, your life is a direct result of what you are envisioning and believing to be true for you. So, if you want to change your circumstances, you must first change what you are judging as "this is the way it is."

First, imagine you can change your circumstances. Then tune yourself into the creative power of infinite spirit. Allow the flow of ever-expanding possibilities to enter your mind. Realize that you are not your circumstances; you are an infinite being with the power to overcome all challenges. Tell yourself the truth!

Today ask

Make the effort to find that starting point, and ask:

"What can I change, that I thought I could not?"

"What can I do that has never been accomplished before?"

"What is possible if I just stop thinking: "This is the way it is"?"

Actions

Contemplate the above questions and allow yourself to tap into your imaginative soul and open up to the possibility of doing something you have never done before.

Day 33

"True courage is found in those who follow soul guidance and let go of compulsive desires and habits."

KEN D FOSTER

Do you have projects that have remained incomplete for long periods of time? Have you ever wondered what it would take for you to complete them promptly with effortlessness actions?

I have seen time and time again clients who have over-committed. They've promised to complete projects yet never anticipated the time and effort involved. Other times, they are good at finishing other people's projects on time, but can't seem to complete their own. So, what do all these people have in common?

Both groups are not aware of how their choices and actions are impacting themselves negatively. They are lowering their self-esteem and confidence in their willpower by making commitments to themselves or others that they cannot or are unwilling to keep.

Most unsuccessful people use only about one-tenth of their attention. They focus their will on trying to do too many things at once and as a result just complete projects half-heartedly. Instead of saying "No" to others and focusing their energy on projects that are key for their future; they divert their strengths and get little done on things that matter to them the most. These unsuccessful people may be very busy but nothing much of significance gets completed.

It doesn't have to be this way. You must take back your power, keep your commitments, use one hundred percent of your awareness and complete your projects.

Today ask

"What must I be aware of to complete these projects?"

"What must happen for me to prioritize my projects and get rid of any beliefs, choices or actions that may block my success?"

"How can I quickly and easily complete my most important projects?"

Actions

Determine the most important project you have and set a completion date.

Day 34

*"Is he alone who has courage on his right hand
and faith on his left hand?"*

CHARLES LINDBERGH[17]

You are the bedrock of success in your own life. You are the master of your fate. What you do today will either propel you forward, or stifle you, the choice is yours! (And yes, the decisions you make today will determine who you will be one, five, or ten years in the future).

So what stifles your success? There are many ways you can repress your progress. One is thinking you know more than you do. Two is assuming you don't know what you do.

When you have all the answers, you will limit any new possibilities from showing up. This can be devastating for business and all areas of your life. If you are doing things the "same way it has always been done" and not questioning how it could be better, you will fall prey to stagnation and limitation.

If on the other hand, you don't use your intuition and mind to find solutions to all your challenges and rely on others to do it for you, you will experience poor choices, lack of success and a roller coaster ride in life.

Today ask

"In what areas of my business or life can I invite others to help me find solutions?"

"Where have I tried to go it alone and caused problems for myself?

"What can I do to surround myself with people who will help me grow?"

Actions

Think about a past failure, where adding a team member would have created greater success.

Day 35

*"It takes courage to love yourself as much as God loves you.
But once you do, everyone benefits."*

KEN D FOSTER

When I work, I live by a motto that I learned from the spiritual leader Sri Daya Mata, which is to "have a mindset of love combined with service, and give the rest to God." Imagine approaching work every day with this attitude!

Many times, we become frustrated when things don't work out the way we planned, but if we step back and look for the good that has come out of even these frustrating times, we can truly learn and become stronger the next time around. As Maya Angelou says: "God puts rainbows in the clouds."

Also, it isn't so much about what you accomplish, but what you learn because of who you are being and what you are doing that matters. Because, the more you are connected to your inner wisdom, the more successful you will be.

Today ask

"What can I do to bring more love and service into my business and life?"

"What insights am I willing to receive that will change my life forever?"

"What memories can I stop judging myself harshly about and allow more love in?"

Actions

Determine if the path you are on is leading to self-actualization or something less. For those of you who need examples of empowering questions to move toward self-realization I encourage you to get my best-selling book; Ask and You Will Succeed, 1001 Extraordinary Questions to Create Life-Changing Results. It will expand your consciousness and show you how to tap into your genius. You can find it on KenDFoster.com or Amazon.

Day 36

"A man of courage is also full of faith."

MARCUS TULLIUS CICERO[18]

Who influences you in a deep way? Who would you feel honored to have as your mentor and friend? Who is your source of inspiration as well as an example of how you want to run your business and life? These are questions that are designed to help you find your mentors.

Mentors are important because they have walked the paths that you are ascending. They can illuminate the challenges you are facing and help you avoid pitfalls. And in many cases, quicken your success.

I have a few select mentors in my life. These are people living in the body and ascended, who help me expand my awareness of what is possible, encourage me to contribute more of my soulful gifts into the world and be the best I can be.

I have found the best way to find amazing mentors is to first get in touch with who the ideal mentor is for you. Make a list of their skills, characteristics, and values. And then determine your strategy for reaching out to your ideal mentors.

Today ask

"What are the highest qualities and greatest skills my new mentor should possess?"

"By having a mentor, what is possible for me?"

"What are the steps I can do today to find the perfect mentor for me?"

Actions

Make a list of your top ten qualities and/r skill sets of your new mentor.

Day 37

"I count him braver who overcomes his desires than him who conquers his enemies; for the hardest victory is over self."

ARISTOTLE[19]

Discrimination is the soulful power that leads to success. We can always use reason to find the pros and cons in any situation. We can stack the deck for one choice or another, or rationalize why one option is better than another, but how do you really know which course to take?

It is through the power of soulful discrimination that the right choices can be found. Use your discrimination to look at each situation from a dispassionate point of view.

Keep your emotions calm and then ask; "What is the truth about this situation?" or "Truth, what is the highest and best for everyone concerned?" Decisions that lead to success are commonplace when you are willing to calmly seek the truth.

Today ask

"What can I do to increase my resolve to overcome my challenges?"

"Where am I blocking my success?"

"In what areas can I expand my awareness to see the truth?"

Actions

Ask the above questions until you get the answers. You will know when the answers are right because you will have a sense of peace about the situation.

Tap into your higher-self and increase your intuition with Ken D Foster's guided meditations on Business, Wealth, Expanding Possibility, Peace, and Health. Yours for free at couragetochange.us/meditation

Day 38

"To see what is right and not do it, is the want of courage."

CONFUCIUS[20]

Darkness may fill a cave for a thousand years, but as soon as light shines the darkness disappears. So too, when you acknowledge what you need to change by shining the light of introspection on it, you will unleash a power within you that will consume unconscious parts of yourself.

It is only when you are not afraid to acknowledge the areas in your life where you feel powerless that things can change. If you tend to deny regions that aren't working, then this is the first place to start.

Don't gloss over challenges you are having. Every problem is there for you to overcome it. This is how we grow! Instead, embrace challenges the same way you embrace things you like. If you do, you will grow beyond your problems quickly.

Today ask

"In truth, what areas of my business or life do I need to acknowledge and make changes in?"

"What am I not seeing that is stopping my success?"

"How can I increase my success today?"

Actions

Today, commit to making the changes necessary until things turn in your direction. Note: (This may take everything you have. But, so what, you must be doing something today, why not be bettering your life).

Day 39

*"Playing it safe does not take courage, but doing
what needs to be done despite great odds against
you is the courageous path to success."*

KEN D FOSTER

Thinking positive is a good thing, but if you don't look at where you have failed and learn from your mistakes, you are bound to repeat them. The most positive success habit you can quickly put into practice is to look at your business or life from a dispassionate, introspective point of view and... Question everything!

The business person who asks where they and their team are frustrated or dissatisfied, and then turns those challenges into goals to overcome them, is one who is consistently successful.

They are not afraid to take on big or small challenges and find the solutions to success by asking questions and probing the infinite solutions. Circumstances rule the weak-minded, but problems build strength and character for those who are up for generating lasting success.

Today ask

"What choices will I make that allows success to flow my way?"

"What am I committed to improving and changing no matter what?"

"When I am facing challenges, what will I remember that will help me overcome them?"

Actions

Pick one mistake you have made in the last week, and figure out what you could have done differently.

Day 40

"With courage comes the determination to focus your whole mind on what you are doing and hold it there until you succeed."

KEN D FOSTER

Will you be better at fighting your adverse circumstances tomorrow than you were today? Of course not. So why not make up your mind today and double your efforts to overcome your challenges?

The mistake most people make is thinking that somehow things will be easier tomorrow, even though they are not doing anything to effect change today. That is just fantasy thinking.

You can change any situation by focusing your brain power on the situation until change is affected. Remember, it is an inside job! You must first change your inner focus for outer circumstances to change.

One of the most significant truths is not to pray for your challenges to go away, but to pray for increased personal power so you can overcome any obstacles. This is the path of success that leads to greatness. Are you up for the challenge?

Today ask

"What does my inner guidance tell me is the best way to overcome my challenges today?"

"What can I do today to find the courage to conquer the unconquerable?"

"How can I be greater than any challenge I am facing?"

Actions

Decide on three action steps to overcome your greatest challenge.

Day 41

"To look at something as though we had never seen it before requires great courage."

HENRI MATISSE[21]

Have you ever noticed that when you start something, there seems to be a grace period when ideas flow, things go easy and then after a while, there appears to be resistance to your success?

The resistance may come in the form of a co-worker who disagrees with you, a government agency with rules you didn't expect, or maybe it is your mind telling you: "This is too much to accomplish." Whatever the resistance, believe it or not, it is there to help you!

Within you is the power to overcome anything that comes your way. Nothing can stop you from succeeding unless you give it the ability to stop you. Resistance is there to strengthen you. Nothing in the world grows without it. A seed must overcome the resistance of the soil to burst through to the sunlight.

You must overcome your resistance to challenging circumstances to obtain what you choose in life. But not in the way you have done in the past. Try opening up to receive the resistance instead of trying to block it. Allow yourself to receive your challenges with a mindset of ease and grace instead of telling yourself a story about how hard it will be.

Today ask

What are three challenges I can embrace today with a positive attitude?"

"How can I be non-resistant, even embrace resistance if it shows up?"

"How can I be more courageous when challenges arise?"

Actions

Make up your mind that you will quickly move past anything that is standing in your way of success.

Day 42

"No matter how serious your problems are, with courage and daily perseverance to find solutions, your problems will eventually be solved."

KEN D FOSTER

Many people try to please their families, friends and employers to their own detriment. They typically don't take time for themselves and say "Yes" too often to the wishes of others. This type of other-centered thinking leaves clues.

These behaviors lead to overwhelm, resentful and an unfulfilled life. Steve Jobs once said: "Your time is limited, so don't waste it living someone else's life. Don't be trapped by dogma and let the noise of other people's opinions drown out your own inner voice."

Life isn't a dress-rehearsal; so why would you generate your life from other people's points of view? Circumstances don't get better unless you put your full force and wisdom behind making them better.

Why do you suppose there are problems and challenges in life? Are they just a fact of life that you must put up with? No way! They are a sign that you need to become determined to overcome them by changing, improving, developing, growing or doing something different.

You don't have to live with people pleasing. You can start now to live an inspired life by asking new questions and making better choices right now.

Today ask

"What will it take for me to overcome this challenge now?"

"What have I been unwilling to perceive, do, change or receive that is stopping me from overcoming my challenge with_____?"

"How can I live an inspired life and overcome my challenges infinitely quickly?"

Actions

Determine to let go of people pleasing permanently and take two actions toward it.

Day 43

*"Indecision dampens courage and creates
lost opportunities."*

KEN D FOSTER

Procrastination is a symptom of a soul that is unwilling to value what it has been given. And with procrastination comes stagnation. There is a lack of caring, laziness and chaos. Although procrastinators may be very busy doing things, it doesn't mean that they are doing things that will expand their spirit and grow their success!

If you are putting off doing what needs to be done, you are probably distracting yourself with less important things. Most procrastinators believe that they will get things done tomorrow.

But unfortunately, without targets to shoot for and a strong commitment to change, tomorrow never comes. There always seems to be something in the way. But who is creating the something in the way? The procrastinator!

The good news for procrastinators and everyone else is: "You are not your thoughts or behaviors." You are a powerful spirit that can create change when you put your awareness to the test.

Use the power of your mind to take empower your life. Affirm: "I am a powerful spirit who has control of my destiny," and "I am God's child. I have inherited the power to move the mountains of procrastination out of my life."

Today ask

"How can I be the white tornado of accomplishment that I am?"

"What energies am I willing to be which will blow procrastination out of my life?"

"Truth, am I willing to delete, destroy and remove all distractions from my life that stops my success?"

Actions

Decide on what goals you will accomplish today and take immediate action.

Day 44

*"Courage comes with action. The minute you step forward,
the minute you declare your decision, the minute you say,
"This is how it's going to go," courage comes. It floods
through you and energizes every single fiber of your
being. You don't have to wait for it. It'll be there."*

GAIL BLANKE[22]

Are you the master of your destiny, or will the circumstances of life master you? We all have had setbacks, hurts, and failures in the past. These challenges come and go, so why let your mind be disturbed by them?

It is only when you think you are a victim of circumstance that you react unfavorably. The more you realize that you are the master of your destiny, the less you will choose to react.

By so doing, your mind will remain calm allowing you to connect with the infinite Spirit and make right decisions. As a result, your success will increase. How can it get better than that?

Remember, challenges can help you grow, develop, improve and increase your awareness if you are not judging them as right, wrong, good or bad. Instead become aware of what is happening and ask Infinite, awareness, possibility, and success-questions to move you forward.

Today ask

"In what areas have circumstances overwhelmed me?"

"What steps can I take to get out of overwhelm?"

"What is possible for me, when I overcome my challenges?"

Actions

Take two action steps to get out of overwhelm and then with poise and courage prioritize your daily activities and open to receive more success.

Day 45

We become filled up with happiness when we are aligned with spirit and allow our life to follow the natural rhythms of the Soul. Happiness is not dependent on getting more things, doing more or being around more people, but on the development of profound wisdom.

Think about the times you have been the happiest in your life. If you are anything like me, it is usually the times when you are doing things you love to do and have let go of worry, fear, or stress.

When you are in a peaceful state of mind and committed to being peaceful, have you noticed that many times you get the answers to your greatest problems or know the right steps to take? I submit that when you are in a peaceful state your inner wisdom naturally flows into your conscious mind.

Today ask

"What is possible for me if I permeate my mind with peaceful thoughts?"

"How can open up to greater wisdom and make better choices?"

"What are the benefits to me by staying peaceful all the time?"

Actions

Come up with two ways you can have more happiness in your life.

Day 46

*"Two things run through the lives of great people; problems
and courage. The great ones focus on courage."*

KEN D FOSTER

Do your senses rule your life or are you a master of the senses? In other words, are
you being governed by your appetite for food, money, sex, fame or maybe a little
drama? If so, today is a good day to reflect on what is running your life.

Past the voice of the senses is the wisdom of the ages—the voice of reason. Who
is the voice that tells you to overindulge? Who is the voice that says: "I am angry/
hungry/ lonely/ tired"? That is not you! You are an amazing infinite being with more
strength, courage, and wisdom within your soul than you can imagine.

You don't have to be run by your senses nor let negative thought-habits get in the
way of bringing forth your inner wisdom. It is time to set a new course, reclaim
your spiritual wisdom and find your authentic voice!

Today ask

"What would my life be like without being a slave to sense habits?"

"What strength do I have, that I can use to overcome my negative habits?"

"How can I increase my resolve to overcome all negative habits?"

Actions

Pick one habit that you would like to change and then come up with a plan to do
it. Note: (By acknowledging the strength that lies within and opening new possibilities, you will overcome any negative thought-habit).

Day 47

"If you listen to your fears, you will die never knowing what a great person you might have been."

ROBERT H. SCHULLER[24]

Are you caught up in the success game? Are you chasing success only to be disillusioned time and time again? You have success in one area of your business or life, and then things change for the worse in another area, so you try to fix that area then things stop working in the area that you were having success.

On and on it goes and where it stops no one seems to know. It may seem like you can never win, and you are right. It is not wise to chase success only for the sake of success. It is like trying to make money for money's sake; it is an empty game. In the end, you may have some success or money, but little else.

You will most likely feel an emptiness inside which can only be filled by getting off the success train and getting into the game of bringing out your greatest gifts, talents, and abilities and doing what you were born to do.

Real success comes when we make a concerted effort to realize the mental, spiritual and physical laws of success that govern our lives and everything in it. In this world of relativity even what appears to be true one day can be gone the next day.

There are lots of illusions, but illusions do disappear when we can see reality clearly. And the only way to do that is to seek the truth behind the illusions.

Today ask

"How did I become the person that I am?"

"What do I consistently think that creates the world I live in?"

"What actions can I take which will bring out my greatest gifts, talents, and abilities?"

Actions

As you ask the questions above, ask from a place of your highest knowing that what you ask for will be revealed to you!

CHAPTER 3

INNER REFLECTIONS

Day 48

"The simple step of a courageous individual is not to take part in the lie. One word of truth outweighs the world."

ALEKSANDR SOLZHENITSYN[25]

No doubt there is more than enough fault-finding in the world. Some people do little else because it is easy to see others' faults, but more difficult to see your own. But to grow and increase success it is imperative to know all of you, including your shortcomings, and the easiest way to access them is to look at your results.

If you are not getting the results you want, the chances are that you have a few blind spots that are blocking your success. Everyone has areas that they are blind to, but with a non-defensive mind, you can determine where they are and what you need to change.

The first step is to listen and watch closely how people respond to you. Are they pleasant or defensive? Are they wanting to be around you, or choosing to keep their distance? Also, notice where you get defensive or are resistant to receiving advice or change; these are usually the areas you may need to improve upon and make proper adjustments.

Today ask

"If I were coaching someone else on how to see their blind spots, what would I tell them?"

"If I did know the areas of my personality that truly needed to change, what would they be?"

"How can I become more aware every day to behaviors that limit my success and drive people away from me?"

Actions

Reflect on areas in which you may have blind spots, and those in which you can improve.

Day 49

*"Admitting mistakes takes courage along with
insight to understand how your behaviors impact
others and what you can do to change."*

KEN D FOSTER

For your success to be lasting you must be compassionate and loving. Have you ever thought about how many people quit their jobs or leave their relationships, because they don't feel loved? Too many people use facts and force to get their point across and even though they may seem to be right at the time, no one ends up happy.

A business or relationship without compassion is harsh and callous and undermines cooperation. It is filled with false control, demands and manipulation which are repelling to most healthy people. Healthy people are attracted to love and compassion. In fact, they thrive on it!

Listen, everyone makes mistakes, blames others, sabotages their success, and falls short now and then. It takes courage to confront our failures and make the appropriate changes. It is the compassionate leader that understands this and brings forth wisdom and empathy which inspires change when people make mistakes. This is the mark of a real leader bound for success!

Today ask

"Where can I have more compassion and love when others make mistakes?"

"How can I be more compassionate with myself when I mess up?"

"What changes can I make to be a better leader?"

Actions

Make a list of three changes you can make to become more compassionate.

Day 50

*"To him, that waits all things reveal themselves,
provided that he has the courage not to deny, in
the darkness, what he has seen in the light."*

COVENTRY PATMORE[26]

Business success requires not only the ability to know your strengths and weaknesses but to have the capacity to make honest assessments of current reality. Being honest about what is happening will give you the understanding of what adjustments need to be made.

It is easy to be caught up in delusional thinking unless you are vigilant about watching your thoughts and noticing your results. Results will nearly always tell you when you need to adjust your thinking.

Most businesses and people fail when they can't see what is most obvious. The reason this happens is because of rigid thinking stuck on the way things "should be" instead of how things "really are."

Many people judge people, places, and circumstances not from a place of reality, but from past experiences or stories they have heard. This gives a distorted view which can result in poor decisions.

Be secure in knowing that when you strive to see the truth in each situation, you will thrive and be a conqueror of illusions.

Today ask

"Are there any areas in my life where I do not see reality clearly?" If the answer is yes, ask:

"What do I get out of living in delusion?"

"What changes in thinking will I make immediately?"

These may not be easy questions to answer, so if you are having trouble answering them, ask a friend who has your best interest at heart. By being courageous, you will create more success in your business and life.

Actions

Come up with three actions that will bring more courage into your life.

Day 51

"Courage is grace under pressure."

ERNEST HEMINGWAY[27]

I have found in business and life that everyone deserves our compassion and love. We don't need to condone negative behaviors to have compassion for others. We only need to relate to the human condition to genuinely feel the love from a deep place, no matter what is going on.

Everyone has gone through situations where we haven't performed at our best. We all make mistakes—big ones and small ones. We are all learning and growing. Believe it or not, most people are doing the best they can with the mindsets they are operating from. This is important to consider because, the more compassion you have the better leader you will be.

If you lead from a place of compassion and can be dispassionate when disruptive circumstances arise, you are bound to have more success. Why, because with emotional upsets comes disharmony, which can blind you from seeing reality clearly and making the best choices. But with a compassionate mind, you will have less stress, more clarity and be available for solutions to your challenges.

Today ask

"What's the best way to increase compassion in my business and life?"

"When disruptive circumstances arise, what can I do to stay calm?"

"How can I bring more harmony into my business and life?

Actions

Take two actions today to bring more love and compassion in your life. One of those actions can be to quiet your mind and give yourself permission to slow down and withdraw from the hectic pace of life. Also, are you open to going deeper in meditation today than you did yesterday? If you need help with this, get Ken D Foster's The Science of Meditation Guide for FREE. www.kendfoster.com/resources.

Day 52

"We must make an effort to go from misery to happiness, from despondency to courage."

PARAMAHANSA YOGANANDA[28]

Most people have self-limiting ceilings on their successes. Do you? If so, have you realized that these limitations were accepted as real and put in your mind by you?

And only you can undo your limiting idiosyncrasies. You must redirect your intentions, affirm your greatness, tune into your intuition and choose to expand your consciousness into unlimited possibilities.

Everyone has streams of thought passing through their minds. But few understand they are choosing the ideas they are focusing on—constructive or not. Be still for a few minutes and see what thoughts are bubbling up in your mind right now. Notice if they are empowering you or disempowering you. Then choose which thoughts you will allow in.

Remember, if you want to change anything in your life, you must choose different thoughts. And the easiest way to do that is to ask unlimited questions. These are questions that will not limit your thinking. This is the key to living the life of your dreams.

Today ask

"What would a person have to believe to keep getting poor results?"

"What new questions can I ask daily that will drive me toward unlimited success?"

"What three new beliefs am I choosing to embrace?"

Actions

Come up with a plan to change your disempowering beliefs.

Day 53

"The courage to be brilliant, talented, and successful isn't given to the top ten percent of people. It is given to everyone who chooses to delve into the unknown parts of themselves and share their gifts, talents, and abilities with the world."

KEN D FOSTER

Within each of us is an unstoppable spirit waiting to unleash its majesty into the world. Most people don't know it exists or don't know how to release it or won't do what it takes to experience a life filled with unending success.

What do you think has been holding you back? Wouldn't you like today to be amazing? Wouldn't you like to live a created existence where your activities yield whatever you want? It will happen if you believe in yourself.

Fill your mind with success thoughts starting the moment you wake up. Then focus on what you will accomplish for the day and don't let doubt or uncertainty keep you from fulfilling your dreams.

Today ask

What can I do today to tap into my creative self?"

How can my life get better today?"

What courageous act can I do today to create more success?"

Actions

Only focus on positive thinking that will move you forward.

Tap into your higher-self and increase your intuition with Ken D Foster's guided meditations on Business, Wealth, Expanding Possibility, Peace, and Health. Yours for free at couragetochange.us/meditation

Day 54

*"The great virtue in life is real courage that knows how to
face facts and live beyond them."*

D.H. LAWRENCE[29]

One of the greatest success-stoppers is arrogance. It is a false feeling of superiority that is built on presumptuous claims and misguided assumptions. It separates people from their true spirit and blocks the sunlight of the spirit from shining through them.

Unfortunately, arrogant people seem to be the last ones to know that they are overconfident. The false pride and self-importance which seems to accompany them wherever they go sets them up for eventual failure.

The opposite of arrogance is humility, which is the ability to be modest. It lacks pretense and tends to result in seeing reality clearly. Truly successful people develop humility and practice it daily.

They realize life isn't about how good you look or how great you are, but how much you contribute to making the world a better place.

Today ask

"What can I do to have greater humility?"

"How can I change the unchangeable with humility?"

"What has to happen for me to see reality clearly?"

Actions

Come up with an action plan to have more humility.

Day 55

"It takes courage to pick yourself up when you are tired,
fearful, and worn out and do what needs to be done anyway."

KEN D FOSTER

The right attitude is everything! Do you wake up in the morning feeling inspired with a mindset of success? Or do you wake up struggling to get out of bed with not much enthusiasm?

Did you know that you can set your intention before you go to bed at night, to wake up feeling refreshed with an amazing attitude? It is simple to do! Before you go to bed, take out a piece of paper and write out what you are frustrated with, then your fears, then your challenges.

Next, make a choice to clear these concerns from your mind by asking: "Truth, am I willing to let all of this go now?" and "Truth, when now can I let this go?" Then allow yourself to release them from your thoughts.

Then imagine what you would like to tell yourself these thoughts when you wake up in the morning. Thoughts like: "This is going to be an amazing day, for I am creating great memories filled with happiness and success." And: "I am attracting happiness and success in everything I do." And: "I am focused on creating a beautiful life."

Keep these thoughts in your mind until you fall asleep. It may take a little practice, but before long you will wake up feeling refreshed and inspired, and you will realize that you are the master of your thoughts and destiny.

Today ask

"How can wake up every morning refreshed and ready to have a wonderful day?"

"What can I do to assure I wake up daily feeling joy in my heart?"

"What three things can I do today to enhance my joy-filled life?"

Actions

Create a new success habit by redefining how you will wake up each day.

Day 56

*"Great spirits have always encountered violent opposition
from mediocre minds. The mediocre mind is incapable
of understanding the man who refuses to bow blindly
to conventional prejudices and chooses instead to
express his opinions courageously and honestly."*

ALBERT EINSTEIN[30]

Conventional thinking has us believe that we must pursue our business and life success through a series of logical steps. The "one-step-at-a-time method" seems to be the standard, but how is this conventional thinking working in your life? For most, it keeps them in mediocrity. It is like crossing the United States in a covered wagon, when jets are available.

Have you ever heard that meditators can concentrate more effectively than others? This is a well-known fact among long-term meditators. They have used the power of their mind repeatedly to concentrate on the spiritual eye, and have not only opened the pathways to the superconscious mind but understand this is where all great ideas come from.

These long-term meditators have developed their mind-power to such an extent that they attract into their lives what they need almost instantly. They realize that the only real relationship is the relationship between your soul and spirit.

Today ask

"How can I get deeply in touch with the relationship between my soul and spirit?"

"What new information or book can I find to further my education on the relationship between soul and spirit?"

"What do I need to do, to let go of doing so much?"

Actions

Find some quiet time and contemplate weather your life is getting better or not. If not, then take two action steps to make it better.

Day 57

*"It takes courage to realize you have the power to change
your life. And with this realization comes the responsibility to
change everything that blocks your happiness and freedom."*

KEN D FOSTER

If you were not born rich, have you ever wondered why? Is there something wrong with you? Or is life just unfair? I can tell you that neither is true.

From wealth, you have come and to wealth you are going. As an infinite being you cannot help but live in wealth. It is an abundant universe! But the question is: *"Are you experiencing abundance daily?"* If not: *"What will it take for you to realize your connection to the abundance of the universe?"*

If you look to nature you will notice there is no lack, therefore the only lack there is has been generated from lack-thoughts crossing your mind and you making them real.

Why not slow down your mind with mindful contemplation and become the observer of each moment. It is in the moment that you can expand your awareness and tap into a power that is much greater than your mind.

This is the power of what is sometimes called the superconscious mind. It is always there waiting to be accessed with infinite, powerful, positive, possibility-questions.

Today ask

"What will it take for me to stay conscious and make brilliant choices?"

"How can I handle all circumstances with ease and grace?"

"Where can I expand the presence of my awareness for increased success?"

Actions

Come up with three questions you have never asked that will increase your self-love and awareness of what is possible for you.

Day 58

"Courageous people build on their strengths. Accept nothing less than the best of you to come forth and build a life of excellence."

KEN D FOSTER

Finding out the true meaning of your existence and where you can add the most value to others in business or life is essential for enduring success. Because you won't find lasting success by doing things that aren't in alignment with your greatest gifts, talents, and skills. And you won't find the essential drive for success by undertaking things that you have no appetite for.

Many people have been told to develop their weak points. While this may work in athletics and some specific situations, most of the time this is a poor strategy for creating ongoing success.

The right strategy is to notice your weaknesses and to build on your strengths. Develop your strengths and become a master at them. They will lead you down the success road. In other words, if you are good at doing something, then do more of it.

We are all given many gifts, talents, and skills to make our Earth journey meaningful to our evolution and help us create spectacular success. Your job is to discover the brilliance of you and then share it with the world.

Today ask

"Which of my gifts, talents or skills can bring me the victory of success and joy?"

"How can I let go of building up my weaknesses and focus on mastering my strengths?"

"What am I committed to changing as of right now?"

Actions

Contemplate your greatest strengths and then apply them today.

Day 59

"When one has nothing to lose, one becomes courageous. We are timid only when there is something we can still cling to."

DON JUAN[31]

Often challenges show up in our lives as a signal that it is time for a change. And what does change represent? It's a soul calling to experience more of yourself by being or doing something different! You may realize that the time has come to let go of old ways of thinking and behaving.

Have you ever stayed in a relationship or work environment too long, thinking that things will get better, only to find that things seem to get worse no matter what you do? When you resist change, things get worse. The world is set up this way.

Have you noticed that pain is a great motivator? Whatever we resist will persist until we recognize and acknowledge what is not working and remember that we have the power to take charge of our lives and change.

I am not saying to leave your relationship or job, but I am saying: look at your part in creating your circumstances and then earn your way out by doing what it takes to recreate your relationships or work environments in a positive new light. You do this by tapping into your personal power and taking time to deeply connect with yourself.

Today ask

"Why am I committed to changing this area in my life no matter what?"

"What has to happen for me to change?"

"How can I free myself from circular thinking, so I can be the change I am choosing?"

Actions

Think about what you want. Then prioritize what you need to change to get it. Note: (Remember, at first it may seem like things are not moving as quickly as you would like them to, but with commitment, persistence and asking empowering questions you will produce incredible success).

Day 60

*"Courage comes in different forms. There's strength—
that's the muscle. But love is the heart. When you
put them together, you can do anything."*

NORA ROBERTS[32]

Today is the perfect day to stay present in all activities. But being present and staying focused on the moment-to-moment tasks can be a challenge. Do you ever find your mind wandering and notice you have lost your focus? It happens to most people, but that doesn't mean you must put up with a wandering mind. You can take back control!

But how can you take back control of your mind when you are rushing from one task to the next trying to keep up? You can't! So, why would an intelligent, powerful, infinite being, be running around like there is no tomorrow? Does this make sense to you? Of course not!

What if it was the constant doing that is stopping you from having what you want? Well, it is! When you end overdoing and slow down, you will have more success.

If you just stop for a few minutes and reconnect with yourself (the infinite being you are), you can become present again to the essential tasks, which ultimately will lead you to success.

Today ask

"How can I become present to the most important tasks?"

"How can I focus my attention consistently?"

"What has to happen to let go of distractions to my success forever?"

Actions

Take some time to contemplate the distractions that are blocking your success and commit to letting them go. Also, allow yourself to go deeper in meditation than you did yesterday. If you need help with this, get Ken D Foster's The Science of Meditation Guide for FREE.www.kendfoster.com/resources.

Day 61

*"Courageous hearts sleep peacefully knowing
they have done everything possible to live a
prosperous life that has benefitted many."*

KEN D FOSTER

Death should not be feared, but it is wise to fear not knowing yourself. Many people view life as a playground, but truly life is a school. Sure, we get recess and time off for vacations, but, if you are not learning, growing and evolving, you're dying. "What part is dying?" you may ask. It is your spirit, your joy, your abundance, your happiness.

When you are feeling empty or disillusioned, it is a sign to stop the busyness and slow down. It is a time to reconnect with your spirit. You cannot know yourself when you are running from place to place trying to fill up the emptiness with other people, places or things. To get to know yourself, you must take time to connect with yourself.

All of us have the answers to life's most significant problems within ourselves, but if you don't take time to be still, meditate, introspect and contemplate you will never realize the potential for a fantastic life that is waiting for you to claim.

Today ask

"Who am I becoming?"

"What is the next step in my life?"

"What am I here to contribute?"

Actions

Think about the direction your life is going. Contemplate on the changes that you can make to make it even better.

Day 62

*"It takes courage to let go of having all the
answers and open the mind to receive instructions
from higher realms of consciousness."*

KEN D FOSTER

Introspection is the way to have an incredible business and life because by assessing what is working and what is not, you can improve, grow and evolve.

Each morning, take some time to decide what direction you will take for the day. Set up the right attitude and then determine what is most important to accomplish. Then, in the evening honestly evaluate what you have achieved and where you need to improve. If you follow this simple formula, life will get better and better.

Even if you have convinced yourself that you are a failure, by using this formula you will consistently improve until failure is a thing of the past. There is no judgment from God or fate. It is your judgments that keep you miserable, poor and unfulfilled. Success is determined in your mind and then accomplished by introspection and inspired actions.

Today ask

"What is not working in my life that I am committed to improving?"

"What are three action steps I will take to increase my success?"

"How can I improve every day in every way?"

Actions

Be relentless in asking questions to improve your life and combine it with two to three action steps.

Day 63

"I learned that courage was not the absence of fear, but the triumph over it. The brave man is not he who does not feel afraid, but he who conquers that fear."

NELSON MANDELA[33]

Have you ever thought about what a miracle your life is? I may not know you personally, but I do know that each one of us has gifts, talents, and skills that are God-given. In fact, we are all equipped with everything we need to succeed in life.

Every person has challenges, and even if you have repeatedly failed, as long as you pick yourself up and try again you will someday succeed. The failure season is the best time to sow the seeds of success. Here is how:

Learn to use the psychology of success to increase your prosperity. It starts with waking up with the right attitude, determination, a clear vision, and daily targets to keep you on track. It also includes daily meditation, healthy eating, exercise and introspection of what is working and what's not.

Today ask

"What is right about my attitude?"

"What is my unflinching vision for success?"

"How can I connect with my mind, body, and spirit to assure lasting success?

Actions

Come up with two ways to have a great attitude today.

Tap into your higher-self and increase your intuition with Ken D Foster's guided meditations on Business, Wealth, Expanding Possibility, Peace, and Health. Yours for free at couragetochange.us/meditation

Day 64

"With the willingness to blaze the unknown, courage becomes an intimate friend."

KEN D FOSTER

Insight is a quality that we all have the potential to tap into, but sometimes we don't use it and end up far from success looking back and wondering what happened. Can you relate?

When insight is missing, most of the time people try to accomplish life on their own without the benefit of intuitive guidance. This is like running a car on only four cylinders instead of eight.

You are only using half of your God-given capacity and are sputtering down the highway. In other words, you have failed to spend enough time connecting with your intuitive inner wisdom and are bumping along in life on your ill-logical thinking.

Intuitive thought is developed by quieting the mind and soulfully connecting with inner guidance. Radical changes are possible, and success can be yours if you take the time to illuminate your infinite mind.

Discard from your mind any doubts or fears, and remember that as a child of Infinite Spirit you have access to the same superconscious intelligence and infinite potentialities as the most brilliant people in the world. As an infinite being, you are neither greater nor less than anyone else. You have the potential to succeed at whatever you choose!

Today ask

"What is it that I want out of life?"

"How can I tap deeper into the mind of God?"

"What will it take for me to improve my intuitive abilities to the point where I am aligned with the highest choices?"

Actions

Attune yourself to be guided by your inner wisdom until you get the answers to your most in-depth questions.

Day 65

> *"As the essence of courage is to stake one's life on a possibility, so the essence of faith is to believe the possibility exists."*
>
> WILLIAM SALTER[34]

There are unlimited possibilities to create the life of your dreams. They are all around you, but you must be able to tap into those possibilities if you are to change your life for the better. To do this, open to expanding your awareness and have the nerve to receive new wisdom.

I say it takes nerve to do this because with an awakened consciousness you will consistently be tapping into your inner wisdom and be receiving guidance that will change the perceptions of how you have understood life. This will take you out of your comfort zone and put you into the zone of the unknown. For many, this is a scary place to be, but in truth, it is where you will grow the most.

The zone of the unknown is the place where all greatness is born. All great people and inventions come from here. Why? Because when you are tapping into soulful thoughts, you do not limit yourself to narrow selfishness or limiting views.

You include others in your successes and achievements and are in harmony with your nature. It starts a cycle of daily living with a sense of purpose and unconditional love. It ultimately evolves your thinking and develops your understanding of how life works to the point where immense success can be yours for the choosing.

Today ask

"What is my purpose for living?"

"In what ways can I expand my connection with spirit?"

"How can I make it possible to let go of limiting beliefs forever and connect with the infinite presence of my soul?"

Actions

Come up with three action steps to connect deeper with your infinite Wise-Self.

Day 66

*"Courage is holding on one minute longer than everyone else.
Courage is stepping forward when every fiber of your being says
step back. Courage is being willing to do
the impossible because it is the right thing to do."*

BLAINE LEE PARDOE[35]

Mahatma Gandhi said, *"There is more to life than increasing its speed."* Many times, we are caught up trying to obtain more, by doing more and doing it quicker.

We try to speed up because we are feeling we need more time, more money, more friends, more, more, more. But this can be a trap resulting in the sense of overwhelm and lack of fulfillment. What we are longing for is a sense of peace, harmony, and happiness.

To create sustainable success, you must know when to slow down, be still, and listen to your inner voice. This is the voice of the Wisdom-Self which will guide you through the chaos if you give it a chance.

As you have realized by now, the Wisdom-Self is filled with unlimited potentialities which can assure your success. But to tap into the Wisdom-Self requires you to be still.

Without stillness and focused attention, you will not perceive the immanence of opportunities that are surrounding you.

Today ask

"Where can I simplify my life?"

"What can I do to still the mind when it becomes conflicted?"

"How can I enjoy my life more while creating success in all areas of my life?"

Actions

Determine what you can take off your schedule to create more space in your day. Note: (It will also help to book time in the future for downtime. A calm, free mind is a powerful mind, so as you do this you will accomplish more).

Day 67

"Where there is love there is courage, where there is courage there is peace, where there is peace there is God. And when you have God, you have everything."

LOUISE PENNY[36]

If you believe that peace and harmony are essential for mental stability, then this is an important question to ask: *"What has to happen for me to live peacefully and in harmony with my nature every day?"*.

It is important because, without a sense of peace and harmony, you will most likely make poor decisions, based on a reactive consciousness which will limit your success.

Peace isn't something that only a few saints possess; it is something you discover and manufacture. It is within each of us, and you were born with the right to tap into is.

To give peace free rein will take a commitment to let go of any beliefs, choices, or actions that produce disharmony in your life. This is easier said than done, but you can do it! Every day you awaken after sleep and have 15 to 18 hours of time to enjoy your life.

For some, the waking hours are filled with drama, for others with peace and harmony. What side are you choosing? If it isn't the side of peace, then you are probably glorifying the dramas in your life by creating them. Lasting peace comes when you take time to connect with your Wisdom-Self and still the busyness of your mind.

Today ask

"What can I let go of that will bring more peace into my life?"

"How can I deepen my peace today?"

"Who can I give my peaceful thought to?"

Actions

Set aside time to journal about how you can genuinely have more peace and prosperity in your life.

Day 68

*"Anyone can stay busy and distracted from what is important
in life. But it takes courage and fortitude to slow down
and connect soulfully to fulfill your life's purpose."*

KEN D FOSTER

Life can get very hectic if we don't watch the choices we are making. Have you noticed that with increased busyness comes the feeling of being out of control, overwhelmed, or a sense of stress? Ouch! How can it get better than that?

Speeding up is not the end game in life. You can be much more productive when you slow down and consciously make choices to take care of your priorities first. I tell my clients: "slow down to succeed." When they do it, the generates more success.

Have you ever wondered what stops you from completing your priorities each day? Most people allow distractions to be more critical than their primary objectives. They like to be comfortable and take the "easy" way.

But if you turn that way of thinking around and do "the worst tasks first," you will become more productive. Slowing down and getting the most challenging things off your plate early in the day will make the day go easier.

Today ask

"Where can I slow down to succeed?"

"What is most important for me to accomplish today?"

"What will I accomplish today that will change my life for the better?"

Actions

Come up with three things you can take off your schedule, so you have more time to plan.

Day 69

"Courage without wisdom is like thoughts without action, nothing much happens until you marry the two."

KEN D FOSTER

Are you consistently connecting to the guiding voice of truth, or are you just getting by, doing what you can and tolerating way too many things?

The only way to master yourself and overcome all challenges is to realize your spiritual nature and to make choices from your intuition which is the fountainhead of lasting success. But it is no small feat to know yourself as spirit and to tap into your intuition. It takes work to let go of ego consciousness.

We all have hunches and sometimes get it right using our gut, but this is undeveloped intuition. Wouldn't you like to have one hundred percent of your choices be right?

This could be a great quest for you. And all you must do is commit to the journey and take time daily to quiet the mind, calm your busy life and practice making choices from listening to your intuition.

This is the path that leads to greatness. The opposite is also true. The most self-defeating way you can choose is to refuse to quiet your thoughts and stay busy because you are ignoring the connection with your Wisdom-Self.

Today ask

"What would be possible for me if I lived from intuitive guidance?"

"What are three steps I can take today to connect with my intuition?"

"How can I get closer to my Wisdom-Self and realize that I am an infinite being who has the power to live an extraordinary life?"

Actions

Determine to realize your full potential and connect with the truth of who you are.

Day 70

*"Real courage is when you know you're licked before you begin,
but you begin anyway and see it through no matter what."*

HARPER LEE[37]

Real success is defined by how much happiness you have, and one way to have happiness every day is to celebrate your life. Your life has been given to you to transcend anything that is creating unhappiness; so, make a conscious effort to uplift your spirit. You don't have to wait for your birthday or a special occasion to celebrate. You can do it now.

How about declaring that today is a day you will celebrate all of you; who you are, where you have contributed, what you have mastered, how you have evolved, where you have loved the most. All of you!

Think about how much has been given to you and then celebrate your relationships, your mind, your health, your friendships, your home, your finances, your family, your spiritual path.

And most of all celebrate the amazing being that is you. Think about who you have become, what you have learned, what you have shared, who you have empowered.

Be willing to put a smile on your face and transcend into happiness anything you perceive as unhappy and start living your life in utter amazement and joy for the life that has become you.

Each day we have a choice to look for all the good in our life or all the things that are going wrong. So, doesn't it make sense to focus on celebrating your life and feeling happy?

Today ask

"What are three things that you could celebrate right now?"

"What will bring more joy and happiness into my life?"

"How can I stay happy all the time?"

Actions

Set your intention to have the happiest day of your life. Imagine how this can change your life for the better.

Day 71

*"With every failure comes the courage to
try again and succeed."*

KEN D FOSTER

If you do not fail, you will never succeed, and if you succeed, failure will become your friend. Why, because failure breeds wisdom and right choices for future actions. In reality, there are no failures; only lessons that are waiting to be learned and applied so that success becomes inevitable. Think about this!

No successful person in the world has not failed many times. Those who succeed look at what is working or not working and make the necessary adjustments. They do not dwell on past mistakes. They move forward with the spirit of courage. They do what they must to succeed despite what circumstances come their way.

Successful people not only take outer actions they also do the inner work. They notice beliefs, choices and activities of the past that are blocking their forward momentum. They remove the blocks to success from their minds. They assess their personalities and how they show up, and they forgive themselves and others quickly.

They also embrace their gifts, talents, and skills and are open to higher abundance flowing their way. And they are willing to receive critical feedback from others by dispassionately contemplating the comments given.

Today ask

"What have my greatest "failures" taught me?"

"What stories have I told myself about past failures, which I am now committed to releasing?"

"When failures come, what am I committed to doing differently?"

Actions

List three failures you have had and then determine how each one has strengthened you.

CHAPTER 4

RECIPES FOR WELL BEING

Day 72

*"When you are struggling, there is nothing more courageous
than asking for a helping hand."*

KEN D FOSTER

Overwhelm is prevalent in this century. It seems like the more you do, the more there is to do. Many people think they will never get caught up. Can you relate? This is just a symptom of saying "yes" too much to the whims, desires, and demands of others and not enough saying "yes" to your soulful self.

When we start doing more than we should, the first thing to go is our intuition. And when our intuition goes, so make right choices. Change your habit of giving yourself away, and you will change your frenetic, out-of-control mind and life for one that works.

When the cluttered mind becomes still, and you stop for a moment to connect with the infinite being that you are, you will hear the precious presence of your intuition guiding you calmly to the next step. This is how the Wisdom-Self is felt and heard.

Today ask

"What is possible for me when I stay connected to my soulful self?"

"What boundaries will I put in place to take care of my interests first?"

"After I have taken care of my primary interests, who can I serve powerfully?"

Actions

Make some time for yourself and then commune with your inner wisdom.

Tap into your higher-self and increase your intuition with Ken D Foster's guided meditations on Business, Wealth, Expanding Possibility, Peace, and Health. Yours for free at couragetochange.us/meditation

Day 73

"Courage has to be cultivated rather than uncovered, and to harvest, the crop of courage takes unquestioning faith in God."

KEN D FOSTER

If a close friend or family member was injured, wouldn't you give 110 percent of your efforts and do everything you could to help them? Of course, you would!

Would you do the same for yourself? I am hoping you said "yes," because it is time to heal whatever has been ailing you, mentally, emotionally, physically or spiritually. Are you aware that you can heal almost anything? I say, "almost anything" because there are diseases that have gone too far and only divine intervention will create the healing.

But, for the most part, you can heal! Some people have been given forty-eight hours to live, such as Anita Morjani, who write a book after her near-death experience called Dying to be Me. And there is countless evidence of others who have healed anything you can imagine.

So, why don't most people heal their diseases? Because most people don't stay committed to their healing, they lack faith and don't realize they can improve. Of course, faith is the foundation of all healing.

If you want to heal whatever ails you, then approach healing as a quest. Think about the multitude of possible solutions to heal. It is rare to find one doctor or healing technique that solves the problem. It takes commitment, determination and consistent efforts to recover. But you can do it!

Today ask

"What areas of body, mind or emotions do I most need to heal?"

"What steps am I committing to take, starting right now?"

"If I allow nothing to stand in my way of healing, how will my life be different?"

Actions

Come up with three possibilities on how you could heal. Then make a supercharged commitment that you will do whatever it takes to improve yourself.

Day 74

"The secret of happiness is freedom;
the secret of freedom is courage."

CARRIE JONES[38]

True happiness eludes most people because they are looking for others to make them happy. But those who understand that nothing outside of themselves can make them happy, keep their minds focused on inner peace, joy, and love.

Happiness is principally a state of mind and conditioned only slightly by outside circumstances. Your happiness doesn't have to fade when things don't go your way. You have more strength in you than you will possibly need, to overcome all obstacles that seem to block your happiness.

Have you ever wondered what permanent and lasting happiness would be for you? It's a good question to ask, because it will start you on a journey to actually have it.

Today ask

"How much of the day do I feel happy?"

"How much of the day do I feel unhappy?"

"How much of the day do I feel neutral?"

Actions

Make a determined decision to remain happy no matter what happens today. Note: It is only when you lose your natural happiness that you are subject to anguish and stress. If this happens, either change what you are doing or make sure you have the right thoughts permeating your mind. Otherwise, your happiness will not be your daily companion.

Day 75

"The minute a person whose word means a great deal to others dares to take the open-hearted and courageous way, many others follow."

MARIAN ANDERSON[39]

Do you understand that business is a means to an end, not the end itself? I have worked with many millionaires over the years. The happiest ones were the ones that understood that there is much more to life than working until they drop. Balance is a success principle the wealthy practice because true wealth brings happiness.

Do you feel consistently calm, peaceful and productive? If not, then you are most likely out of balance and out of touch with the importance of this success principle.

Take some time to go back to the basics. Slow down, quiet your mind, meditate, let go of thinking you must do everything yourself, stay in the present moment and know that no matter what you are going through, "This too will pass." It always does!

Then make balance a priority in your life and ask: "What will it take to bring about a more balanced approach to life?" When you do, you will get the answers that are right for you and your reward will be peace of mind and abundance.

Today ask

"What is important for me to have more happiness in my life?"

"What has it cost me not to have balance in my life?"

"How will my life improve when I am happier? "

Actions

Make a list of five reasons why you will create a balanced life from this day forward.

Day 76

"You have to be courageous about your instincts and your ideas. Otherwise, you'll just knuckle under, and things that might have been memorable will be lost."

FRANCIS FORD COPPOLA[40]

It isn't how educated you are, or how fantastic your ideas are which create a tremendous life, although you may think this is the source of building success. It is your everyday habits that control your destiny.

So, the most important habit you can develop is to find joy in everything you do. If you do this, you will be energized, and your creativity will soar. Through this simple habit, your life will get better and better.

When you are doing what you love or doing things that are challenging to you with the right attitude, you feel good. It is when you feel connected to life that you become more productive and focused on doing things that empower you. This is the foundation for your success.

Today ask

"How will I start my day? Will it be with gratitude in my heart, prayer, meditation, nurturing foods and exercise?"

"What will I accomplish today that I have not accomplished up to this point?"

"At the end of my day, what empowering thoughts will I be telling myself?"

Actions

Pick one new success habit and make it your priority for the next fourteen days.

Day 77

"Everyone has talent. What's rare is the courage to follow it into the dark places where it leads."

ERICA JONG[41]

Today is all about action! It is time to wake up the power within you and bring about some overdue changes. Nothing is stopping you from taking steps that will bring more joy, fulfillment, and abundance into your life but you.

I have seen in my own life the many seemingly relentless obstacles that are put into my life by me. Not someone else, it is I (the ego) who creates these, and it is I (the soul) that overcomes them. Can you relate to this? If so, it is imperative to bring in more awareness of what you are generating in your life that is stopping your success.

Think about what changes you will make to achieve your greatest dreams. Ask: *"What tendencies do I have that stop my success?"* By identifying tendencies like procrastination, overwhelm, over-commitment, under-commitment, apathy or any other trend that is stopping your success, and making a commitment to let go of it, your life will change for the better.

By the way, when you let go of a tendency, all the beliefs that have been supporting it will also collapse, and you will be in a higher state of success, isn't that exciting to know?

Today ask

"Would an infinite being have any problem letting go of negative tendencies?"

"What is the most important change I can make in my life today?"

"What actions will I take today that will maximize my success?"

Actions

Commit to taking two new steps daily which will change your destiny.

Day 78

"Real courage is doing the right thing when nobody's looking."

JUSTIN CRONIN[42]

Wouldn't you like to smile much more? You can! Start by asking this question. What do you believe people who smile a lot focus on? I can tell you. They focus on what makes them happy.

They look for the good in every person and circumstance. They find the lemonade when they are given lemons in life. They have given up the notions of critical thinking and focus on what it the highest and best in each situation.

People who are truly happy and smile often are a unique bunch of people. They are committed to being happy no matter what comes along. Wherever you find them, they have one thing in common. They are making a difference big or small each day. They look for opportunities to help others put a smile on their faces and they contribute to making the world a little better for all.

Saint Thomas of Aquinas was asked at the end of his life how he loved so much. He said, "I willed it." You too can use the power of your dynamic will to smile much more. It's easy, just put a smile on your face and see how many people you can make smile today.

Today ask

"What am I willing to be more aware of so that I can smile more often?"

"What has to happen for me to smile more?"

"How can I use my will to create greater love and wealth in my life?"

Actions

Make a list of what you will use your willpower to generate.

Day 79

*"Making mistakes is part of life, but it takes courage
to stop repeating habitual acts and do what it takes
to mold your life into an amazing success story."*

KEN D FOSTER

The energy that we use to create joy and happiness is the same energy we use to create disappointment and failure. It doesn't matter if you are active doing things that lead to success or failure; since you alone choose how to use your energy, you alone will decide your fate.

There are always opportunities for success, but we must increase our awareness, if we are to see them. Most people consistently judge what is right, wrong, good or bad in each situation which can shut down their awareness, limits their thinking, and drain their energy. Instead of thinking in finite terms, practice thinking in terms of what is possible.

Imagine suspending your judgments for a day. Think about how much more energy would you have. What could show up for you different? If you short circuited the power to your home, your lights, television, washing machine and anything else electric would stop working. Judgmental thoughts to the same, they short circuit your power.

Why don't you try letting go of making yourself or anyone else wrong and just imagine what is possible for you each day. Start your day out imagining how much joy, love and productivity you will generate. This is the path to success.

Today ask

"Is my life getting better and better, or do I need to make adjustments?"

"What have I been judging that is blocking my energy?"

"Am I happy with how I show up or is there need for improvement?"

Actions

Take some time to step back from your life and notice the direction you are going.

Day 80

Have you ever wondered; "What is the point of being successful if you are stressed out all the time?" So many people sacrifice their inner joy for outer striving. They strive for one desire after another only to find themselves miserably busy at the end of the journey.

It doesn't have to be this way even amid success. Although you cannot buy peace, you can cultivate it by quieting your mind with daily meditation, contemplation, and introspection. Today, after meditation, resolve never to lose your inner peace. Keep a chamber of silence within you no matter what is happening.

Don't let moods, challenges, trials or battles defeat you. You are more powerful than any of your problems, and you can remain peaceful no matter what happens. Keep in mind, what most upsets you the most is most likely the belief that you won't get what you want, or you will lose what you have.

Today ask

"What is possible for an infinite creative being like myself?"

"When I am at peace, how much more clearly do I think?"

"How can I generate more peace today?"

Actions

Challenge yourself to only focus on peaceful thoughts today.

Tap into your higher-self and increase your intuition with Ken D Foster's guided meditations on Business, Wealth, Expanding Possibility, Peace, and Health. Yours for free at couragetochange.us/meditation

Day 81

"Courage is the atom of change."

BETTINA R. FLORES[44]

Have you cleaned up your environment yet? Neatness is a success law. Whenever I visit a highly productive entrepreneur's office, one of the first things I notice is simplicity and order. There is a sense of peace and tranquility that comes with order, not to mention harmony with the universe.

Would you like to have that in your life daily? It is simple to achieve because it starts from the inside out! Commit to simplify and clean all the clutter out of your life.

Then become determined to bring more harmony into your life and do what you need to do daily: balance your checkbook, tidy your home, file your paperwork, organize your office, clean or complete any unfinished projects that have been weighing on your mind.

You will find that by doing consistent actions to clean up the clutter daily, within a few weeks or even days, you will be living in a more harmonious environment and have some much more energy.

Affirm what you would like to have, saying: *"I am one with harmony. It permeates every particle of my being. I reflect harmony in everything I think, do and say".*

Today ask

"What does the harmony I choose to have for my life look like?"

"What are the most important steps I can take to bridge the gap from chaos to harmony?"

"How can I reflect harmony in all areas of my life?"

Actions

Pick an area of your home or office and clean it up within twenty-four hours.

Day 82

"The most courageous people don't look for someone to open doors for them;they look for doors to open for others."

KEN D FOSTER

Today is a fantastic day not only to take care of your welfare but to find others and give them some of your wisdom, love and money. As you probably realize, what you give unconditionally to others seems to come back to you in many plentiful ways.

There is nothing in this universe that goes unnoticed. In fact, you can break the mold of failure if you consistently give away your gifts, talents and abilities. Why? Because through the laws of karma (cause and effect) you are continually reaping your rewards. The more you give the more you receive.

I have practiced this formula in my Coaching Business for many years. I don't charge an initial fee for those I feel called to support. I give them all I have to offer. Some eventually work with me and others don't but, either way, I am always giving my gifts, talents, skills and love away. It always comes back in many ways, which creates abundance and richness in my life.

Today ask

"What can I do that will help others improve their life?"

"What is possible for my family and friends if I increase my contribution to their lives?"

"How would my business benefit if I developed a plan to contribute more to my customers?"

Actions

Do you believe that giving to others is giving to yourself? If there are any doubts make a list of these thoughts, then make a conscious choice that you will not be limited by these thoughts. Note: (Increased wealth can happen for you if you will make the effort by freely giving away what you would like in your own life).

Day 83

"Your time is limited, so don't waste it living someone else's life. Don't be trapped by dogma—which is living with the results of other people's thinking. Don't let the noise of others' opinions drown out your own inner voice. And most importantly, have the courage to follow your heart and intuition. They somehow already know what you truly want to become. Everything else is secondary."

STEVE JOBS[45]

Making money is easy, but finding happiness while you are making money is an art. Many people achieve substantial monetary success, yet they are miserable. They are ever striving for more, but rarely do they unconditionally share what they have accomplished with others.

It is only by taking ambition and topping it with service to others or by working for a great cause that true happiness can be found. If you want to be fulfilled in life, then find out what makes you happy and serve others. In other words, you must give away your brilliance, talents, gifts and skills to others for you to have lasting happiness.

We are all linked together so whenever you are helping others you are helping yourself. It seems kind of selfish, but it's by giving away what you have that you become all you can be, and in the process, you will find true happiness and wealth.

Today ask

"What truly makes me happy?"

"What are my greatest talents that I can share with others to help them?"

"How can I stay happy while making money to support myself?"

Actions

Find one person to help advance their greatest dreams.

Day 84

*"The bravest are surely those who have the clearest
vision of what is before them, glory and danger alike,
and yet notwithstanding, go out to meet it."*

THUCYDIDES[46]

Do you realize that life is not meant to be lived in stress, uncertainty and overwhelm? Of course, you do! It is to be lived in peace, faith, and ongoing happiness.

This doesn't mean you won't have challenges along the way, because without them how would you ever grow? But it does say you can handle them with a calm mind knowing you have the resources to overcome whatever comes your way.

I have found that when we look within to find the source of our happiness, outer stresses seem to fade away like wetness in the sunshine. Happiness is a symptom of living a courageous and harmonious life, but harmony can't exist simultaneously with stress and chaos. So, you get to choose what side you want to live on when challenges come your way—the side of courage and harmony, or the side of stress and chaos.

Try taking some time to slow down and become aware of your thoughts. Then affirm everything is perfect in this moment. Let all the stressors fade from your mind as you claim again and again everything is perfect in this moment. It is the ideal moment to create harmony. It is the perfect moment to learn and grow.

When you know that you are being supported in every moment of the day and when you realize that there is nothing that has come your way that has not been placed there to help your evolution, life becomes more comfortable.

Today ask

"What is possible if I allow peace to shine through me in every moment?"

"How can I be more harmonious in my business?"

"What will help me to remember that everything is showing up perfectly to support me in every way?"

Actions

Take three actions steps to bring more peace into your life.

Day 85

"Courageous people take the time to tune in and then turn out consistent wise choices for the good of all concerned."

KEN D FOSTER

When I was young, all I did was play. I went from one thing to the next, enjoying my life and loving every moment. Then, I decided that just playing wasn't enough. I wanted more things to play with! I decided I would get a job so that I could make money to get more things.

So, I go the job and bought a hot car. But then the car wasn't enough, I wanted someone to drive with me, so I found a girlfriend. But she wasn't enough, so I decided I wanted more. I wanted a wife, so I found a wife. And then I wanted more, so I thought I would buy a house.

Then I wasn't satisfied with just the house, I wanted beautiful things to go in the house. Then I wanted children. Then I wanted to travel but then I had all these bills and I was stressed out and my health started to fail, so then I just wanted peace and my health back. Finally, I saw the folly of my ways and chose to invite happiness and joy back into my life and guess what showed up? I simplified my life and began to play again.

Has your life been on the treadmill of wanting, wanting and wanting more? Are you sick and tired of chasing your dreams rather than living them? If so then make a resolution today to be free. Define what real freedom means to you and then start on a quest to make it happen.

Today ask

"Where have I been unwilling to enjoy my life?"

"What must happen to bring more joy and play into my life?"

"What are three steps I can take today to simplify my life and play more?"

Actions

Determine where you are resistant to enjoying your life more

Day 86

"It takes more courage to reveal insecurities than to hide them, more strength to relate to people than to dominate them, more 'manhood' to abide by thought-out principles rather than blind reflex. Toughness is in the soul and spirit, not in muscles and an immature mind."

ALEX KARRAS[47]

In a general sense, people who are contributors are the biggest winners in life, but those who give too much of themselves find that they have no time to take care of their business.

Many people give to get attention, or give to please people, or they give to distract themselves from doing what they need to do for themselves. This type of giving eventually leads to an overstressed and an under-accomplished existence. If you are a business owner with these qualities, I dare say you are most likely on a sinking ship.

When giving gets out of balance, over-givers seem to attract takers. They find themselves surrounded by these people who will take all they offer and then some. The more they give, the more others take advantage.

Giving is an excellent quality to have but you must have reasonable boundaries and take time to provide yourself with downtime, quiet time, meditative time, planning time, exercise time and play time. In other words, tithe to yourself first and then you will have reserves of wisdom, energy and everything else you need to contribute to others.

Today ask

"How much time will I consistently schedule on my calendar to properly charge my batteries, before I start giving to the world?"

"What am I now willing to receive about myself, that if I were willing to receive this, I would stop looking for others to fulfill it for me?"

"Where has my giving been taken advantage of and what am I willing to do now to stop it?"

Actions

Think of a new personal boundary you will put in place.

Day 87

*"Dwelling on the past deflates courage
and numbs the creative spirit."*

KEN D FOSTER

All that you have acquired over the years will someday disappear but all that you have become will be yours to keep forever. The best gifts we can give ourselves cannot be purchased because they are gifts of the soul. They must be developed through consistent actions to create daily success habits.

Any habit can be formed for good or naught by taking consistent actions. By doing this, it forms neural pathways in the brain. Old negative habits can be broken, and new ones formed in just a few days. It only takes a willingness to change.

Years ago, I decided to start running for exercise. I hadn't run in ten years because I had a knee injury that was still painful. Over the years, I had bought into a lot of people's opinions that running put a lot of pressure on your joints and was a bad idea for me to run. These were not runners giving me this advice, these we "rocking chair experts," and I bought into their ideas.

About this time, I ran across a person who told me that not only could I run but that if I could move the pain in my knee even a millimeter, I could move it out of my body. So, I committed to 21 days of running and the possibility that I could move the knee pain out.

The results were astounding, not only did I become a runner and have run 3 to 10 miles a day for the last 19 years, the pain disappeared. Because of finding my courage and forming a success habit of running, my life became much richer.

Today ask

"What new habit will I form starting today?"

"If I commit to never giving up until I realize this new habit how will my life be richer?"

"Who will I become by implementing this new habit?"

Actions

Find a book or article that will support you in developing a new habit.

Day 88

*"Courage brings a spring to your step and a smile on your
face evenwhen everything appears to be falling apart."*

KEN D FOSTER

Everyone has good times and difficult times. Have you ever complained to someone when things are not going your way, only to find your friend compounds your misery by telling you about their problems or, worse, they decide to judge you and fix you? Pretty soon, you are so immersed in the limitations of what is wrong that you forget what you can create.

Remember, the moment you go into critical judgment, you stop the endless flow of abundance. I mention critical judgment because while noticing what is not working or getting positive feedback on what needs to change is essential, negative mind chatter stops the flow of success.

I have noticed that most children under seven years old can completely change their state of being within three minutes. They can be crying and whining one moment, and almost instantly they can shift their state and be smiling and playing. How would your life be different if you could shift your states that quickly and live moment to moment?

You can! Just make a point to let go of any emotional upset within three minutes. It may take a while to accomplish this goal, but imagine the benefits over a lifetime.

Today ask

"What is possible for me when I let go of emotions within three minutes?"

"How can I be ever aware of the infinite joy and abundance that surround me?"

"What do I have to know, without a doubt, to be victorious in letting go of my emotions within three minutes?"

Actions

Practice letting of your emotional states within three minutes.

Day 89

*"Courageous people create a wake of
inspiration for others to follow."*

KEN D FOSTER

Are you surrounding yourself with amazing people who support and encourage you in all areas of life? We are constantly influenced by those around us. We all pick up other people's moods, thoughts and points of view. But you must be stronger than other people's vibrations and points of view if you want to succeed.

Have you ever walked into a room after two people were arguing and felt the negative energy? And have you been in situations where you took on someone's negativity? It wasn't your stuff, but you walked away feeling downbeat and heavy because you took it on and lived as though it was real.

If you want to stop this from happening, I will give you an insight I received from Anthony Robbins when I was working with him: The person who is feeling more certain about his state of being is the one who will influence the other person to move toward that feeling.

In other words, if you set your intention that no one is going to upset your happiness, no one can, because other people's thoughts are just their point of view. Your point of view, as an infinite being, is that you are stronger than anyone else's point of view and you are choosing to remain happy. Get it! Your point of view will create your reality.

Today ask

"Whose point of view am I choosing to remain in harmony with?"

"What am I choosing to feel consistently today?"

"What can I do to remain calm in the face of other people's upsets?"

Actions

Set you intention to make this the happiest day you have had in the last month. Watch your thoughts and realize you can be happy no matter what happens.

Day 90

*"Courage is vulnerability. Vulnerability is courage. Like
shadow and light, neither one can exist without the other."*

WAI LAN YUEN[48]

Happiness is the natural state of being, and if you are unhappy, you most likely have forgotten that you have the power to be happy all the time.

No one can make you unhappy if you make up your mind that you will not let anyone take away your happiness. If you don't believe this, don't take my word for it, try it! You will soon see you have the power to be joyful all the time.

But are you ready to be happy all the time or are you stuck in a pattern of remembering past hurts or hanging out with people that remind you of how limited you are? With this going on, you will only be as happy as your saddest memory, but that is no way for an infinite being to live and you can change that today.

Unhappy people live with sad stories and limited choices. They live in ignorance of their power to change and move on. They focus on thoughts of loss from the past, and believe a bright future is impossible for them to achieve.

Focusing on these types of thought will disempower anyone. The truth is many options can be tapped into by asking questions to redirect your mind and focus on the infinite possibilities that are available to everyone.

Today ask

"How can I learn to be happy and content all the time?"

"What books can I realize to increase my happiness?"

"What stories can I let go of that will immediately grow my happiness?"

Actions

Contemplate an area of your life that seems to impact your happiness. Note: (If you don't evolve your happiness, you'll eventually evaporate the joy in your life).

Day 91

*"Courage propagates life-force energy surging through the body
ever lifting us upward toward the greater good."*

KEN D FOSTER

Many spiritual teachers promote living a simple life, but living a simple life does not mean living in poverty-consciousness. It means living a balanced life by being self-controlled.

When you are focused on doing too many things, life can get very challenging. You may find yourself in overwhelm and worn out. This is no way to go through life! By balancing your time with quiet moments of self-reflection, time doing things that enliven the spirit, you will find peace, happiness, and ongoing success.

Spending time and money on things that you do not need is also foolish, even when you have the means to do so. It is a sign of weakness. Why do things that bring temporary pleasure, but long-term emptiness? It is better to forsake the immediate gratification for the long-term satisfaction.

It requires a strong will and masterful mind to live simply. It also takes wisdom to be content with what you have, instead of continually chasing what you think you need. Practice self-control, and do not live beyond your means.

Today ask

"How can I simplify my life?"

"What can let go of that will empower me?"

"What can I do less of that will enrich my life?"

Actions

Determine one goal which will help you have more harmony in your home and business.

Tap into your higher-self and increase your intuition with Ken D Foster's guided meditations on Business, Wealth, Expanding Possibility, Peace, and Health. Yours for free at couragetochange.us/meditation

CHAPTER 5

INSPIRING PASSION

Day 92

"If you have not the courage to step past what you think is possible, you will never experience the magic in life."

KEN D FOSTER

Do you love what you are doing? If you do not love what you are doing, why are you doing it? Life is not a dress rehearsal. Why not do the things you love now?

So many people get caught up in doing things they think they "should do" instead of doing things that bring fire to their soul. This is no way to live because if you continue doing the infinite amount of "shoulds" that come your way, one day you will wake up stressed out, angry, empty, and unfulfilled.

So, why not start today and become aware of what you would really like to be doing and then start doing it. Why not bring forth your greatest talents, gifts, and abilities for an amazing professional and personal life? Is it possible that within you is the power to generate an extraordinary life? Of course! It is evidenced by all the great men and women that have ever lived. They utilized their potential, and so can you!

Today ask

"How can something greater than I can imagine show up for me?"

"What can I do to leverage my strengths?"

"Where can I blow through the limitations that I have set up?"

Actions

Try taking a new approach and focus your mind in the direction of what you love to do. Then take two steps in the direction of creating an amazing life. This is sure bring out the genius in you!

Day 93

"The two hardest tests on the spiritual road are the patience to wait for the right moment and the courage not to be disappointed with what we encounter."

PAULO COELHO[49]

Everyone has a "calling" to be all they can be and bring forth their amazing selves. It is your job to find yours because your "calling" is what will evolve you and your life. It is the doorway to your infinite spirit and ongoing success.

You can start your march toward freedom right from where you are today by finding your "calling." I encourage you to start by asking three questions: "What am I doing that I truly do not want to be doing?" "What am I being called to do differently?" and "If I were fearless, (that is, unrestrained) what would I be accomplishing in my life?"

Knowing what you don't want to do is just as important as knowing what you want to do. Doing what you don't want to do on a consistent basis is a way to get caught up in "victim-mode." Thinking that you have no choice is no way to live.

To be truly successful it is important to find the path that leads to fulfilment and joy. This is what will expand your brilliance. The great unspoken truth is "as you expand your spirit you will find your calling.

Today ask

"What fills my spirit and brings me joy?"

"What am I not getting about myself that, when I do, will inspire greatness?"

"What am I committed to doing consistently, so I tune into my spirit?"

Actions

Take some time to still your mind and contemplate the above questions and then take three action steps which reflect your greatness.

Day 94

"One need not live like a victim of fate, as long as
one has the courage to overcome limited thinking
by never giving up on their dreams."

KEN D FOSTER

Are you in tune with being all you can be? I see people rushing from one task to the next without any real understanding of how powerful they are, nor how their choices are impacting their lives. Many times these people are in overwhelm running at lightening speed and often changing careers, friends, cars and houses, but in reality their lives stay much the same.

They have lost sight of their life purpose. Don't do that! Otherwise, you will create your life from the place that most people do: The confining thoughts and habits of the past that limit your Wisdom-Self.

Wouldn't you rather be creating your dreams from the infinite opportunities that are available to you? And wouldn't you like to evolve, change, develop and grow?

So, would you an infinite being, lack anything if you started asking infinite, powerful, positive, possibility questions that would be answered by the Universe? No way! Then why have a lack of anything? Why not start today on a new journey by allowing the Universe to work for you?

Today ask

"Where have I stopped myself from being all I can be?"

"What can I do to let go of any limitations I have placed on myself?"

"What will it take to receive increased prosperity into my life?"

Actions

Spend time tuning into where you have limited yourself. Notice: the jobs you are doing, the people you are surrounding yourself with and the ways you show up. Then resolve to change whatever is not working for you. Remember: This isn't a "pity party" exercise, you are doing this so you can improve.

Day 95

*"Those who lack the courage will always
find a philosophy to justify it."*

ALBERT CAMUS[50]

What is your major aim in life? In other words, when you come to the end of this lifetime, what will it have all been for?

Most people go through life with little sense of the direction as to how their life will turn out. This is problematic because if you don't know where you are going, most likely you won't get there; you will just drift with the whims of circumstances and wake up someday wondering, "What happened?"

But this isn't the way to find fulfillment in life! If you drive from New York to Chicago, most likely you would use a GPS. Navigation, is the key to success.

Know where you are going and what you want out of life. If you want to be fulfilled, then decide on your direction and navigate with continual realizations, improvements, and evolution of soulful wisdom.

This can happen for you through continued questioning of how things are working and deciding where you would like to improve, change, grow or evolve daily. If you follow this formula, one day you will wake up fulfilled in every area of your life.

Today ask

"Who have I become at the end of my life?"

"In what areas of my life have I evolved and changed for the better?"

"What was my life all about?"

Actions

Spend some time with these questions and see if by answering them you can set a true course for the rest of your life. Note: (You don't have to go into massive detail over this. Just come up with a general theme about what you would like to accomplish, and what values you would like to live from. Then map out your life course).

Day 96

*"All our dreams can come true, if we have
the courage to pursue them."*

WALT DISNEY[51]

Endurance combined with commitment is a powerful combination that leads to ongoing success. Without this combination, any good endeavor has no chance of lasting success. But how do we endure and commit if we don't believe in what we are doing?

The answer is we don't, so the first step in creating lasting success each day is to make sure you are aligned with your dreams. To draw yourself into your future, you need to see straight into your soul and connect deeply with your deepest desires.

When you align with your dreams, you will be inspired to create them. You will wake up and want to do what it takes to make them come true. Just wanting them to come true is where a lot of people believe the process stops but that is inaccurate.

You must also be determined to go all the way no matter what obstacles come. Why? Because this is where you grow and become all you need to become to make your future come true.

Why live an uncontrolled existence, blowing willy-nilly through life by the vagarious winds of time? Why not take charge of your fate by using your inner strength to bring forth your power, and make your life yield what it should?

Today ask

"What are two dreams that I have put on hold?"

"How will my life improve as I remember my infinite self and accomplishing my

 dreams?"

"What are three steps I can take today to generate my dreams?"

Actions

Take two courageous action steps toward a dream you have put on hold.

Day 97

Inspiration is the path that leads to greatness, but many people are uninspired and looking for people, places or things outside of themselves to inspire them. This is not where inspiration is founded. It is an inside job!

Inspiration is a gift that we give ourselves when we connect with our higher selves because it opens the doors to our creativity. It's a state of mind where limitations vanish, and everything becomes possible, and there is a broad sense of peace or oneness with the soul.

So how is this accomplished? By slowing down and reconnecting with yourself, your dreams, and the magnificence of who you are. It can also happen quickly by asking inspiring questions or by sitting still for a few minutes and contemplating what inspires you.

Today ask

"What inspires me?"

"What motivates me to be all I can be?"

"What commitment can I make that will open the doors of my creativity and expand my business and life?"

Actions

Take a courageous action towards what inspires you.

Day 98

"We must substitute courage for caution."

MARTIN LUTHER KING JR.[52]

What are you devoted to? Are you devoted to your family, friends, business or spiritual success? Have you noticed that whatever you are devoted to seems to get better and better and what you are not devoted to seems just to stagnate?

I have found that devotion is the key to success and it goes hand in hand with commitment. It takes a commitment to increase your devotion because there are always success stoppers waiting to derail your devotion. So, use the success stoppers to strengthen your resolve to overcome them.

Do you know any successful entrepreneurs who are not devoted to their business? I don't, and I don't know any long-term, happy marriages where both partners are not devoted to each other.

Nor do I know of any scientists, doctors, lawyers, ministers or any other professional who are successful that are not devoted to their practice. Devotion is the key to long-term success, and without it failure is certain.

Today ask

"What am I devoted to?"

"Why am I increasing my devotion?

"What can I do to become even more devoted to my business and life?"

Actions

List three areas of your life that you will commit to increasing your devotion.

Day 99

"I have found the most courageous people on the planet are those who give of themselves to others in unexpected ways."

KEN D FOSTER

Success happens quicker when you are in service to others. Many would argue that this is the wrong area to focus on when building a business or a life, but if you think about it logically, it makes perfect sense.

When you know what your customers, friends, or family want, and you can help them achieve it. Doesn't that inspire them to want to be around you more? Sure, it does!

A big mistake people make is focusing on what they want rather than concentrating on being of service and helping others get what they want. Service is the key to success that many people just miss.

I once created a mastermind group filled with takers. They all showed up trying to get contacts, ideas, and support from each other without contributing back. The result was a valuable life lesson.

I noticed that I had no desire to meet with the group. Then the light bulb went on! I then asked the group to show up each week with ways we could give to each other. A few people dropped out, but those who stayed were empowered, and everyone benefited.

Today ask

"Where am I being called to serve in a greater way?"

"In what ways will I increase my service to others?"

"Who are three people I can be of service to which will grow our relationship?"

Actions

Notice how you feel when you give unconditionally.

Day 100

"We are not weak if we make a proper use of those means which the God of Nature has placed in our power. The battle, sir, is not to the strong alone; it is to the vigilant, the active, and the brave."

PATRICK HENRY[53]

Rid your thoughts of limited thinking and realize that you were made in the image of your creator with the power to reach for the stars. No matter where you have come from, huge things can happen for you. The only thing that stops you from having the life of your dreams is your limiting and judgmental thoughts.

Have you ever thought that things are just too tough? Or that things will not work out for you? Cast out those limiting thoughts and make up your mind to succeed.

Be determined to remold your consciousness and ask questions such as: "What has to happen for me to know that I have what it takes to create a wonderful life?"

Today ask

"As an infinite being, why is my life getting better and better?"

"What is right about what I have made wrong about my life?"

"What brilliance is flowing through me right now?"

Actions

Choose thoughts that support you in knowing things are getting better and better. Then watch your thoughts carefully and if you slip into any sort of negative thinking ask some empowering questions. Note: (It may be tough to ask questions each time you slip into negativity, but soon you will be programming your mind for success. Remember, live life in the question, not from you having all the answers!

Day 101

"We must have courage to bet on our ideas, to take the calculated risk, and to act. Everyday living requires courage if life is to be effective and bring happiness."

MAXWELL MALTZ[54]

Success is more than money in the bank, nice cars and a big home. True success brings the joys of health, happiness and fulfillment. An important question to ask is: "What is the blessing that I bring to the world?" Based on the answer to that question you may also ask: "What is the legacy I will leave?"

We all have gifts and talents, but if we keep those to ourselves, we will most likely miss the joyful adventures that life offers. I have seen many people who, despite apparent handicaps and would-be limitations, make up their minds to succeed and accomplish amazing feats. They are driven by a sense of purpose to be the best they can be.

True success is waiting for you to find your purpose and do whatever it takes to step into your greatness. Finding your life purpose is a deep question that we all must answer for ourselves. But by doing so, you will find meaning and fulfillment in your life.

Today ask

"What am I being called to do differently?"

"What would I like to accomplish which will give my life more meaning?"

"How can I deliver my gifts to the world?"

Actions

Explore your life purpose and make a list of what you think it could be. Note: (it is important to connect with your soul and passionate dreams because life is a soulful journey.

Day 102

Did you know that death is your friend? Death teaches us that everything is temporary in this world. It helps us not to be attached to people, places or things. It clarifies that it is truly important to live from faith, courage and love. If you would like to have a richer and simpler life, try living like you are dying.

Imagine that you have thirty days to live. How would you show up each day? Would you be worried about the future? Would you complain about others? Would you be upset when things didn't go your way? Would you keep yourself in overwhelm? Or would you live life to the fullest and have blissful, orgasmic experiences every day doing what you love to do?

Most likely, you would appreciate what you have in your life and simplify the activities that you do daily. You would probably complete what you felt strongly about, and you would let go of those things which are unimportant.

You would also most likely spend time with those who are close to you, and not persist in being busy all the time. Life would be richer because each moment would be precious to you.

Today ask

"If I had thirty days to live, how would I design my life?"

"What will bring more bliss into my life over the next thirty days?"

"How can my life become the glorious life I was meant to live?"

Actions

Decide what you stand for and what is important to you right now. Then take the steps to simplify your life, so that each day you can live like you are dying, and experience much more fulfillment and joy.

Day 103

*"There is no one obstructing your success but you, so
find the courage to overcome your small self and tap
into the unlimited power of your soulful self."*

KEN D FOSTER

It isn't so much the big things you do that determine your success, but the small and daily consistent actions that you take with the right attitude. The performance of small tasks builds strength and discipline that is needed to create the big dreams, right?

So, try doing the small things you don't want to do first! "Do the worst first," as my friend Paul Freedman would say to me.

It is foolish to expect that you can obtain everything you want by only doing the things you want to do. The wise person finds as much joy doing the things they don't want to do as in the things they love to do, because they are aware that joy is where the power of creation sits.

Yes, creativity follows a peaceful, joyful mind!

Today ask

"How can I be more joyful every day?"

"What has to happen for me to be the energy of joy?"

"What is possible for me if I choose to live in joy daily?"

Actions

Right now, put a smile on your face and see how you feel. Do you feel your state of mind change? Does it feel lighter, maybe happier? Try bringing your consciousness to your lips and smiling more. Then, watch your day become brighter and brighter, filled with joyful energy and creativity flowing through you.

Day 104

"Without courage, wisdom bears no fruit."

BALTASAR GRACIAN[56]

Is the pursuit of happiness the highest goal for mankind? I believe it is a high goal, but I am also aware that there is something higher, and that is called self-realization—the foundation of enduring success.

As you realize who you truly are by connecting deeply with your soul, you will start to bring your greatest talents, abilities and gifts into the world. You will become aware of yourself as an infinite being connected to every person, place, animal, and things in this universe. And you will know at the core of your being that you can make a difference and contribute to making this world a better place.

In other words, as you evolve the wisdom starts flowing, the joy starts growing, and you will begin to know who you are and what is truly important in your life.

Today ask

"What will it take for me to expand my awareness and contribute more?"

"How will I evolve and become a magnet for conscious success?"

"Being the infinite spirit that I am, what am I choosing to bring more awareness about?"

Actions

Contemplate what areas of your life you would like to evolve. And then when the insights come, take three steps toward evolving your life.

Tap into your higher-self and increase your intuition with Ken D Foster's guided meditations on Business, Wealth, Expanding Possibility, Peace, and Health. Yours for free at couragetochange.us/meditation

Day 105

"If you listen to your fears, you will die never knowing what a great person you might have been."

ROBERT H. SCHULLER[57]

Are you caught up in the success game? Are you chasing success only to be disillusioned time and time again? You have success in one area of your business or life, and then things change for the worse in another area, so you try to fix that area then things stop working in the area that you were having success.

On and on it goes and where it stops no one seems to know. It may seem like you can never win, and you are right. It is not wise to chase success only for the sake of success. It is like trying to make money for money's sake; it is an empty game. In the end, you may have some success or money, but little else.

You will most likely feel an emptiness inside which can only be filled by getting off the success train and getting into the game of bringing out your greatest gifts, talents, and abilities and doing what you were born to do.

Real success comes when we make a concerted effort to realize the mental, spiritual and physical laws of success that govern our lives and everything in it. In this world of relativity even what appears to be true one day can be gone the next day.

There are lots of illusions, but illusions do disappear when we can see reality clearly. And the only way to do that is to seek the truth behind the illusions.

Today ask

"How did I become the person that I am?"

"What do I consistently think that creates the world I live in?"

"What actions can I take which will bring out my greatest gifts, talents, and abilities?"

Actions

As you ask the questions above, ask from a place of knowing that what you ask for will be revealed to you!

Day 106

*"It is curious that physical courage should be so common
in the world and moral courage so rare."*

MARK TWAIN[58]

Have you given some thought lately as to who you are and what you stand for? Are you a person of high conviction or do you have double standards? These are questions every successful leader eventually asks!

Many people apply their standards to others but neglect to use the same criteria for themselves. I see this time and time again where a leader sets one standard for their subordinates and lives by another. The same shows up with parents who tell their children to live one way while doing just the opposite.

Double standards are what being out of integrity is all about. How can anyone be in integrity if they don't walk their talk? Now, this is not an easy thing to do always, but it's not about being perfect, it is about setting a standard and doing your best to live up to it.

If you get off track, then reset the standard and start over again and again until it becomes a part of who you are. This is the way to build a successful and fulfilling life which is beaming with lasting friendships, wealth, health, and happiness.

Today ask

"What are my greatest convictions?"

"Do these convictions align with my values?"

"Where do I need to set higher standards?"

Actions

Make a list of what you stand for and see if it aligns with what you are doing.

Day 107

Gratitude is one of the most empowering forces in the universe. It fills our hearts with joy and essentially lifts our consciousness to a state of appreciation. Without it, you will be destined to live a dull existence without the life-force of a healthy spirit.

It is gratitude that makes our hearts sing and uplifts the spirit. It empowers us to live a life filled with grace, and delivers the promise of a joyful existence. Gratitude will get you where you want to go! Why?

Because with gratitude you can immediately shape-shift your mind into a positive state. And when you are in an affirmative state you will make better decisions, plus have more energy to accomplish your goals.

Today ask

"What am I truly grateful for?"

"How can I increase my gratitude?"

"What can I do to remember to be in gratitude every day?"

Actions

Make a list of five things that you are grateful for, and then also choose two steps that will have a positive impact on your life. Note: (If you would like to increase the gratitude experience, even more, find someone whom you can serve unconditionally. There is nothing in the world more powerful than gratitude combined with service).

Day 108

*It takes great courage to expand our love when
others have not been kind, and yet it is love
that is needed in these circumstances."*

KEN D FOSTER

Love is the key to living a happy and prosperous life. And only you can turn the key to your heart's desire. Yes, love is a choice, and the decision is yours. To feel more love or not, this is the question for today.

When most people think of love, they think of family, friends, places or things they enjoy, this is human love, but there is more profound love. It is love within every heart and soul on the planet. It is a love that longs for peace, oneness, and connection.

And we all have the choice to tune in and expand our love, or pretend it is gone and shut it down. But if we choose to extend our love, we become magnets to love, and our businesses and lives get better.

I once gave an assignment to a client to expand her love for seven days. She told me what happened was astounding. Conflicts with her family disappeared, her business picked up, and little children started coming up to her in the marketplace just wanting to touch her and be with her.

This is the power of love that awaits us all. When you choose to love, love chooses you. As Mother Teresa said: "It's not what you do that is so important; it's how much love you put into the doing."

Today ask

"How can I increase my love for everyone?"

"Who can I love more?"

"Where can I bring more love into life?"

Actions

Deeply contemplate the areas of your life you could choose to bring more love in and take one action step toward it today. Then make an effort every hour to check in and see how much love you are feeling.

Day 109

*"Courage helps us let go and suspend belief so that the
impossible can become possible."*

KEN D FOSTER

Children laugh between two and four hundred times a day; most adults laugh fifteen to twenty times a day. Do you wonder why? It is because most adults have forgotten who they are, and how much joy resides within them.

They make life a struggle and take it way too seriously. Instead of laughing at their mistakes or the mistakes of others, they turn them into judgments, criticisms, or something negative.

But this isn't how to approach mistakes. Challenges are there to strengthen and enlighten us. Errors are of the same nature. Don't let your mistakes take away your happiness.

Remember what a fantastic being you are. Remember that you are learning and growing. Be kind to yourself. Be easy on yourself.

You can have consistent happiness if you prepare each day. Upon waking, decide to be happy no matter what comes your way. No one can take away your joy unless you give them the power to do so.

Also, decide how you will give happiness to others and give it unconditionally; because when you can give unconditionally and let go of any expectations, happiness flows your way too.

Today ask

"What can I do to increase laughter in my life?"

"What am I taking too seriously that, if I lightened up, could enable me to find more happiness?"

"Who can I bring happiness to?"

Actions

Keep track of how many times you laugh today, then set a goal to increase that number over the next week.

CHAPTER 6

DREAM BIG DREAMS

Day 110

*"Have courage for the great sorrows of life and patience for
the small ones; and when you have laboriously accomplished
your daily task, go to sleep in peace. God is awake."*

VICTOR HUGO[60]

We do not become wise or successful by dwelling on the past, but by knowing who
we are, in the moment. If you are consistently identifying yourself with what you
have accomplished in the past, you are most likely missing what you are capable of
in the future.

So, what are you focused on? Is it leading you to the future that you want to build,
or just distracting you from creating your dreams? Steve Jobs, the co-founder of
Apple asked himself a life-defining question daily: "If today were the last day of my
life, would I want to do what I am about to do today?"

As you answer this question for yourself, determine what you really what you want
to be doing and do it! Remember, the future is created in the present moment.
Decide what your future will look like and generate it with the consistent actions
you take moment by moment.

Today ask

"What is the vision of the brightest future I can imagine?"

"What has to happen for me to start creating an amazing future?"

"How can I empower myself to take daily actions toward my greatest dreams?"

Actions

Take some time to meditate and then tune into your future and define what you
truly want it to look like. Also, allow yourself to go deeper in meditation than
you did yesterday. If you need help with this, get Ken D Foster's The Science of
Meditation Guide for FREE.www.kendfoster.com/resources

Day 111

"Courageous actors in life do not make excuses. They create plans to improve their lot in life daily."

KEN D FOSTER

What is it going to take to accelerate your success? One of the ways to increase the speed of success is setting up targets of achievement. We are all given reason, intuition, and willpower to bring out our best, but many people run their lives by the "seat of their pants" and only use a portion of what is available to them.

Let me explore a question you may want to ponder: Would an infinite being (that is you) who has genius within them, choose to go through life only using a portion of their power? Of course not! That would be like driving a sports car and never accelerating over five miles per hour. Most people don't see their true potential, but the secrets can be unlocked. This book has the keys.

So, what will it take for you to step up and reclaim all your brilliance? If you are serious about seeing how far you can go, then set up unreasonable goals, and set about achieving them with indomitable will. This is the starting point of reclaiming your power.

Today ask

"How am I achieving my goals with ease and grace?"

"What has to happen for me to increase my resolve and hit my goals?"

"How can I increase my willpower and accomplish what I set out to do?"

Actions

Focus on one area that you have been neglecting and set up a powerful goal that will stretch you in its accomplishment. It can be finance, health, relationship, spiritual, friendship, etc. Make sure your goals are specific, measurable and truly stretch you.

Authors Note: For those of you who would like to expand your knowledge on how to ask the right questions to set up goals, I encourage you to get my best-selling book; *Ask and You Will Succeed, 1001 Extraordinary Questions to Create Life-Changing Results*. You can find it on KenDFoster.com or Amazon.

Day 112

"It is with courage that we heal the sour places in our mind and allow the sunlight of the spirit to shine through."

KEN D FOSTER

Right choice is a function of living from awareness; so too, it is the key to a business well run, and a life well lived. But how can you make proper choices if you don't really know what thoughts are running your mind and your behavior's? You can't.

So, try a new strategy like asking: *"What am I not aware of that, if I were aware of it, would immeasurably increase my success?"*, or *"What is blocking me from having a more amazing life?"*

Questions like these help you tap into the infinite or super-conscious mind of all possibility and move you past your limited thinking. To increase your awareness of how to generate more success, you must tap into your immeasurable knowing of what to do next.

You can do this by asking powerful questions and then continue asking them until you get the answers that are right for you.

Today ask

"If I were to accept all aspects of myself, how will I show up differently, starting now?"

"What are the most important choices I can make to infuse my soul with passion?"

"If I were one hundred percent committed to accomplishing my greatest dreams, what would I be doing today?"

Actions

Form your own powerful questions that will expand you in positive ways. Note: You are the creator of all your successes and failures, so start being aware of how much more success you can have if you are aware of each choice you are making.

Day 113

Most people don't get what they want because they put up barriers up to getting it. For example, they are determined to make more money but believe they are not worthy to have it. This is what I call dual thinking or having the foot on the gas and brake at the same time.

If you are ready to dream bigger dreams and allow yourself to have what you want, then let go of thinking: you can't have it, you don't deserve it or any other thoughts that cross your mind and stop you from getting it. By uprooting your subconscious thoughts of doubt and uncertainty you will recreate a bright future.

Would an infinite being be thinking they don't deserve to have what they want? Of course not. There isn't anything limiting yourself but you! If you're going to change your life for the better, then do it! Don't make any excuses, just start now by letting go of any thoughts that say you can't.

Today ask

"What can I let go of now that will expand my awareness?"

"What is going to happen for me when I stay focused on "I can"?"

"How can I open to my dreams so wide that I intuitively get the next steps?"

Actions

List two dreams you will accomplish in the next year. Then come up with one limiting belief that would stop you from accomplishing these dreams. Then choose to reset your thinking, let go of the limiting belief and focus on what is possible for you now.

Day 114

*"Courage is more important than to be deceived by
shallow victory—waiting for a delayed defeat."*

DEJAN STOJANOVIC[62]

The concept of tomorrow is an illusion. Tomorrow doesn't really exists. The only thing that really exists is this moment. Your future is created the moment that you choose and act. It is only in the present moment that you create your future. If you are thinking of what you will do later or what happened earlier, you are not really in the moment.

Have you been around people who always tell you that they will do this or that, tomorrow? Maybe you even made the mistake of believing these people. If so, you have probably been disappointed time and time again when nothing happened.

There is an old saying; "good intentions pave the way to hell." It is true. Intentions without actions don't usually manifest.

Today ask

"What are the three most important actions I can take to create a bright future?"

"How can I increase my resolve to accomplish my greatest dreams?"

"What will it take for me to overcome any obstacles on my path to success?"

Actions

Don't waste time, make your thoughts your ally by determining what you will accomplish; and then go after it.

Day 115

*"Courageous people don't excuse their behavior,
they acknowledge when they are off track
and make proper adjustments."*

KEN D FOSTER

You know, it can be done—you can create your most fabulous dreams! But what stops most people from creating their dreams? Excuses! They excuse themselves because they don't feel like doing things, or they use the reason that others aren't doing things so why should they, or they allow their insecurities to hold them back rather than allow their greatness to move them into their future.

Expand your awareness to include what is possible and the best course of action for you. It may consist of doing things that you don't want to do and that others wouldn't do.

Most people live insipid lives because they won't step out into the unknown by taking consistent action until their dreams are created.

The "3 B's of Success" is written in the minds of those who are successful. What are the 3 B's of Success? Just Be it; Be someone powerful, and Be it now. This is a foolproof formula to become all you can be and to get you to take the actions you need to.

Today ask

"Who am I when I am feeling empowered?"

"How can I tap into my empowered self consistently?"

"How can I increase my life starting now?" Then apply the *"3 B formula"*.

Actions

Look into your soul and bring out your strengths and will power. Then, look at anything you have been putting off that will propel your success and then take immediate measures to fix it.

Day 116

"We are divine travelers here for a brief period in our infinite lives, so be bold and live from courage."

KEN D FOSTER

Never think of yourself as weak. When you do, you are programming your subconscious mind for failure. *Your power is unlimited, and you have everything you need to create your dreams.*

There is enough nuclear energy in each atom of your brain cells to light the city of Los Angeles many times over. But you will never know how powerful you are until you bet on yourself and release that power.

You can do this by setting your sights on the largest, maybe scariest dreams you can think of. Why? Because it will take everything you have, to accomplish them, and in the process, you will release your greatness.

Many people talk a big game, but very few bring their unstoppable spirit into play and train their mind, body, and emotions to accomplish what they choose. To do this, you must let go of judgments about what you can and cannot accomplish. Then, become aware of your infinite capacity to be, do and have what you choose.

Today ask

"Who am I, and what can I accomplish today?"

"What has to happen for me to stop limiting myself?"

"How can I have a quantum breakthrough and increase my success exponentially?"

Actions

Set your intention to be unstoppable and make up your mind to let your greatness shine.

Tap into your higher-self and increase your intuition with Ken D Foster's guided meditations on Business, Wealth, Expanding Possibility, Peace, and Health. Yours for free at couragetochange.us/meditation

Day 117

"Courage is being scared to death, but saddling up anyway."

JOHN WAYNE[63]

What are you dreaming about? Is your mind focused on external affairs that you have no power to control, or are you positively concentrating on mastering yourself and bringing your greatness into the world?

Too often, people spend their time thinking about what they could, should, or would have had if only.... But this is no way to use your God-given creative power. Why use your energy to recreate what you don't want repetitively? Isn't it far more productive to focus your awareness on how you can generate your dreams and make this world a better place at the same time?

If you will only look around and ask, "What is possible?" You will find there is no shortage of vital improvements to be made in this world. If you focus your gifts, talents, and abilities on finding ways to align what you pay attention to with who you are and what you were born to produce, your life and the world will get a little better.

Today ask

"What is one thing I can improve upon to make this world a better place?"

"What is the brilliance that I have been given to bring to life in this world?"

"How can I increase the possibilities of success in my life, now?"

Actions

After answering the questions above, take three action steps that will generate success in your life.

Day 118

"Courage and perseverance have a magical talisman—before which, difficulties disappear, and obstacles vanish into air."

JOHN QUINCY ADAMS[64]

Real success comes as you become more authentic and real with yourself and others. When you allow yourself to bring forth your brilliance by mastering yourself, you will realize who you truly are and what you are capable of accomplishing.

I have found that dreaming big and committing to creating those dreams is the quickest way to unleash the attraction power that is within all of us. You will attract exactly what you need to create your dreams, but you must get real with yourself, acknowledge your magnificent self and name any success-stoppers daily.

I am not talking about becoming an "egomaniac." I am talking about acknowledging the greatness of who you are and allowing more of that brilliance to improve the world.

If you set meaningful goals for yourself and then use those goals to self-actualize, at the end of the day, you will not only accomplish the goals but become the person with the qualities and accomplishments you would like to have.

Today ask

"Who do I have to become to achieve that dream?"

"Where can I open up to receive more?"

"Who can I invite to mentor me in the process of becoming all I can be?"

Actions

Make a list of the qualities you would like to improve upon and then take three action steps to achieving it.

Day 119

*"You will never do anything in this world without courage.
It is the greatest quality of the mind next to honor."*

JAMES ALLEN

To bring a more magnificent future into your life, you must awaken your initiative. This is the power of readiness in action—a spark from the infinite being that you are. It is your sustaining force which will drive you toward success.

For the next few days when you wake up, take some time to go within and ask for your initiative, your creativity, your resourcefulness to be increased threefold. This is not something to take lightly. This practice was given to me by a friend and my life changed dramatically for the better when I asked for my initiative to be increased three-fold. Was the new pathway easy? No. Do I regret it? Never.

While you are doing this practice keep your mind positive and affirm to yourself something like: "I have never-ending energy", or "I will accomplish all I set out to do", or "My initiative is increasing every day in every way". Keeping your mind focused on truthful statements like this will accelerate your success.

Today ask

"What has to happen to increase my initiative?"

"What is the greatest vision of success I have for myself?"

"When I awaken my initiative what dreams will I awaken?"

Actions

No matter what "reality" looks like in the moment, never give up on your dreams. Note: (Evoke initiative with unflinching steadiness toward your goals until you reach success).

Day 120

"There is no courage in bouncing from one project to the next without completing what you started. But it does take courage to prioritize and follow through with your commitments."

KEN D FOSTER

To succeed in anything, you must have definite priorities. Without them, nothing much happens, but with compelling preferences, you can move any mountains that are blocking your success.

Living your priorities will ignite the heat of inspiration and fire up your imagination for your next steps. This thinking makes it easier to persevere with sustained effort. First, decide what you want; then ask for inner awareness to direct your priority-driven actions. As you move forward with essential soul-directed steps, you will surely meet and exceed your goals.

Take some time to quiet your mind in meditation, and then use the power behind your mind to answer the questions that you have about achieving success. The answers will always come if you ask the questions, and are determined to find them.

Today ask

"If I don't give up on my dreams, who will I become as a result of achieving them?"

"What do I know to be true about myself, that will help me accomplish anything?"

"What are my most important priorities that I am committed to living?"

Actions

Find the fire in your belly and take a commanding step that will increase your success.

Day 121

"When you have the courage to move forward despite daunting circumstances confronting you, Providence provides the answers."

KEN D FOSTER

Goal setting is the key to any successful business or productive life. Most people only see goal setting and accomplishing them as a task-oriented exercise. In fact, most people don't like to set goals, because it launches them into actions they may or may not feel ready to take, and if they don't accomplish the goals, they label themselves a failure.

It doesn't have to be this way! What would be possible if you started thinking that setting up your life for success is fun? Goals are only intentions to expand or improve the way you perceive your situation.

Aren't you excited to carve out an amazing life? Wouldn't you like to succeed beyond your greatest expectations? Sure, you would, and goals are the stepping stones that will help you get there.

How about committing to setting targets that will take your business and life to the next level? It may take everything you must accomplish this, but so what, you are always doing something, why not put your energy and passion toward generating more happiness, fulfillment, and success?

Today ask

"What is one area of my business or life that I am committed to evolving?"

"Who do I need to become now to evolve my business or life?"

"What areas of myself do I need to align with to generate ongoing success?"

Actions

Determine one obstacle that could come between you and your success. Note: (Whatever obstacles come between you and your goals are only there to strengthen you. It isn't what happens to you that matters, it is who you become that will determine your success.

Day 122

"The essence of the courageous isn't found in books, workshops or advice from others, it is built one step at a time by being in integrity with yourself."

KEN D FOSTER

Great minds have learned to say "yes" to their dreams while saying "no" to distractions that get in their way. Whether your goal is exceptional health, a deep and loving relationship, an amazing career or a multi-million dollar business, know this: When you tune into your inner wisdom and fore go diversions, you will have success uncommon to most.

So many people avoid conflict at the expense of creating an exceptional life. They appear to be weak by saying "yes" to everything and everyone. These interruptions take them away from their dreams.

Instead of living an uncreated existence, it is important to set boundaries and to keep commitments not just to others but to yourself as well. The old saying about being able to "Disappoint others to be true to yourself" applies here.

Today ask

"How can I say no to distractions and say 'yes' to my dreams every day?"

"As an infinite being, what is available to me?"

"How can I stay true to myself and my dreams?"

Actions

Reflect on where you have let down your boundaries, and what you need to do to have stronger boundaries.

Day 123

"Why burden yourself with black-and-white
thinking about the way things should be?
Why not unshackle yourself by finding the courage
to open up new possibilities and demand
the impossible show up for you?"

KEN D FOSTER

Every regret and shattered hope of success must be transformed into new dreams, goals and positive actions. The past does not equal the future unless you continue to think and act the same as you did in the past.

Don't burden yourself with restricted thinking. If your logical mind could have liberated you from all your problems, don't you think you would be free by now? Liberate yourself by connecting to the awareness of who you are as an infinite being with unlimited energy and power.

Just behind your thinking is the boundless power of spirit, just waiting for you to connect. Why be disenchanted when things don't go your way? You can turn things around in an instant by asking infinite, powerful, positive, possibility questions and by making new choices. Boundless opportunities await.

Today ask

"What is one opportunity available to me now that will boost my success?"

"What can I do to increase my determination to succeed beyond my wildest dreams?"

"What is the path of least resistance to generating massive success for me?"

Actions

Contemplate the above questions until the answers come. Note: (As the insights and answers come, take the required actions to put those opportunities in motion).

Day 124

"The flame of courage is not brightened by being in the company of those who are self-centered; it is ignited by the company of those who are making positive changes in themselves and making a difference in the world."

KEN D FOSTER

Have you ever started working on a project and heard others express their opinions in a negative way, which caused you to doubt yourself or the project's validity?

Sometimes, doubt is a good thing because it helps us to get clear on whether we are doing the right thing. But often, doubt is a destructive force that stops us from creating our dreams.

When you are starting a new project, the last thing you need around you is a "doubting Thomas." It is better to surround yourself with positive people or no one at all.

Many times, I'll start a project and won't let anyone know about the project until it is well on its way. I call it holding "Sacred Silence." This gives me time for the ideas to be formed, before other people's opinions may dilute the original inspiration.

Today ask

"What is my next project that I am choosing to manifest?"

"Why am I inspired about this project?"

"How will this inspiration empower the project?"

Actions

Take a few moments, think about your project and allow inspiration to permeate your thinking. When you know the direction you want to take, push out any thoughts of doubt and follow the guidance you have been given. By doing this, you will be more successful at creating your dreams.

Day 125

"Within each one of us is a creative force that can generate our greatest dreams, it is called courage."

KEN D FOSTER

Those who live on the creative plane of life are tuned into the infinite mind of the creator. They are the truth-seekers, ever seeking new ways to create instruments of health, happiness, and prosperity for all. They are in service to humanity in many ways and are always looking to better themselves and others along the way.

When you focus on opening your creativity, you are focusing on the abundance of the universe. This is no small force, for it is the power that created everything you see.

Appropriately used your greatest dreams will come to pass; misused, your greatest nightmares may unfold. But it isn't dangerous to use this power when you are a force for good and consciously create goodness in the world.

To tap into this power, quiet your mind and get yourself to a place where creativity can open. Then let go thinking about the past or future and be completely present at the moment. Take a few deep breaths in. Then think about one area of your business or life that you would like to expand.

Use your power of imagination visualize what is possible as this dream comes to pass. See it, feel it, and expand it within your imagination. After you have done this, come up with a minimum of fifteen ideas that will propel you towards this Vision.

Today ask

"If I had no limitations such as money, time or energy, what would I like to create?"

"Why would it be important for me to create this dream?"

"What are the three most important steps I can take today to generate that dream?"

Actions

Spend some time in awe of your life. Be amazed at how much goodness there is and how much you are in gratitude for all that you have.

Day 126

*"Like gaining confidence, finding one's courage is
gradual rather than all at once."*

BARBARA BARKSDALE CLOWSE[66]

Wouldn't you like to honor and cherish your greatest dreams by creating them? You have been given specific gifts, talents, and skills to bring forth your dreams into the world. These dreams haven't been given to everyone; they have been given to you to bring your brilliance into the world and be all you were meant to be.

I can't tell you how many people I have coached over the years that were wondering if they should move forward with a dream. They were stuck contemplating whether their dream was right for them to do.

But, as you know, doubt is the biggest stopper of dreams around! It is like having one foot in the ocean ready to play in the waves and one foot out thinking "I must keep dry." But if you keep dry and don't peruse your dreams, you will never know what you missed, or worse: live a life filled with regrets.

So, what must happen for you to start dreaming bigger and generating those dreams? It will take commitment, belief in yourself and the trust that you either have what it takes right now or that you will be guided along the way to make your dreams come true. But mostly it happens when you take the first step, which can be today.

Today ask

"If I were to accomplish my dreams, what would my life be like in three years?"

"What could possibly stop me from manifesting my greatest dreams?"

"If I were brave, what would I do today to start generating my dreams?"

Actions

Use your imagination to expand what is possible for you and then take immediate measures to generate your dreams. Note: (You cannot *think* your way into your greatest dreams, you have to live them).

Day 127

"Courage is developed in stillness and out pictures in the lives of those who let love flow through them."

KEN D FOSTER

As you evolve yourself, it is essential to allow yourself to dream your biggest dreams and then go after them without attachment of how they show up. Open yourself up to find out what is inside of you and realize just how much you can enjoy life when you take off the limits of what you think is possible.

Achievement of your dreams will follow the commitments you make. So, it seems fitting that as you make promises and keep them, your dreams will start to generate. But commitments alone may not keep you on track.

What is needed is to let go of the desire to succeed. This is counter logical, but letting go of the attachment to how the success comes is critical. Some might even say it is wrong not to have desires and attachments to your dreams, but if you have been in a stop/start pattern for a while; starting a project and then stopping when something seemingly better comes along, try letting go of the desire to succeed and see what happens.

What will most likely happen is that you will accomplish your goals consistently because you have no attachment to the outcome; therefore you will enjoy the journey by doing what is in front of you step by step.

Today ask

"What is possible for me to create when my mind is focused on the joy of creating?"

"How can I detach from emotions that may stop me from creating something new?"

"How much joy will I allow myself to feel today?"

Actions

Make a point today to stay present to the task at hand and enjoy the journey.

CHAPTER 7

INFINITE POWER UNVEILED

Day 128

"He who is not courageous enough to take risks
will accomplish nothing in life."

MUHAMMAD ALI[67]

Set expectations of yourself high and move forward with continuous integrity. Most people have it backward: they set expectations high for others and don't' pay much attention to how they show up. How many people do you know who complain about others but rarely look at themselves?

Of course, this is probably not you, but it is important to take time daily and notice what you make judgments about, whether about yourself or others. Imagine what it would be like to stop thinking in terms of right, wrong, good and bad, and started thinking in terms of acceptance and understanding?

Accepting the others point of view can be difficult if you are attached to being right. So just for today, see what it is like to make everyone you come across right about their opinions. Notice if you have less conflict and possibly more harmony in your relationships.

Today ask

"What is possible for me if I stopped judging myself or others?"

"What can I become more aware of?"

"What can I do to improve, develop and change for the better?"

Actions

Often others reflect our negative qualities, which can give us insight into what we need to change. So, make a list of what you most often judge about others and then reflect on whether you have these qualities within yourself. If so, resolve to overcome them.

Tap into your higher-self and increase your intuition with Ken D Foster's guided meditations on Business, Wealth, Expanding Possibility, Peace, and Health. Yours for free at couragetochange.us/meditation

Day 129

"There are moments in our lives when it takes courage to move forward; these are defining moments that strengthen and fortify our resolve."

KEN D FOSTER

You will grow by either pain or insight. Pain comes through ignorance—insight, through experience and wisdom.

Many people have a high threshold for pain and misery. They can stay in unhealthy relationships, with crummy bosses, poor health, or disempowering environments for years.

But, being able to stand disharmony doesn't mean you are on the right path. It only means you haven't realized there is something better for you which will take courage to act upon.

You weren't created for a life of suffering and misery! You were created to bring forth your brilliance and find lasting happiness. No one is given more than they can handle. Within each one of us is a spark of spirit that will guide us through the dark times into the light of success.

But, you must set your sights to better yourself, have faith in yourself, and move with courage when things get tough. It may take all the strength you have to move past failures, but these can be exactly what you need to strengthen your resolve. And if you have right mindset you may feel some pain and discomfort, but you won't suffer.

Today ask

"What can I do to improve, develop and change for the better?"

"What is one way I been limiting myself?"

"What is possible for me, when I get out of my comfort zone?"

Actions

Make a list of where you stay in your comfort zone. Then, remember it is best to learn how to be comfortable in uncomfortable situations. Take off your limits!

Day 130

"With indomitable willpower and unbridled courage your soul will glow bright, and you will be unstoppable."

KEN D FOSTER

There is a goldmine of power that lies dormant within you. This power can be accessed at any moment by stopping what you are doing, quieting the mind and asking powerful questions like: "What can I do immediately to feel more connected to my authentic power?" and "What will I do today to blast past the limits in my life?" and "How can I open myself up to receive more energy and abundance?".

By asking these types of questions and staying in the questions until you get the answers, you will bring more energy and enthusiasm into your mind, body and spirit. If you do this consistently, you will have the energy you need to succeed.

Today ask

"When this day is through, what will I have accomplished?"

"What is possible for me, if I stay connected to my soul?"

"Who am I becoming?"

Actions

Increase your personal power and determine to have boundless energy and focused attention to create your dreams.

Day 131

"It doesn't take courage to take the easy way. Moreover, the path of success is filled with courageous acts of those who struggled and persevered until they achieved their greatest dreams."

KEN D FOSTER

Are you ready to push your limits and break through the bondage of past habits? One of the illusions in life is to think that you are powerless over circumstances. As soon as you hold onto the thought that "It will always be this way" or "There is no way out of this mess," it becomes real for you and you are now stuck.

To break free of this kind of thinking, you must use your willpower, creative thinking and a little dab of faith. Don't be afraid to cut the cords that bind you to the past. The past doesn't equal the future unless you continue to dwell on it. Don't! Within you is the wisdom of the ages, but you must tap into it by asking the right questions, keeping your mind positive and taking immediate actions to break free.

You will be amazed at how much you can accomplish when you light up your mind with questions that empower you.

Today ask

"What is the most powerful thing I can do today to overcome my problems?"

"What actions can I take today to overcome any obstacles to success?"

"What can I think about to have a great attitude no matter what happens?"

Actions

Pick an area where you have been feeling helpless, and then determine to change things around.

Day 132

*"Courageous people look at what is impossible to do,
and then find a way to do it anyway."*

KEN D FOSTER

You must increase your awareness and realize you have the power to achieve your dreams. The only thing that can stop you is doubt and disempowering beliefs about yourself and your abilities.

So, if any doubts or negativity arise in your mind, re-direct your mind by asking questions like: "What can I do differently?"; "How can I increase my power right now?" You always have a choice about what questions you ask and what your focus will be.

Today ask

"What is the quickest and most positive way to achieve positive results today?"

"How can my life get better right now?"

"What do I have to remember, when challenges come, that will aid me in blowing right through them?"

Actions:

Set up a positive, energetic vibration of success thoughts so powerful that this dynamic force influences your mental, emotional and physical states so much so that you set up a rhythm of success that is unrelenting.

Day 133

"Life grows and blossoms in relation to one's courage and connection to God."

KEN D FOSTER

Do you ever feel that you are being blown around by life's circumstances like a piece of paper in the wind? If so, the way out is by seeking the truth and finding out why you're challenging problems are happening specifically to you. Nothing happens by accident.

You are exactly where you are because you put yourself there. If you don't like what is happening to you, then you must look for the beliefs that are keeping you stuck. But don't worry, you must dissect everything you believe.

I suggest you take another route and search for the brilliance that is "you". You can do this by discovering your true nature. It is by finding your true self that you will find the keys to lasting success. It is embedded in all of us and you will find it, if you look.

Although, what I am suggesting is uncommon to most, just because it takes discipline to still the mind and tune into the higher consciousness, if you do, the freedom to create lasting success will be yours.

Today ask

"What can I do to connect deeper with my "true nature?"

"What can I do to create unlimited success and freedom?"

"What am I being called to do differently?"

Actions

Take some time to still your mind and tap into the source of your greatness. Also, review some of Ken D Fosters other programs for creating success at KenDFoster.com/our-products.

Day 134

*"It is with courage and faith that you can develop your
intuition and live life from the inside out."*

KEN D FOSTER

Living a victorious life is not created from studying books, taking seminars or listening to enlightened teachers. You cannot pump wisdom from the outside in. Victory over circumstances is an inside job! It starts with quieting your thoughts, tapping into your soul and opening the doors to unlimited possibilities.

Why tap into the soul? Because this is where the ever-knowing source of unlimited knowledge and all the answers to any question you may ask will emerge. It takes more than willpower to generate a victorious life. Human drive only takes you so far, but by combining intuitive guidance with a soul-powered will, you can become the master of your destiny.

Remember, it is the extent of your ability to listen and receive the intuitive voice of the soul, which determines how much success you will have. So, are you ready to accept more? I hope you said *"Yes"*!

Today ask

"What has to happen for me to open up to receive more?"

"What are three new beliefs I can embrace to change my destiny?"

"What thoughts am I willing to give up, to expand my presence and increase my success?"

Actions

Visualize how the three new beliefs will change your destiny.

Day 135

"Courage is not the absence of fear, but rather the judgment that something else is more important than fear."

AMBROSE REDMOON[68]

Love is the single most powerful and necessary component of business success. If you bring love into what you are doing, even though you are doing something that seems painful at the time, you feel empowered and will evolve.

Yes, life and business are challenging at times, but love allows us to reach beyond ourselves, to stretch and experience all that we have within us. It gives us power to see past what is wrong to take the next innovative step toward your success.

Today ask

"How can I deepen my capacity to love during an unloving situation?"

"How can I bring more love into my business?"

"How can I be more generous with my time, energy and money to foster love?"

Actions

You are either fear-driven or love-driven, you choose. Decide which side of the equation you will live from, and then live it fully!

Day 136

*"Don't give up, don't give in. This is easy to say, but
to do this takes courage and fortitude, of course,
the payoff is a satisfying and joyous life."*

KEN D FOSTER

No matter what your state of being, you can always turn things around when you put your full soul power into it. It takes discipline, self-control, and daily actions but nothing is impossible for you to accomplish.

In fact, it is your spiritual duty to manifest your dreams. They weren't given to everyone. Your dreams were given exclusively to you. They are there to help you bring forth the glory that is you—the infinite being and to realize your divine nature.

There is a secret cause of most failures, and it is mental laziness. Sure, it is easier to watch TV or spend time with friends than to do things that will move you forward with your business or life.

But what will happen if you distract yourself from generating your dreams? You will end up a slave to disappointments. It doesn't take any more effort to have a fantastic life compared to the effort it takes to live a mediocre life. The choice is yours!

Today ask

"Who am I when I bring the full force and power of my attention to create success?"

"How can I bring my soulful energies into generating an outstanding day?"

"What has to happen for me to let go of distractions and succeed in all my dreams?"

Actions

Watch your mind and actions. Notice if you are progressing and how much you are accomplishing. Don't hide from yourself. Be aware and notice any thoughts or habits that are keeping you from staying focused and making your dreams come true.

Day 137

*"You have been called selfish for the courage of acting on your
own judgment and bearing sole responsibility for your own
life. You have been called arrogant for your independent mind.
You have been called cruel for your unyielding integrity."*

AYN RAND[69]

Are you taking fully responsible for your thoughts and emotions? Can others make you happy or upset? In truth, no one has the power to make you feel happy or upset, unless you give them the power.

You have two choices: Either blame others for your problems and stresses, or take full responsibility and be the awareness that can change your circumstances. This may seem like a strange concept, but think about it. When you become aware that nothing can upset you unless you decide it can, then nothing can.

The reason this concept is so important is that when you think others have the power to impact your choices or attitudes, you will be very vulnerable emotionally. It can be like a roller coaster ride. One moment you are up and the next you are down.

To create your greatest dreams requires consistent energy and a peaceful mind. Therefore, it is essential to increase your awareness of just how much power you have, to strengthen your resolve not to let others impact you in a negative way.

Today ask

"What would it take to acknowledge the power that is at my command and be the master of my thoughts, feelings and emotions?"

"What can I do to increase my resolve to live in peace, harmony and joy?"

"How can I be even-minded every moment today?"

Actions

Contemplate the above questions for a minimum of 15 minutes today.

Day 138

"Each mistake teaches you something new about yourself.
There is no failure, remember, except in no longer trying.
It is the courage to continue that counts."

CHRIS BRADFORD[70]

Would you like to increase your personal power? There can be no ongoing success unless you are present and available to receive the unlimited possibilities that can be generated by the creative force within you.

Are you ready to allow the greatness within you to reinvent how you perceive reality? Try reconnecting with why you are committed to creating your dreams, and decide what is most important to you.

Then meditate and ASK for divine aid to direct your thinking and to make the right choices. The inner soul direction combined with persistence will truly increase your personal power and lead you to success.

Every problem can be overcome, and every goal can be accomplished by this method. By tapping into the superconscious mind, all that power and creativity will flow into your life.

Just behind your thoughts is infinite intelligence, just behind your heart is divine love, and just behind your soul is unending joy. Doesn't it make sense to take some time to meditate and ask for guidance in what you are doing?

Today ask

"How can I achieve success beyond measure?"

"What will it take for me to increase my knowing of how to succeed?"

"How can I realize that I have within me the power to achieve anything?"

Actions

Being afraid or pretending not to care will never get you where you want to go. Make the effort to find the key to lasting success for yourself.

Day 139

"Challenging problems are no match for a courageous heart that is fired up with an unstoppable will."

KEN D FOSTER

True teachers never teach you to become an automated machine, only focusing on creating health, wealth or success by their "proven methods" or personal points of view. Instead, true teachers guide you to your own answers.

They help you tap into the infinite wisdom that is within you. They help you increase your inner awareness and become more conscious on multiple levels.

It has been said: "Consciousness includes everything and excludes nothing." As you live more and more from the infinite, powerful, positive, possibility questions and give your soul the chance to answer them, your consciousness will open to the endless possibilities available to you.

Today ask

"What will it take for me to be in harmony with my spirit?"

"How can I increase the time to do the things I love?"

"What can I release to increase my receptivity to spirit?"

Actions

Get serious about having more time for your inner reflections and spaces between your busyness. Note: When you are in harmony with your spirit and doing things that enliven the spirit life gets better and better.

Tap into your higher-self and increase your intuition with Ken D Foster's guided meditations on Business, Wealth, Expanding Possibility, Peace, and Health. Yours for free at couragetochange.us/meditation

Day 140

*"Wisdom and courage go hand in hand. It takes courage
to overcome major challenges, and wisdom to know what
underlies the challenges, so they don't keep showing up."*

KEN D FOSTER

Your greatest thinking got you where you are in life. If you feel stuck, your greatest thinking will not get you unstuck. Because if you could have thought your way out of your messes, don't you think you would have done that by now?

Most people focus on the superficial parts of their life, not delving into the depths of
who they are. Nor do they find out the causes of their successes or failures. But this information is available to you by asking your WisdomSelf infinite, powerful, positive, possibility-questions.

Try doing this: Quiet your mind by taking a deep breath in, hold and tense your body for ten seconds and then release all the tension in your body. Do it six times while closing your eyes and gently raising them to the spiritual eye. After inhaling, pausing and exhaling the six breaths, then sink deep into silence and ask: *"Infinite Spirit reveal yourself?"*

Don't look for answers, but connect with the peace and tranquility even if only for a moment. Then, affirm: *"I am one with the infinite spirit,"* and *"I am courageous, and I will do more than survive, I will thrive."*

Today ask

"What do I need to know to overcome the challenges facing me?"

"How will I connect deeper and deeper with Spirit and my intuitive wisdom?"

"How can my life get better and better starting today?"

Actions

Take two courageous steps toward your dreams that you have not done before. Note: (The courageous person is an increasingly happy person, because they assess the answers of how to improve, grow, change, and develop daily until things get better and better).

Day 141

*"We must have courage to bet on our ideas, to take the
calculated risk, and to act. Everyday living requires
courage if life is to be effective and bring happiness."*

MAXWELL MALTZ[71]

The worst thing that can happen in your life is not poverty, loneliness or ill health, but lack of peace of mind and a sense of joy. Why limit yourself to a busy mind and chaotic life with no sense of fulfillment? This is no way to live, yet millions live this way.

Whatever your circumstances are, it is you who put yourself there. And since it is you who got you into your messes, it is also you who can change your destiny. But if you don't change your thinking, choices, and actions, your life will be the way it is forever. That isn't good news for some!

There is a power that you can tap into right now, and that power brings forth the greatness in you. It has been there since the beginning of time. All you need do is quiet your restless mind and focus on importance that resides in your thoughts.

Think about being great in all you do. Do the little things in front of you now with greatness. By doing so, you will strengthen your resolve and become more powerful.

Today ask

"What are the three most important steps I can take to bring greatness to into everything I do?"

"How can I become unstoppable in bringing greatness into my life right now?"

"What can I do to remember to always tap into the force of greatness behind my will?"

Actions

Take three action steps which will propel you to victory over your goals. Note: (Always check in to make sure what you are focusing on is right for you to have and when it is, use all the forces of your willpower to obtain your goal while continually keeping your mind on the greatness within).

Day 142

"Take chances, make mistakes. That's how you grow.
Pain nourishes your courage. You have
to fail to practice being brave."

MARY TYLER MOORE[72]

Problems are static and limited, but solutions are limitless when you tap into your soul and step into the unknown. Never admit defeat when your brilliance is challenged, but take full responsibility for your circumstances and surrender to what you have been holding on to.

Find out who you are being called to become, or what you are being called to do differently. It has been said that "Boldness has Genius" and it is true because behind all genius is the courage to let go of all that is known and dive into the unknown.

As Einstein said: *"Problems can't be solved with the same mindset that created them."* To change a problem into a victory, you will have to change you and your point of view.

Problems are not put in your life to overwhelm or crush you. They are gifts which will strengthen you and help you be all you were meant to be. They are the secret source that all greatness is born from. And the way to approach all problems is with a peaceful heart and a calm mind trusting the solutions will come.

Today ask

"What are five solutions to my greatest problems?"

"What are the most important shifts I can make to solve my problems now?"

"Who must I become to solve my problems?"

Actions

Make a list of what you are learning from overcoming your problems.
Note: Do what it takes to realize that issues are not there to crush you, but to strengthen you.

Day 143

"Find the Courage to be open to all possibilities and attached to nothing."

KEN D FOSTER

Your thinking will either empower you or leave you standing still. In other words, if you use your mind correctly, you will have everything you need. If not, you won't. It is that simple!

Every object you see in the world started from a thought by people who are no smarter than you. They just asked different questions and focused their minds on generating what they chose to have until it manifested. You can do the same; because what one person has done, you can duplicate.

Your creative thoughts have magic in them. But if you haven't learned how to focus the mind consistently on productive actions, then the mind is like a wet match which can't be lit. Your mind should be charged with infinite power and detached from any past unpleasant experiences. Fear, harms, resentments, misinformation, guilt, or shame will all stop the creative force from flowing through you.

If you create the determination now to focus your mind on your greatest dreams and withdraw your attention from all objects of distraction, soon you too will be able to attract to you the object of your concentration.

Today ask

"What am I choosing to focus on and bring into my life?"

"What are courageous actions I can take to have more ease and grace?"

"What can I do to increase my initiative and willpower to concentrate?"

Actions

List two dreams you have set aside and decide if you are ready to manifest them now.

Day 144

"Truth is never afraid of courageous questions, so ask what you have never asked before, and then find the courage to act when the answers come."

KEN D FOSTER

When a man stops thinking in limited terms, he starts knowing himself in unlimited terms. But how is that possible? Most would say we are limited as mortal humans and limited in many ways.

But I say: *Forget limiting thoughts!* Success is an "inside job"; it is not found outside of you in a seminar, book, or school. These can help guide you, but ultimately success is found inside of you by tapping into the genius of your soul.

Am I saying you have genius in you? Absolutely! We all have genius within us, but most remain unconscious of this power. We are socialized to think we are limited in our abilities to use our souls to accomplish our dreams.

This is evident because most people only use their minds and bodies to generate success, but when you can use *soul*, mind, and body, true success will come your way. You can let go of your limitations by deep meditation, then contemplation of whom you are and why you have come here.

It is by asking these types of questions, and then staying in the questions until the answers come—and they will come—that you will tap into your genius and bring your greatness into the world!

Today ask

"Where have I stopped the unlimited source of my genius?"

"As I consistently tap into my genius, how will my business and life be different?"

"What is my soul's mission in life, and what steps can I take to bring it forth?"

Actions

Focus your attention on brining awareness to the power of your soul to manifest your greatest dreams.

Day 145

"We ought to face our destiny with courage."

FRIEDRICH NIETZSCHE[73]

With the expansion of the mind and the use of willpower, you can realize your destiny. So, try this on for size: Ultimately everything in this universe has been born from, or comes out of Spirit. And out of Spirit come individual Souls. So, the Spirit is over the Soul. Out of Souls comes consciousness.

So, the Soul is meant to rule the mind. The mind is over your feelings. What you think you will feel. Feelings are over actions. How you feel will, to a large degree, determine the actions taken. Actions are over results and results are over your destiny. Therefore, no one is destined or fated for lack, or failure. You create your destiny by your thinking and actions.

You are unlimited, but if you are not connecting with your source, then as a mortal you have become limited. Try to focus your attention on the Soul and Spirit, and you will have all the power you need.

In willpower lies the power to pour out your soul when taking actions. In this power sits the keys to accomplishing whatever you choose. And when you persist refusing to accept failure, the object of your desire must appear.

Today ask

"What is my greatest challenge that I will turn into a great accomplishment?"

"How can I increase my willpower threefold?"

"If I connect several times a day to Spirit, how much more success will I have?"

Actions

Take time today to tune deeply into your soul and feel the power that resides within yourself.

CHAPTER 8

REACHING NEW HEIGHTS

Day 146

"The most courageous act you can do is master your mind and then master yourself."

KEN D FOSTER

Today is the day to take your life to new heights. It is time to make new choices. It is a time of renewal and rebirth. It is a time to let go of the past and those things that have not served you well. It is time to throw off the portals of limitations and open to new possibilities. It is the time to set intentions and breath new life into your greatest dreams.

Imagine if you could really start over, what changes would you make? How would you remake your life? Well, now is the time to answer those questions and more! Are you done playing small? Are you sick and tired of living in mediocracy? Then, fear not, but realize you have some work to do.

Every human being is here to evolve their consciousness. But how can you evolve if you are not making courageous choices and brining more "You" into the world. I am talking about aligning "You" (the Soul) with your Nature (highest qualities) by manifesting your greatest dreams.

Try taking on a New Point of View. "Beginning today, I will create a new future by creating a new me. I will do what it takes to remold my thinking and become all I was meant to be. I will bring forth my brilliance and create excellence in all areas of my life. I will change my perceptions, words, and actions again and again until I have found the road to success by evolving myself into being the change I want to see in this world."

Today ask

"What is the core of who I am?"

"What am I being called to do differently?"

"How will my business and life evolve so that I have the greatest year ever?

Actions

"Your future is as bright as you proclaim it to be. Repeat the "New Point of View" affirmations above six times until you feel a sense of empowerment.

Day 147

"Courage doesn't happen when you have all the answers. It happens when you are ready to face the questions you have been avoiding your whole life."

SHANNON L. ALDER[74]

Positive thoughts are always stronger than negative ones because they vibrate within us at a higher resonance, energizing us and making it easier to stay focused on generating success.

Positivity happens when you become aware of your thoughts and the effects they have on every aspect of your life. When you are upset, your thoughts act as a magnet drawing to you people, places and things you genuinely don't want. But the opposite is true also: When you choose to stay positive and focused on overcoming any challenges that come your way, you attract the resources you need to overcome and achieve success.

It sounds simple, right? Just remember this. When you focus your mind on a situation and keep dwelling on it repeatedly, you will create an emotion—either positive or negative. What you focus on you will feel! So, if you are feeling upset, most often you have been dwelling on something that is upsetting. When you are dwelling on the positive, you will most likely feel empowered.

Today ask

"What are the most important goals I can focus on to stay empowered?"

"How can I feel powerful even when I am doing things I don't like to do?"

"What is it possible for me to generate if I stay positive most of the time?"

Actions

Take some time and tune into what you are spending your time on the most, then decide if this is bringing you closer to what you want or not.

Day 148

*"Unspeakable things may happen to courageous people,
but their courage carries them through to accomplish
their dreams despite their circumstances."*

KEN D FOSTER

Have you mastered setting up targets of achievement, prioritization, and delegation of tasks? So many people go through life thinking they do not have what it takes to do this. But let me ask you this: Do you know any successful people who have a no-choice point of view that limits what they are capable of? No way!

Are you willing to acknowledge and own the fact that you have what it takes to set up achievable goals, prioritize and delegate them as you need to escalate your success? I hope you said "YES" because you can truly have your greatest year ever if you will do this.

Imagine setting aside time each morning to organize your day for success. How would your life be different in the next year? Would you have more wealth, health and happiness? Of course, you will! So, how about embracing the consciousness of setting up daily targets, prioritizing them and, if need be, delegating them?

Today ask

"What must happen for me to embrace setting daily targets, prioritizing them and then delegating them?"

"If there was a block in setting daily targets, what would it be and how can I overcome it?"

"What can I do today to accelerate my effectiveness?"

Actions

Decide on two things you will accomplish in your business and/or personal life

Day 149

"It may take courage to embrace the possibilities of your own potential, but once you've flown past the summit of your fears, nothing will seem impossible."

MICHAEL MCKEE[75]

It is much easier to create success if you are not doing it alone. I run across many entrepreneurs who are trying very hard to create success in their businesses. They seem to have mastered doing many things simultaneously but most of these "masters" have one thing in common, they are struggling.

One of the fastest ways out of the struggle is finding a coach or mentor that has experience in doing what you are doing and is willing to help you figure things out. It is important to find a mentor who is committed to helping you find your own answers and not just giving you their answers. There is a big difference.

On the one hand you are empowered to go within and find your own path, on the other you are getting someone else's advice, which may or may not be right for you. Just because someone accomplished goals a certain way may not be the way for you to attain success.

Creation is a dance with many steps. My research with millionaires showed me there are multiple routes of attaining wealth. The commonality is in the thinking habits, not the means of achieving the goal.

You didn't come into the world to lose yourself but to find the greatness that is within you and to win victory over life. Don't let what has limited you in the past stop you now. There is nothing you are fated to become or do; you are the master of your life! Choose now to become the Master of your destiny

Today ask

"How will I find a great mentor that will help me succeed?"

"If I were to stretch my limits, what questions can I ask that will blow the doors open to great success?"

"How can I let go of struggle and bring in the boldness of effortless action and joyful accomplishment?"

Actions

Make a list of what you need support in, then determine who your coach or mentor will be and make the call to ask for support.

Day 150

*"Keep your fears to yourself, but share
your courage with others."*

ROBERT LOUIS STEVENSON[76]

Why do limitations rule some people's lives more than others? All of us have conscious and unconscious beliefs that stop us from creating the life of our dreams. But most people are not aware of their limitations; therefore, they live them day in and day out.

You don't have to be limited by past thinking or programming. These limitations can come to light very quickly when you set goals and keep promises to yourself, as you complete the goals you set. The reason is simple: goal setting helps you to get in touch with the beliefs and habits that have stopped you in the past.

Why? Because when you set goals beyond what you think is possible to achieve, they drive the creative force within you to come out. Also, your "stinking thinking" will start to surface. In other words, when you put a little pressure on yourself to succeed, out will pop what has stopped you in the past.

Beliefs that keep you being afraid of failing, or of having too much success, or of abusing power, or, "I'm not good enough," or "I don't have what it takes," or "I am too old" or "too young," are limiting beliefs.

You can move past this 'stinking thinking' when you choose to release these thoughts and keep focused on your goals. This is how to create a beautiful life, where your values and contributions make this world a better place.

Today ask

"What new goal can I set that will stretch me beyond my comfort zone?"

"What have I realized, that will propel me forward quickly?"

"How can I stay focused on my goals to bring out my greatest good?"

Actions

Decide what your most important goals are and prioritize them.

Day 151

"It takes strength and courage to admit the truth."

RICK RIORDAN[77]

The noblest visions of life are within our reach, because they are sitting in our souls. Within all of us is a blueprint of our most fabulous aspirations and these desires will bring you great joy if you dare to realize them.

This blueprint can be accessed daily by calming the mind and remembering who you are—an infinite being. I would like you to think of what you are about to do today. Is it something that you can hardly wait to do? Or is it something that you "have to do"? Either way, if you find the good in it, you will have a sense of happiness and fulfillment.

That is not to say, you should consistently do things that bring you misery. Many people have lost the joy in their lives because they continually do things which they think they "have to do." On the surface these "have to do's" seem important but as you delve deeper, they are mostly just staying busy. This is no way to live! If you want to feel the joy, you must do things that bring you joy. How simple is that?

Today ask

"Will what I am about to do today bring me closer to achieving my goals?"

"How can I find joy in doing things I don't want to do?"

"What is on my "to do list" today that I can let go of, or delegate, to find more joy?"

Actions

You are a powerful being; you can figure out how to have more joy. So, make a list of what brings you joy and then take some immediate action to bring in more joy.

Tap into your higher-self and increase your intuition with Ken D Foster's guided meditations on Business, Wealth, Expanding Possibility, Peace, and Health. Yours for free at couragetochange.us/meditation

Day 152

*"It takes courage to never give up on yourself and
your dreams no matter what happens."*

KEN D FOSTER

Are you honestly getting the desired results that you want in life? Why be satisfied with a mediocre life? Your greatest aspirations are given to you for a reason. Meditate on what you really want to do, be and have.

Your dreams are given to you, not to frustrate you, but to empower you in bringing out your greatest qualities and generate a fantastic life. They are there to provide you with the courage, confidence, and consistency in fashioning a life filled with ongoing success.

But this won't come to pass if you accept mediocrity and rest on your laurels. Eventually, this attitude will bring dissatisfaction to your life. So why not become all you were meant to be, right now, by conquering your imperfections and drawing all your dreams to you?

Today ask

"If I let go of all the ways I have defined my life as a limited being, and become aware of how powerful I truly am, what could my life be like?"

"What three actions can I take that will bring out the magnificence I have to offer the world?"

What can I focus on that will inevitably transform my life to fulfill all of my dreams?"

Actions

Take three action steps that will bring out your gifts, talents, and abilities in a more significant way.

Day 153

"Being deeply loved by someone gives you strength while loving someone deeply gives you courage."

LAO TZU[78]

Do you wake up each morning with lots of energy and enthusiasm or do you wake up wishing you didn't have to get out of bed? Each day is either a gift or a curse; depending on your attitude.

Wouldn't you like to start every day with the right attitude? Of course, you would! So, commit to challenging yourself for the next seven day by doing the following:

1. Each night before you fall asleep, set your intention to wake up feeling energized.

2. Upon waking in the morning, come up with five things you are grateful for having in your life.

3. Meditate for ten minutes or more.

4. Set your intention to have the best day ever.

Today ask

"What are five things in my life that I am truly grateful for?"

"What do I love about my life?"

"What am I excited to accomplish today?"

Actions

Follow the four-step process and journal your results. (You will be amazed at how much energy you have when you develop a waking routine).

Day 154

*"It is easy to live an unrestrained, unorganized life, but it takes
courage to simplify your life and focus on your dreams."*

KEN D FOSTER

The most successful people in the world demonstrate that order is imperative. No one can be his or her best in a chaotic environment. Over the years, I have seen time and time again that those who are the most productive have implemented order in their home life, business, office, garages, desks, etc.

I have often wondered why it is so vital to be clutter free and organized. Here is what I have found. By letting go of clutter, you will be clearing up the clutter and confusion in your brain. Did you know that your subconscious mind is keeping track of all the stuff in your life?

When you let go of clutter and organize you will have more peace. Arranging your environment also creates efficient routines that will increase your productivity.

Order is something that must be worked on daily. If you didn't empty your trash cans but once a month, you would quickly pollute your environment with flies, ants, roaches and a great smell. It is the same with order. You must work on it daily. It starts with a commitment to tidy up and get your life in order.

Today ask

"When will I start to put my home environment in order?"

"What areas of my home will I concentrate my efforts on simplifying first?"

"By when will I have my home and business environments cleaned up?"

Actions

Take two steps toward improving and organizing your environment today.

Day 155

"All happiness depends on courage and work."

HONORÉ DE BALZAC[79]

Wherever you are in life, it is you who put yourself there, and only you can turn the key and unlock the door of abundance.

Ongoing success is driven by an energized body, mind and spirit. But the human will, when led by the ego causes nothing but troubles and the lack of a completely fulfilled life. It is only when you turn toward your inner wisdom, guided by deep intuition, that real success comes.

It is by attuning your will to the unstoppable will of spirit and choosing to concentrate on thoughts that strengthen your intentions that unlimited power flows through your body, mind, and spirit accomplishing your greatest dreams.

When your power is developed to that extent, you control your destiny. So infuse your spirit with thoughts of success and life will get better.

Today ask

"What will strengthen my resolve to succeed?"

"What has to happen for an infinite being like me to align my thoughts and actions with divine will?"

"How can I attune myself to soulful intuition and increase my power?"

Actions

Ask these simple questions above and keep asking them throughout the day, until you feel inspired. Note: (You may notice you are more powerful, balanced and productive. Also, note how others respond to you today when you are positively focused).

Day 156

"There are thousands of places to feel the warmth of the sun and thousands of ways to live a courageous life."

KEN D FOSTER

Today I am asking you to dare to be aware. I would like you to bring to the forefront of your mind your biggest dream. Picture it and then feel it. Imagine standing in this dream that you have just accomplished. Intensify your feelings! What are you saying to yourself? What are your family and friends saying to you?

It is equally as easy to create a dollar as a million dollars. And anyone who has built a small dream can create a much larger vision. All you must do is apply the same principles you used to create the small dream. Are you aware of this?

So, if you've generated a dollar and are interested in opening the door to earning a million dollars; start by becoming aware of your dream and then open yourself to receive the gifts of this dream.

Spend some time looking at how you bring your dreams to life, then commit to being even more aware of what you truly want in life. You can do this because it is based on natural laws. We all have the innate ability to create our greatest dreams and hone our consciousness of what is possible.

Today ask

"Where can I let more of my brilliance shine and generate my greatest dreams?"

"How can I increase my awareness of what is possible for me?"

"Who am I being when I am generating my greatest dreams?"

Actions

Take some time to meditate today. Commit to one of your greatest dreams and start making it a reality today. Also, think about what it would take to go deeper in meditation than you did yesterday. If you need help with this, get Ken D Foster's The Science of Meditation Guide for FREE.www.kendfoster.com/resources

Day 157

*"Courage questions everything, is attached to nothing,
and welcomes change with open arms."*

KEN D FOSTER

When you can access a feeling of peace in any given circumstance, and tune into your intuition, right choices will be yours consistently. Inner peace is the gateway to success and happiness. It is the gateway to becoming unstoppable in business and life.

The opposite is also true; when a person consistently makes decisions when feeling negative emotions such as anger, sadness, revenge, jealousy, etc., they are destined to make poor choices which lead to binding failures and chaos.

Why? Because their restless mind has blurred their discernment, so they consistently make poor choices. Intuition on the other hand is born in the bosom of peace and tranquility. Those who trust it are bound to succeed.

Today ask

"What has to happen for me to consistently make choices from a peaceful state?"

"How can my life get even better than it is?"

"What choice will I make today which will grow my life in a dynamic way?"

Actions

Practice making decisions only when your mind is free of harmful emotions, then watch how much less drama and how much more positive outcomes consistently appear in your life!

Day 158

"Wisdom equals knowledge plus courage. You not only have to know what to do and when to do it, but you have to also be brave enough to follow through."

JAROD KINTZ[80]

Visiting the big picture on a consistent basis will help assure your success. What is the big picture? It is your vision for success in both business and life! Many times, we get bogged down in the details. We sometimes get way too focused on the small things, and forget to stand back from our challenges and give ourselves time to relax and see things in a new light.

Success comes consistently to those who are willing to let go of how they think things should be, and open themselves up to how things indeed are. When you can see reality clearly without filtering it with false judgments, you will make better choices that will ultimately lead to greater success.

Today ask

"What am I not seeing, that if I did see, would open up new possibilities for me?"

"Where is my judgment getting in the way of my success?"

"What can I do to see reality clearly and make better choices?"

Actions

Make a success list of three areas in your life that you are committed to bringing in greater awareness, letting go of seeing things as they currently are and opening up to a brighter future.

Day 159

*"It is easy to judge people, places and things as less than
or more than you, but it takes courage to look through
eyes that choose to see beauty, love, and truth."*

KEN D FOSTER

Did you know that 'fault-finding' will stop your success? Fault-finding comes from a judgmental mind, and if you are going through life judging others, you will eventually see only the negative in every situation. The leads to worry, stress, and it will limit your success.

You have probably heard what goes around comes around, this is just a success principal called the Law of Karma. Simply stated, what you put out, you get back. In this case, if you are judgmental, you will get back critical judgments.

The amazing thing is that you may be the last to know that you are the one starting this vicious cycle and are attracting negative judgment to yourself.

Today ask

"What is positive about this thought or situation?"

"What is interesting about this?"

"How can I instantly change my point of view to see the positive about this situation?"

Actions

Note: (There is a catch to this exercise: If you dwell on the negative thought for more than 30 seconds, you will need to stop this exercise and restart your 24-hour timer. The goal of this exercise is to have 24 hours of continuous positive thoughts).

Continue the exercise above until you have 24 consecutive hours of positive thinking.

Day 160

"What is at the summit of courage, I think, is freedom. It is the freedom that comes with the knowledge that no earthly thing can break you."

PAULA GIDDINGS[81]

Your thoughts will limit you, or they will free you. Your mind is the principal creative instrument readily available for you to utilize and establish your pathway to success. In fact, it will create whatever pattern of thought you attach to it. Here is what I mean.

Right now, in this minute thoughts are floating past your mind. Whatever you decide to focus on will expand. For instance, try saturating your mind with the idea that you are unstoppable and will have the most amazing day ever.

In fact, if you stay focused on being unstoppable long enough, you will unleash an unstoppable force in your life. You will start to feel unstoppable because what you focus on will transform how you feel. And how you feel will change how you act.

The truth is that success or failure is nothing more than a thought. I have carefully watched my coaching clients over the years, and I will tell you this.... It wasn't the best looking, smartest or even the ones with the most money who were successful; it was the ones who developed the power of their minds to break out of their limitations. Once they made up their minds to create something, nothing stood in their way.

Today ask

"What can I do to increase my determination and realize the power of my mind?"

"How can I improve my knowledge and quickly bring forth my greatness?"

"If I stayed focused on being unstoppable every day, what would my life be like?"

Actions

Find the courage to take two constructive actions toward generating your dreams. As you do, notice how your mind power and magnetism increases drawing toward you everything you need to produce success.

Day 161

"Authenticity and achievement beyond measure await those who are courageous enough to find out who they truly are."

KEN D FOSTER

You must increase your personal power if you want to improve your success. The quickest way of doing this is to allow yourself to be who you indeed are. If you are ready to proceed to a new level, you will have to make demands on yourself and the universe to create the changes you desire.

No external circumstance can change unless you change the inner dialogue with a renewed commitment to align your inner self with the outer changes you intend. Just remember that within you is the powerful light of infinite spirit. You are more powerful than you think and more courageous than you know.

Know that the divine spirit is just behind your voice, just behind your mind, and just behind your willpower ready to burst forth in support of your dreams.

Then affirm, "I am submerged in the eternal presence of God. I am filled with wisdom, power, abundance, and love. It infuses every cell of my being. I am living this truth every day in every way."

Today ask

"Where have I defined the limits of my personal power?"

"What can I do today to let go of these limits?"

"What can I do to bring in more wisdom, power, abundance, and love?"

Actions

Meditate and decide on one step you will take to let go of your limiting beliefs. Also, think about what it would take to go deeper in meditation and feel more love than you did yesterday. If you need help with this, get Ken D Foster's The Science of Meditation Guide for FREE.www.kendfoster.com/resources.

Day 162

"It takes courage to let go of your stories of the past, forgive and realize your God-given strengths to overcome every challenge facing you."

KEN D FOSTER

When opportunities come your way, they are your own doing. Don't ever think they don't come by luck or chance. This is also true for problems you create. They didn't come to you by chance.

Instead, they came to you by your misguided thinking, created by you in the moment or by past thoughts you had. In fact, every choice you make is either propelling you to success or blocking it.

So, it is essential to pay close attention to your mind, emotions, and actions. Remember, you are an infinite being with creative power. You and Spirit are indeed one. Therefore, you can generate anything you ask to receive. Don't give that power away.

This doesn't mean you become passive. Don't be afraid to demand anything that is for your highest good. When you do, make sure to use your will and wisdom to take the consistent actions required.

Today ask

"What are the highest and best choices I can make today?"

"What are the next steps for me that will accelerate my pace of success?"

"How can I deepen my self-trust and consistently make the best choices?"

Actions

Take ten minutes three times today to become present and rest in the infinite connection you have with your soul.

Day 163

"Courage is fear that has said its prayers."

DOROTHY BERNARD[82]

Circumstances do not dictate your fate, but what you do with those circumstances will. What you make of your life is up to you, it is not based on where you live, where you went to school, who you know, what you know, how much money you have, or anything else.

Your beliefs, choices, and actions primarily determine your lifestyle. But even your beliefs, decisions and actions will not lead you to success unless you have found the path of inspiration. Because when you are "in-pired" or "in-spirit," you are tapping into the creative spirit where all success lies.

Wouldn't it be great to be inspired every day and bring forth your brilliance? You can do this by finding a cause or project that aligns with your spirit and is much larger than what you think you can accomplish.

You can become inspired at any time. Grandma Moses painted over fifteen hundred masterpieces after the age of seventy. Michelangelo did some of his most magnificent work after the age of seventy.

Louise Hay started Hay House Publishing, the largest publisher of self-help books in the world in her sixties. All these masters had one thing in common—inspired thinking. But why wait until you are in your sixties or seventies, start now!

Today ask

"Where am I inspired the most?"

"What has stopped me up to now from generating my greatest dreams?"

"What has to happen for me to be inspired and complete my dreams

Actions

Contemplate one thing that will inspire greatness within in you today and take massive action to bring it forth.

Day 164

"With courage, you will dare to take risks, have the strength to be compassionate and the wisdom to be humble. Courage is the foundation of integrity."

KESHAVAN NAIR[83]

It is all straightforward; what you put into your mind, body and life plus what you release from your mind, body and life will determine who you will become and how much joy and fulfillment you will have!

Learn to use the psychology of victory. Many times, when people see others, they think they are a failure because they don't have the material possessions, body type, relationship, job status or any number of things that the other people have. They never feel like what they have is enough and feel "less than others." This type of thinking is not friendly to your success.

Most of the time if you knew the other person's consciousness you wouldn't want to have it! The psychology of victory says: "There is nothing that can stop your success but you!" You will either be your own best friend or worst enemy. If you befriend yourself, you will succeed. If you think in negative terms, you become your own worst enemy and will fail. Friends treat friends with kindness and respect. Do you treat yourself this way?

When you talk to yourself in negative ways, think about the impact it has on you! Do you feel joyful and empowered or just miserable? Since your thoughts have energy behind them and this energy turns into vibration, which turns into feelings and those feelings will inspire actions or non-actions.

Today ask

"In what ways can I empower myself and others today?"

"How can I improve my self-talk?"

"What can I do to increase my energy in my mind, body, and life?"

Actions

Decide what you can do differently to bring more harmony into your relationship with yourself.

Day 165

"It takes courage to bring consciousness to what we think, say and do, and yet this is what is needed to find happiness."

KEN D FOSTER

Today's strategy is to become more conscious of how powerful your words are and what you are saying to yourself or others daily. As you may have realized, your words have the power to create happiness and success or misery and lack.

Words spoken in anger or shame can change a relationship forever and words spoken with love and gratitude can do the same. Dr. Masaru Emoto has studied the effect of words on water.

He has made some groundbreaking discoveries that supports the fact that your success or failures reflect your consciousness. And your consciousness reflects the words you speak.

Your words will determine where you live, who your friends are, how much money you have and everything else in your life. In other words, you are speaking your world into existence by what you think and say.

Commit to be fully present to what you are thinking and saying. Notice the effect it is having on you and those around you. Become aware if you are feeling empowered or disempowered after you speak.

Are you telling stories of success and abundance or creating a world filled with misgivings and worry? Remember, when you speak you are either building success or something else.

Today ask

"How can I become more aware of the words I speak?"

"What can I do to speak with clarity, wisdom, and authority consistently?"

"What are the most important words to speak to myself daily?"

Actions

Make a list of the ten most influential words or phrases that make you feel empowered.

Day 166

*"Have courage and a little willingness to
venture and be defeated."*

ROBERT FROST[84]

People whose view of life does not change through time pretty much waste their lives. This is a bold statement, but it is true.

We are here to evolve mentally, emotionally, physically and spiritually. Playing small and staying in your comfort zone is of no use to your advancement. It is only when you stretch your limits and grow your presence that you can become all you were meant to be.

You can become anything you choose. Why not start becoming the master of your life—starting today? You may ask: "How do I do this?" The answer is simple. First, close your eyes and ask: "What is possible for me?" Then let go of what you have imagined yourself to be in the past.

The truth is you are infinite spirit, so why would an infinite spirit limit itself? Now start acting harmoniously with your soul. Who are you without any confining limits? What does your life feel like without any thoughts of your past? The more you stay connected to your spirit, the better your life becomes.

Today ask

"What do I need to accept today that will change all my tomorrows?"

"Where can I find the answers to get what I want in life?"

"What am I willing to take ownership of to increase my success?"

Actions

Make a list of three ways you are limiting yourself and then take actions to change this around.

Day 167

"Do not expect the world to look bright if you don't wear courageous glasses."

KEN D FOSTER

A person without imagination has lost the ability to soar with the eagles of creativity and generate the life of their dreams. As Einstein said, *"Imagination is everything. It is the preview of life's coming attractions."*

Your ability to use the power of imagination will determine to a large extent how much success you have. Developing the habit of daily positive imagination lays the foundation for opening the portals of your brilliance.

The spiritual teacher Yogananda said: *"Consciousness is imaginative, sensitive and pliable; it can think and dream itself into any state."* Take a few minutes and contemplate this statement, then determine what you will imagine into being.

Today ask:

"What are the qualities I possess that will make this dream come true?"

"How will I evolve my thinking to have the life of my dreams?"

"Who must I become to live my dreams?"

Actions:

Close your eyes and take a few minutes to Imagine that your dreams are creating your destiny and then take two action steps to make them come true.

Tap into your higher-self and increase your intuition with Ken D Foster's guided meditations on Business, Wealth, Expanding Possibility, Peace, and Health. Yours for free at couragetochange.us/meditation

CHAPTER 9

UNLEASH YOUR COURAGE

Day 168

"There is within you, waiting to be called, a great source
of power called courage. Call its name, and it will give
you the strength to overcome fear and uncertainty,
and the heart to continue with bold confidence despite
the pain of disappointment and even tragedy."

MICHAEL JOSEPHSON[85]

You are on a courageous journey called life. Life always comes with choice. You get to choose your journey and take full responsibility for what shows up. The journey is set up with losses, hurt, hopelessness, emotional pain, suffering, hardship, challenges and distractions.

There is also love, pleasure and happiness to help soften the journey. But don't be fooled, the journey is there for a reason. You will either evolve which will lead you to permanent victory and unending happiness or not, in which case you will be given another opportunity to try again.

To have a successful journey you will need to remember who you are, how powerful you are, and you must coax your courage to come out. If you don't, sooner or later your dreams will die, and your life's journey will not have been fulfilled.

Today ask

"What can I do to detach from the delusions of the world and see reality clearly?"

"How can I be free from restless thoughts so that I can enter higher states of consciousness?"

"What are the steps I can take today to bring more love, with a service-attitude, into my life?"

Actions

You have a future full of possibilities, so do the best you can and give one hundred percent to making a difference in the world.

Day 169

*"Why trust others for your answers? Why not summon up your
courage, delve deep into the unknown parts of yourself,
and realize what is possible?"*

KEN D FOSTER

If you have not tried to do the impossible, you will never know your limits. Great things have been accomplished by people who have stretched themselves past their limits.

Think about what it took to build companies like Apple, Amazon, and Google, or structures like the Golden Gate Bridge, Statue of Liberty, or the first Space Station.

These are great feats that started with an idea in the minds of the founders. You too have amazing ideas that the world is waiting for! Does this sound odd to you?

If so, then it is time to rethink what is possible for you. No matter what your station in life, there are opportunities waiting for you to explore. So why not start now?

Today ask

"What has been holding me back from bringing my greatest gifts into the world?"

"What am I determined to do, no matter what happens?"

"What will make the biggest difference in determining whether I succeed?"

Actions

Think of two ideas that would truly stretch your limits if you worked them out. In other words, determine two large goals that you cannot possibly accomplish on your own. Journal about these ideas using the power of your creative mind, asking how you can expand these ideas until you get clarity on what the next steps will be.

Day 170

*"You see, to find the brightest wisdom one must pass
through the darkest zones. And through the darkest zones,
there can be no guide. No guide, that is, but courage."*

ADAM GIDWITZ[86]

Have you noticed that one person with courage can change the world? Just look at Gandhi's courage to free his country from British rule, or Mother Theresa's courage to work with the poorest of the poor, or Martin Luther King's courage to stand up against cultural-based prejudice and injustice.

You may ask: "What does courage have to do with changing my life?" I say, *Everything!* When you connect with the courage of your soul, you can change whatever you choose and make it better.

This may seem far fetched when you are struggling with an issue, but it can get better starting today. The first step is to declare that you will be a Victor over the issue and realize nothing can stand in the way of your success.

Today ask

"If I let go of the ways I have limited myself, what would happen?"

"What has to happen for me to make courageous choices consistently?"

"How can I be courageous consistently and manifest my greatest dreams?"

Actions

Think about three areas you are committed to changing. Then decide your highest priority and take two steps toward it.

Day 171

"It is not the size of your goals that matters;
it is the size of your courage."

KEN D FOSTER

Have you ever told yourself that you could not do something that you wanted to do? Maybe you tried to fly a plane, take a trip, have a slim body, overcome some disease, have a fantastic relationship or own a multi-million-dollar business; but you dismissed it thinking it is too wild, or too big, or too unbelievable, or too whatever, to become a reality for you.

Don't believe it! Whatever you focus your attention on and make up your mind to do, you can do! Within you is an unstoppable and inexhaustible power. Nothing and nobody can stand in your way; other than yourself. To tap into this power, you must stretch your limits.

You will never know what you can accomplish until you make up your mind to let go of whatever is stopping you from taking actions toward your dreams.

Today ask

"What is one thing I will accomplish, which will change my life for the better?"

"How can I become unstoppable?"

"How will I put the full force of my will behind every effort, no matter what?"

Actions

Decide what the goal is that you have been putting off and then come up with five ways to generate this goal. Note: (Go ahead and stretch yourself until you are never the same).

Day 172

"Courage isn't having the strength to go on—it is going on when you don't have strength."

NAPOLEON BONAPARTE[87]

Are you playing to win the game of life, or are you playing it safe? People who play to win have a different mindset than those who are focused on being secure. There is a cost to playing it safe, and that cost may be your life's purpose.

If you are not growing and stretching yourself to be all you were meant to be, you may one day look back with regrets and wonder; "If only I would have, or "could have made more courageous choices."

When you play it safe, you are typically more focused on fears than possibilities. If you are wondering if you are playing too small, then take a few minutes and rate yourself by the results you are getting. On a scale of one to five rate these areas: career, business, relationships, health, spiritual, fun and financial life. Then you will know where you need to show up bigger.

One of my early mentors Tony Robbins taught me this. "If you are doing a good job, you will most likely be getting poor results. If you are doing a great job, you will probably be getting good results, but if you are playing full-out and doing what it takes to win, you are getting outstanding results". How are you doing?

Today ask

"What are the results I am committed to getting?"

"What part of myself must I tap into so that I play full-out?"

"How am I choosing my life to be, from today on?"

Actions

Determine where you have been playing it safe and then set a new intention to play full-out.

Day 173

*"Discouragement is not the absence of
adequacy but the absence of courage."*

NEAL A. MAXWELL[88]

There is only one thing that will free you from limitations in your life and that is the truth. And the truth is: you must replace the blind spots in your life with an awareness of what needs to change or improve.

To accomplish this, you must be able to see your actions from a dispassionate point of view. Getting upset with yourself when you don't achieve what you intend; or making mistakes and then beating yourself up will not lead to healthy, productive change. You will only feel disempowered, through shame, guilt or resentment—not empowered to move into success.

It is when you get to the cause of personal friction that you change your perception and release whatever is causing conflict in your life. We are all free to have fantastic life experiences or a life filled with suffering, drama and strife. Which one will you choose? What will you do to evolve your points of view today? What will be better for you from here on out?

Today ask

"What do I need to change, so I can be in harmony with all circumstances?"

"How can I be more accepting of myself and others?"

"What can I do to let go of false expectations of myself and be happier?"

Actions

Dispassionately notice when you walk into a room how your personality impacts others. Also, take note of what bothers you or zaps your energy and then ask: "What must I believe to be impacted by this person, place or thing?".

Day 174

*"Confront the dark parts of yourself, and work to banish
them with illumination and forgiveness. Your willingness to
wrestle with your demons will cause your angels to sing."*

AUGUST WILSON[89]

Right now, you can exponentially change the way you are showing up in life and break the lifelong patterns that have caused you misery. Have you noticed that circumstances change, but your habits remain the same?

Maybe you have the habit of negative self-talk, procrastination, overeating, lack of self-confidence, being easy to anger, lack of self-control, or lack of willpower. For change to take place, you must first acknowledge precisely what you are going to change. Most people take this first step. Just think—New Year's resolutions are filled with people acknowledging habits they want to change, but that is where it stops for most. But not for you. Here is the formula to break your habits.

When you wake up, open your eyes and think of what you experience gratitude for, then meditate for a few minutes. Reflect on what is important to you and who you are choosing to become.

Talk to yourself about who you indeed are, a child of the God. Take a few deep breaths in and feel the presence of something bigger than yourself pulsing through your body. This is your spirit. Connect to it, and then commit to breaking one habit which is stopping your success.

Today ask

"What is the habit I am committed to breaking?

"What steps I can take today that will increase my resolve to break the habit?"

"What new habit can I start today to replace the old one with?"

Actions

"Google" the habit you are going to break. Get information about how others have also broken this habit.

Day 175

*"Find the Courage to know the truth of who "you"
really are, and then live "you" fearlessly."*

KEN D FOSTER

If you take the average of your closest friends and measure their weight, finances, and health, chances are you will be the average of them all. In other words, if your friends have an average weight of 180, an income of $100,000 and are of average health, you will most likely be very close to these statistics.

Why? Because, consciously or not, they have become your mentors and teachers. You have aligned with their vibration and energy. You will have similar fluctuations in thought. They either hold you back, or empower you, or in many cases, both. If you take on their points of view, eventually your lifestyle will be similar to theirs.

If you would like to live an extraordinary life filled with unending joy, happiness, and abundance, set your intention to quicken your success by choosing the right friends. These are friends who have your best interest at heart, who embody your potential and raise you up. This is particularly important if you are to succeed in your efforts.

Today ask

"What are the personal qualities that I am choosing to develop?"

"What are the most important qualities of the companions I am choosing?"

"What will it take for me to attract amazing friends and mentors in my life with the qualities that I need to increase my success?"

Actions

Set your intention to find one new friend or mentor over the next two weeks that will take your life to a new level.

Day 176

Some people wonder when success will finally come to them. Others understand that life is showing up perfectly to teach them what they need to know to evolve and conquer their poor habits. They also develop their gifts, talents, and abilities to make the world a better place for all.

Success is here—living and breathing in each one of us this very moment. If you have eyes to see and a brain to think, you are a success. If you can feel the wind on your skin, you are a success. If you can breathe the air, you are a success. If you can smell the fragrance of a flower, you are a success.

You have beaten the odds of millions of other sperm and egg-cells and have been born in a body that gives you the potential to realize your divinity and tap into your greatest dreams.

Today ask

"What has to happen for me to realize that I am already successful?"

"What will I focus on to bring more of my brilliance out and expand my success?"

"How can I realize my full potential?"

Actions

Meditate and determine what you will do today to bring out more of your brilliance? Also, think about what it would take to go deeper in meditation and allow the expansion of your brilliance to actually happen. If you need help with this, get Ken D Foster's The Science of Meditation Guide for FREE. www.kendfoster.com/resources

Day 177

*"Courage is not simply one of the virtues but the
form of every virtue at the testing point, which
means at the point of highest reality."*

C.S. LEWIS[90]

Since the world you live in is a replica of your thinking, doesn't it make sense that if you don't like your circumstances, it's time to change your beliefs, choices, and actions?

I see so many people going through life stopping their success without any realization that they have a part in it! They seem to be blind to their shadow side until it starts creating immense problems for them.

Why go through life creating havoc and believing that you have no part in it, or that you can't change your conditions? This is silly! It is equally easy to create a life filled with drama as it is to develop a life of harmony.

If something isn't working in life, it has been given to you as a gift to help you overcome your limited thinking and evolve yourself. It isn't there to hold you hostage or crush you. Think about a challenge that has been persistent in your life. Whatever the problem, be it money, business, relationship, friendship or family, you can change it starting now.

Today ask

"If I really knew I could change anything in my life what would it be?"

"Starting today, what am I committed to changing no matter what?"

"How can I change the unchangeable with ease and grace?"

Actions

Make a list of three things you will change for sure.

Day 178

Courage isn't about taking reckless risks it's an inner strength that you can tap into anytime. We all have this capacity—but like a muscle—if it lies dormant and unused, it will become inactive.

The opposite is also true. When we consciously tap into courage, it opens the energetic doorways that power us into action and aids us to overcome any obstacle in our way. You can learn to be courageous at will and hold onto it no matter what happens.

Some people are absolutely crushed when life tests them, while others realize that the tests are there to strengthen them. When the ego surrenders to the soul, that is the true triumph over trials and the overcoming of all obstacles.

Thus, those who are unconquered by tests live in the Wisdom-Self, an ever-expanding consciousness of inner fulfillment. They are indeed successful in life. This is what living a courageous life is all about, coming through the turmoil into the light as a stronger, more confident person.

Today ask

"If I were courageous, what would I do today?"

"How can I become more courageous every day?"

"What are the three most courageous acts I can do to increase success in my life?"

Actions

Make a list of 5 things that will increase your courage?

Day 179

*"To be victorious in life takes a courageous heart
and a mind filled with wisdom."*

KEN D FOSTER

It has been said that to live on planet earth you must be able to see the darkness to realize the goodness. If you deceive yourself by only looking at what you perceive as "good," then you will misperceive life and reap havoc on yourself.

It all starts by shining light on your shadows to illuminate what you need to change, improve and develop. Why? Because if you can't see your darkness, how can you ever change your life for the better? And, how can you know who you genuinely are?

Truly successful people spend time in meditation, introspection and contemplation. They connect to their intuitive self, realize who they are and affirm what is possible for their lives. They are not afraid to look at all sides of themselves and make changes to improve their lives. In fact, they become masters of themselves and their lives.

Today ask

"What shadows in my life are keeping me stuck?"

"Where will I shine the light of introspection to uproot problems in my life?"

"Who am I destined to become when I can see my shadow side and overcome it?"

Actions

Determine one area of life your shadow is stopping your success, then focus on one strength to overcome the shadow.

Day 180

"All men are frightened. The more intelligent they are, the more they are frightened. The courageous man is the man who forces himself, in spite of his fear, to carry on."

GENERAL GEORGE S. PATTON JR.[91]

Fearful thinking will not get you where you want to go. You can't worry your problems out of existence; you must approach your challenges with courage and the spirit of inquiry if you are to overcome them.

Positive questioning paired with right actions is the way to success. No matter how many fearful thoughts come your way, realize they are just thoughts. You can always ask a compelling question to move past a fear, such as: "If I didn't have this fear, how would my life be better?" or "What can I do to overcome this fear immediately?"

There is no better way to build strength and self-esteem than to overcome your misguided fears. Everyone has some built-in fears. They protect you and warn you of actual dangers.

But when your fears start running your life, you must take charge to overcome them. Because most fears never happen. They are no more than a product of an imaginative mind or other people's points of view, so why let them rule your life?

Today ask

"Truth, am I willing to find the courage to let go of my fears?"

"Truth, when will I let these fears go?"

"What will my life be like when I am fearless?"

Actions

Tell a friend your greatest fear and come up with a strategy to overcome it. Your dreams are meant to be realized and you will be much closer to accomplishing them, when you let go of fear!

Day 181

"Too many people have cut out their connection with spirit and are running on logic. It takes courage to go against the herd and reconnect to your inner genius."

KEN D FOSTER

The word inspiration comes from combining the words "in" and "spirit." "Inspirited" meaning you are being inspired by your spirit. For the success- seeker, it is a risk to live from Spirit, because listening to intuition and being natural and authentic in public sometimes feels strange.

In truth, however, Spirit and Courage go hand in hand. When you combine the two, you will find happiness, fulfillment and ongoing success. So, are you ready to increase your inspiration? If you are, here are a few suggestions.

In the morning, upon waking, take some time to connect with Spirit. First, close your eyes and gently lift your gaze to the so-called spiritual eye. Second, repeat the mantra, "Spirit and I are one" until you have a sense of peace. Third, ask: "How can I connect deeper with Spirit?"

(Note: You don't have to answer the question with your logical mind. Allow Spirit to do that for you). Fourth, open up to receive some surprising new insights.

Today ask

"What will it take to have more inspiration in my life?"

"What am I not seeing, that if I did see it, would inspire me greatly?"

"When I am inspired, how much more energy do I have? "

Actions

Meditate on the infinite possibilities that are available to you to realize your dreams.

Day 182

"Do you think courage means being fearless? Or daring?
Courage, real courage, is taking three steps when it terrifies you."

CATHERINE ANDERSON[92]

A competitive mindset combined with wisdom will increase your ability to succeed. Did you know that in some communities, competition is looked upon as something that is negative? Some go so far as to believe that competition needs to be rooted out of a personality if a person is to walk a spiritual path.

I have found just the opposite to be true. Healthy competition builds strength, endurance and good fellowship. If you look upon competition in a way that promotes health and growth, it can increase your connection to the divine.

Of course, competition is not so laudable when it tears down your competitor and creates misery and suffering for others. If you conquer your domain at the expense of others, you are embarking on a path of self-destruction. Eventually, you will burn bridges and lose yourself.

True competition is the ability to conquer yourself and to overcome any obstacles that stand in your way of success. It also builds both you and your competitor to new heights.

Today ask

"What do I love about competing that brings joy to my heart?"

"How can I increase my competitiveness and yet empower others along the way?"

"Where can I win, my competitors win, and the community win at the same time?"

Actions

Resolve to be a better competitor by finding win/win/win solutions in all you do. You win, your competitors win, your community wins.

Day 183

*"Courage, kindness, friendship, and character; these
are the qualities that define us as human beings,
and propel us, on occasion, to greatness."*

R.J. PALACIO[93]

Some people are inspired with large dreams and have causes that are bigger than themselves. They are connected to a worthwhile purpose that enhances their life and the lives of others. Others live for themselves and are always looking to see what they can squeeze out of other people and life.

It doesn't take a genius to know that people who are givers are happier than the takers. But it does take a strong intention and continuous efforts to stay on the giving side of life. It all starts with the right attitude and an optimistic mindset. Optimism is a type of charisma that by its very nature attracts people and good circumstances to us.

Most people don't realize the power of their mind but those who know recognize that when the mind is positively charged, it sets up a vibratory energy that attracts wealth, health, love and everything you are looking for.

Try to surround yourself with those who are positive lights and who are contributing to the betterment of humanity, knowing that this special group is well on their way to lasting success.

Today ask

"What is miraculous about today that I am seeing?"

"How is it that my life is getting better and better?"

"What will positively charge my mind with energy, brilliance and joy?"

Actions

Increase your determination to succeed and follow through with two action steps.

Day 184

"There is a power that is greater than the sun, moon, and stars;
it lives in each one of us, and it is called courage."

KEN D FOSTER

Let nothing stand in your way of being all you can be. You were born to bring forth your greatness. The only thing that stands in your way is limiting self-beliefs. So why let disempowering beliefs stop you from being all you can be?

If something is preventing you from being all that you were meant to be, then it is up to you to transcend the limitation. You may say I don't know what it is or how to do this, but don't let these thoughts stop you.

Within you is brilliance and the power to overcome any limitation. Don't even consider being an ineffectual human being. Cast out of your mind any thoughts of failure. You must not doubt if you are to overcome your limitations and succeed.

Remember you are a child of the Most-High; your nature is success. The Ego may be sensitive and afraid, but the soul is invincible. Know that you are always connected to your soulful self and know you can overcome any limitations; this is the way to ongoing prosperity and success.

Today ask

"What is stopping my success that I am committed to overcoming?"

"What can I do to bring forth my gifts and talents in a much bigger way?"

"How can I transcend every limiting belief I have bought into?"

Actions

The journey begins anew. Decide here, and now you are going to do what it takes to become who you were meant to be.

Tap into your higher-self and increase your intuition with Ken D Foster's guided meditations on Business, Wealth, Expanding Possibility, Peace, and Health. Yours for free at couragetochange.us/meditation

Day 185

*"So long as you have courage and a sense of humor, it is
never too late to start life afresh."*

FREEMAN DYSON[95]

Wisdom is a soul quality which is developed when the truth is sought after. It is a quality that is not just available to a wise few, but to everyone who seeks truth and acts upon it.

I encourage you to take time every day to read books filled with wisdom. Dive deep into the meaning of what you read until you understand your station in life. There is nothing more important than finding out who you truly are and what you value in life. It is by living in harmony with yourself that life unfolds in awe-inspiring ways.

It is also wise to know if you are moving forward, standing still or going backward in all areas of life. For many, this is difficult, because you may fixate on looking good at all costs.

But the wise way is to lower your pride and drum up the courage to look at what is working and what is not, then ask for help from knowledgeable counsel when you don't have the answers. As Einstein pointed out "you can't solve a problem with the same mindset that created it." Wise men and women are all around you, seek them out.

Today ask

"What has it cost me not to seek wise counsel?"

"Who can I approach that will offer me some wise counsel?"

"What is the most important action steps I can take today that will increase my wisdom?"

Actions

Think of an area in your life that challenges you. It may be finances, health, or areas of family or home life. Then make an effort to figure out why you have let this challenge remain with you.

Day 186

*"It isn't for the moment you are struck that you need courage,
but for that long uphill climb back to sanity, faith, and security."*

ANNE MORROW LINDBERGH[96]

Your daily actions express your true commitments. If you want to see what you are committed to, just look at what you prioritize daily. Do you make work more important than your family? Do you make distractions more critical than accomplishing your dreams?

Do you make playing safe more important than playing to win? Are you living your highest priorities? Of course, you are, whether you are conscious of it or not. Your priorities are what you are doing each day, and nothing else.

Every day, through your thinking, choices, and actions, you are either freeing yourself or creating more troubles. You can get off the drama merry-go-round any time, but you must be willing to acknowledge what you want and go after it.

You can't have more if you don't know where you are going.

Today ask

"What is the most important area in my life that needs attention?"

"What am I willing to change, no matter what?"

"What has to happen for me to make choices that consistently lead to success?"

Actions

Think about your three most significant accomplishments in the last three days. How do you feel about them?

Day 187

"Courageous people own their thoughts, feelings and choices."

KEN D FOSTER

Every day is an opportunity to create more joy, fulfillment, and success. You have been given everything you need, including an unstoppable spirit which is there to help you create an amazing life. Your job is to take care of your body, mind, and spirit, so it is entirely functioning, vibrant and filled with happy thoughts.

I am sure by now you realize that your thoughts control your experience in the world. Everyone has their share of troubles, but for those who learn to master their minds and focus on being even-minded in the wintertime of challenges there waits for ongoing happiness.

Don't live in the darkness of mental disenchantment subject to the emotions of worry, stress, and unhappiness. It is essential to dispel every negative thought of discouragement, fear, and discontentment. Instead, drink in the vibrations of abundance, gratitude, and joy.

Mentally nourish your mind with inspiring books and positive affirmations. Feast unendingly on creative thoughts and ever new accomplishments. Take long walks introspecting with your spirit.

Make a difference in someone's life by just loving them. Give away your worries and fill your mind with happy thoughts. Exercise your right to accomplish your highest dreams without interrupting dramas, and genuinely choose to be even-minded.

Today ask

"What can I do to have a more vibrant, healthy, and happy life?"

"Who can I help or encourage to bring more happiness into their life?"

"How can I remain calm in the face of life's storms?"

Actions

Tell a friend or your coach three ways you will take better care of yourself.

Day 188

*Letting go of cultural programming and realizing
your soulful essence takes determination and
courage, but it is worth the effort."*

KEN D FOSTER

Belief in yourself and faith in the Infinite Spirit will meet any challenge you face. Are you truly the master of your destiny or a victim of your circumstances? The choice is yours. The Infinite Spirit lives in you, and you live in the Spirit.

In fact, everything comes from Infinite Spirit: the good, bad and everything else. The good and the bad help you evolve and grow into the awareness of the infinite being that you are.

Take a few minutes and think about where you would like to be in your business or life, one year from now. Allow your awareness of what is possible for you to expand. Once you have determined what it will be like, ask: *"How can it be even better?"* Now consider if you truly believe that you have everything you need to get there. Do you? If not, you are not alone.

When looking at big dreams it can seem daunting, but when you have a strong conviction in your abilities to achieve, and combine that with the realization that you are an infinite being filled with power and wisdom, you become unstoppable.

Today ask

"What do I know is true about manifesting my dreams?"

"What are the most important steps I can take to fulfill my dreams, starting today?"

"How can I ensure that my dreams are realized?"

Actions

Remember the infinite part of yourself and then practice being unstoppable.

Day 189

"You can be victorious in life if you find the courage to change your beliefs, choices, and actions until success is yours.

KEN D FOSTER

Courage is a divine gift that exists within you. It is yours instantly when you are ready to coax it into being. But remember this! It must be savored and developed. When it is, you will experience a sense of greatness within yourself and do things which are impossible for most.

Courage calls all of us to awaken our consciousness to new possibilities. It invites us to start over when everything has fallen apart. It calls us to change when we want things to stay the same. It asks us to accept things the way they are instead of the way we want them to be. It calls us to be better and not bitter about what has gone on in the past. It invites us to awaken to our Spirit and leave mediocracy behind.

Close your eyes and think of a time when you were courageous. What did it feel like? Where do you feel it in your body (head, heart, throat, stomach, legs, arms)? Wherever you feel it, imagine it expanding to every cell of your body. Now imagine that feeling is increasing. Practice this technique several times until you can generate courage instantly in any situation.

Today ask

"What has blocked me from developing my courage?"

"How can I experience a deeper sense of courage within myself?"

"What are two courageous actions I can make today that will evolve my soul?"

Actions

In the next twenty-four hours, connect with your courage and do something you have never done before.

Day 190

"Finding out who you are and what your purpose in life is, takes courageous efforts that are rewarded with wisdom and peace."

KEN D FOSTER

The urge to become all that you can be is universal. So, don't deny that you want to be more, do more and have more of your brilliance come into the world. Focus on expanding the boundaries of what you think is possible, and your life will get better!

Look at your life and decide where you can improve and bring in the mastery of excellence. Setting specific large targets to hit or goals to achieve will help bring forth your greatness and stretch you so that excellence can be born. But excellence doesn't come just because you set up goals; it occurs because of wisdom, determination and focused effort.

It happens in the silence and stillness of meditation. So before setting goals or making any significant decisions, meditate. It will nurture the coming forth of your wisdom.

Also, after meditation, contemplating exactly how you achieve your goals is a good practice. Then determine to generate your dreams no matter what obstacles come your way and take immediate actions to accelerate your success.

Today ask

"What are the standards of excellence I will set in my life?"

"What am I committing to achieve that will stretch me way beyond my comfort zone?"

"What has to happen to keep me determined to achieve my dreams no matter what obstacles come my way?"

Actions

Access higher states of consciousness by meditating for at least ten minutes in the morning and evening.

Day 191

*"Courage is the hallmark of spirituality. Courage comes
when you love yourself for who you are."*

DR. AMIT RAY[97]

Meditation is the door that leads to conscious awakening and ongoing success in all areas of life. You can free your mind of problems and the delusions of the world when you clear your thoughts through meditation.

By clearing your mind, you will be able to tap into the super-conscious mind of unlimited solutions rather than run your life utilizing only the senses. Most people run on whims, emotions, attitudes, and habits. They are not capable of creating lasting success.

However, when you learn to clear the mind and make right decisions based on awareness, your life gets better and a lot more fun. Imagine being calm under fire and coming up with wisdom-guided solutions to your greatest problems.

Today ask

"What is possible for me if I were to make the right choices with each decision?"

"What can I do to stay calm under all circumstances?"

"How can my life get better and better?"

Actions

Schedule some time to connect with your Creator. Then, open to receive the information you need to see things differently and make wiser choices. With the ongoing practice of meditation, you will see that it facilitates your life to get more and more into the flow of who you indeed are.

Day 192

"The essence of courage is the heart saying peruse the unattainable, find your passion, and bring forth your brilliance for all to see."

KEN D FOSTER

Efficiency that leads to success is developed through deep concentration. There is no better way to develop concentration than through meditation. It is by focusing your attention on the "third eye" or "spiritual eye" that develops the focus.

When you can quiet your thoughts and still your mind, you become entirely focused. As you do, you begin to tap into the creative power within you, which is the source to bring forth your greatness.

So, why wait? Start today and find the wisdom, intuition, and brilliance that is waiting for you. When you want to create something that is important to you, sit in stillness and meditate deeply upon it.

As you do, you will be guided by the creative spirit! It is also imperative, once you receive the answers you are seeking, to exert your willpower to accomplish your objective immediately.

Today ask

"What can I do that will increase my wisdom-guided choices?"

"How can I win victory over my limiting beliefs today?"

"What am I being called to do differently?"

Actions

Expand your meditation time today and go deeper than you ever have. If you need help with this, get Ken D Foster's The Science of Meditation Guide for FREE. www.kendfoster.com/resources

CHAPTER 10

UNTETHER YOUR SOUL

Day 193

"To be courageous requires no exceptional qualifications, no magic formula. It's an opportunity that sooner or later is presented to us all and each personmust look for that courage in his soul."

JOHN F. KENNEDY[98]

A focused mind and loving heart will clear the pathway of life for you. It is through the art of controlling the mind that all-around success is achieved.

Although your conscious mind cannot in itself bring about success, when you are tuned into the vibrational energy of the superconsciousness mind—you can be assured of victory. It is within the superconscious state that all wisdom and power flows into your body, mind, and will.

According to Yoga Psychology, there are five primary states of mind: disturbed, bewildered, distracted, concentrated and controlled. Most people spend their days with a disturbed, bewildered or distracted state of mind.

But when—through meditation—the mind is calmed; the higher states of consciousness are attained. It then becomes easy to concentrate and keep the mind focused on superconscious states of awareness bringing in the ideas for unlimited success.

Today ask

"What is possible for me when I consistently meditate?"

"What can I commit to doing that will upsurge my success?"

"How can I consistently make choices with a calm mind?"

Actions

In the next twenty-four hours, tell a friend or your coach what will empower you and change you for the better.

Day 194

"Why trust your senses for answers? Why not summon up courage and delve deep into unknown parts of yourself to realize what is possible?"

KEN D FOSTER

Many people walk around believing they are making good choices only to find that their thinking is flawed. They invest their time, energy and money into people, places and things that they believe will bring them success, only to find failure waiting around the corner for them. Has this ever happened to you?

If you would like to have more success in your life, then take time today to meditate. Quiet your mind and see if you can go deeper today than you have the last time you meditated. In fact, set a goal to go more in-depth each time you meditate.

Let's face it: Life gets better and better when you can tap into your intuition, and since intuition is perfected through meditation, it is wise to commit to meditating morning and evening. Are you willing to do that?

I am hoping you said *"Yes"*! When you sit down to meditate today, just affirm to yourself that: *"I have nowhere to go and nothing to do, but be with God."* This is the right attitude to have.

Today ask

"What has to happen for me to go deeper in meditation every day?"

"How can I become in tune with higher states of consciousness?"

"How can I improve my commitment to meditation?"

Actions

Take one action step to increase your intuition.

Day 195

"It takes courage to grow up and become who you really are."

E.E. CUMMINGS[99]

Have you wondered how you can consistently generate success in all areas of life? I am sure you're now realizing that your circumstances are not dictated by fate rather by every choice you have made! So, now that you recognize this, how can you make consistent decisions that are in your best interest? Are you ready to explore this?

I have found that true success comes to those who meditate and tune into their inner guidance. Once you realize the power of spirit, you can focus it on anything you choose and generate success. Try this; before embarking on an important project, take time to quiet your mind and meditate. Now use the full force of your attention and start contemplating your next steps.

Use the magnifying glass of your thoughts to concentrate on the task at hand. Don't let yourself be distracted by anything until you have determined what your next steps will be. The root cause of many failures is lack of clear direction and focused attention. Greatness is a result of committed care!

Did you know that there is a scientific method of concentration in which results are consistent? What it takes is you disengaging from objects of distraction and placing your complete attention on the task at hand until you get the results you desire.

It requires doing one task at a time and being fully present to everything you're doing. With the power of this concentration, you can tap into the unlimited power of your mind and guard all the doors against any iota of failure entering.

Today ask

"What will I concentrate on to create more success in my life?"

"How will I fully develop the power of my concentration?"

"How can I increase my awareness and disengage from distractions that block my success?"

Actions

Tune into your intuition and solve one of your greatest challenges today.

Day 196

"Through courageous acts and by facing the unknown,
one can tap into their brilliance and generate
products and services that benefit society."

KEN D FOSTER

Every great invention, every amazing idea, and all the brilliance that has ever come into the world comes from the superconscious mind of people just like you. The superconscious mind is all-encompassing and ever-present, but to tap into it, you must learn to still the constant thought chatter and judgments that limit you.

Einstein once said, *"I want to know God's thoughts; the rest are details."* He knew that by tapping into the superconscious mind he could find the answers to any challenge and bring in new information that could change the course of history. You can do the same!

Take some time to still your mind chatter by meditating. Then visualize your greatest dream repeatedly until you can feel the realness of it. Imagine having perfect faith that it will materialize. Then let go of any doubt, fear or uncertainty and bring in only peace, tranquility and a knowing that you are a powerful creative being, ever generating what you need at the time you need it.

Today ask

"As an infinite being, what am I capable of generating in my life?"

"What is the power that dwells in me that will generate my greatest dreams?"

"What am I willing to question, which will bring more abundance into my life?"

Actions

Take some time to make a list of three things you think are impossible to accomplish, then do what it takes to start achieving one of them.

Day 197

"Courage counts when you surrender your old ways in a quest for a new course. But how do you find a new course? It is by communing with the soul."

KEN D FOSTER

Wikipedia defines charisma as a compelling attractiveness or charm that can inspire devotion in others. And this radiance of character or charisma is a master key to business success.

Imagine having enough presence of self to attract what you need when you need it. It can be done! You have the power, but you must develop this trait. Think about it. If you truly make up your mind to be more charismatic, can anyone stop you? Of course not! Only you can stop your success by not tapping into your charisma and allow it to emerge.

But how do you increase your charisma? Since charisma is a soulful quality, the first step is to connect with the soul deeply. A commitment to daily meditation will connect you to your internal beauty and power.

Take some quiet time and meditate on the fact that you are one with your creator because who is more charismatic than a soul connected to the infinite?

As you meditate, try to realize that you are just as close to your creator now as you ever will be. Your charisma comes from this connection, so the more you remember to connect the more you will radiate charisma deeply.

Today ask

"How can I remember who I truly am and express more charisma?"

"As an infinite being, what has to happen for me to intensify my charisma?"

"What shifts in consciousness can I make to use my charisma in more powerful ways?"

Actions

Imagine that you can attract what you need when you need it. Next, set your intention to consistently show up in a charismatic state and see what happens.

Day 198

"Courage is what it takes to stand up and speak; courage is also what it takes to sit down and listen."

WINSTON CHURCHILL[100]

Success isn't about how many things you possess; it is about being able to create what you need when you need it. This is a power that doesn't come from just thinking, but by tapping into the creative force in your superconscious mind.

Possessions come and go. One day you are a millionaire and the next you can be under pressure to find your next meal. This can happen very quickly in this ever-changing world.

Then what? Very few can use their willpower and determination alone to create their destiny. If you were to lose everything you have, where would you be? For those who have learned how to turn on the faucet of infinite creative mind, there is nothing to fear, because they can move all obstacles that stand in their way.

So, how do you tap into that creativity and generate what you need at will? It is through quieting your mind, increasing awareness and connecting deeply with the infinite power within you. There lies the secret of real success.

Today ask

"What choice will I make today to increase my awareness?"

"What am I going to start doing that will instantly make my life better?"

"What is one thing I will stop doing to make my life better?"

Actions

Today, tell your best friend how your life is getting better.

Tap into your higher-self and increase your intuition with Ken D Foster's guided meditations on Business, Wealth, Expanding Possibility, Peace, and Health. Yours for free at couragetochange.us/meditation

Day 199

*"When you let courage permeate your heart you will
generate an unlimited life for yourself."*

KEN D FOSTER

Bringing out the best in ourselves is as much an art as a discipline. It is essential to know when to push and when to relax and enjoy our growth. With all work and no play, we become brittle and too focused on outcomes. With all play and no work, we lose our willpower and productivity.

It is through walking the razor's edge of balanced living that consistent growth takes place. There is no better way to balance your mind and therefore, your life, than by meditating. I have realized this in my own life and have been fortunate to be around many self-made millionaires who meditate daily for a harmonious and balanced life.

By consistently concentrating deeper in your meditations, you will find that you will have an increased capacity to focus your attention on your goals and attain greater success. You'll see steady improvement with this consistent commitment.

Today ask

What can I do to take my meditations deeper?"

How much time am I committed to morning and evening meditations?"

As I feel peace in meditation, how can I expand it to all my activities?"

Actions

If you haven't already, set up a daily meditation routine that includes time for affirmation, prayer and contemplation.

Day 200

*"To be courageous requires no exceptional
qualifications, no magic formula; it's an opportunity
that sooner or later is presented to all of us."*

JOHN F. KENNEDY[101]

There is only one power that can destroy the seeds of failure. That power lives right inside of you. It will never fail you. It is always present and shows up in many forms such as wisdom, courage, strength, insight, and power. It is the guiding light of all.

So, why then don't you still your thoughts and tap into this power continually? What you have been trying to find is close at hand. This power is ever calling you to wake up and become aware of its existence. It waits patiently for you. But, you must make an effort to connect with this power if you want to be free.

I encourage you to double your efforts in meditation. If you have been meditating for 20 minutes, then increase it to 40 minutes. Learn to sit still and quiet the mind. As you do, you will have a greater sense of who you are, and your life will expand.

Today ask

"How can my life get even better?"

"How can I be free of my most pressing challenges?"

"If I let go of negative thinking, what positive things could happen to me?"

Actions

Take a few minutes today to meditate deeply. If you do meditate consistently then what you believe could never change will change. It only takes commitment and consistent actions to live this truth.

Day 201

*"The most courageous people I have come across are those
who are consistently improving themselves."*

KEN D FOSTER

No one should be satisfied until they have sufficiently developed their intuition. When your intuition is developed, you will consistently make wise choices, accomplish more, and have greater focus which will lead you to success.

Clear thinkers should be distinguished from people who think too much. Intuition is developed by calming the mind, because a restless mind does not allow your intuition to surface.

Clear thinkers don't allow their intellect to override their intuition. They listen for guidance and know the difference between rationalizing intelligence and clear direction given through soulful connection.

With undeveloped intuition, you will have limited power to truly succeed, because the intellect cannot truly comprehend all the components and pathways necessary for lasting success. On the other hand, intuition is the guiding force to attain higher states of consciousness, ever-expanding your mind and the capacity for unending success.

Today ask

"What actions can I take to develop my intuition to the point I make clear choices?"

"How will I know when I am intellectualizing or connecting with intuition?"

"What exciting things are possible for me if I make good choices consistently?"

Actions

Allow for some quiet meditative time to connect with your soul and develop your intuition. Note: (One of the goals of meditation is to calm the mind so that without distortion you may hear the infallible counsel of the intuitive soul).

Day 202

"Any intelligent fool can make things bigger and more complex.
It takes a touch of genius and a lot of courage
to move in the opposite direction."

ALBERT EINSTEIN[102]

A small cup cannot contain a swimming pool of water; neither can a small mind contain all the ingredients for success. Meditation combined with introspection contains the formula for unlimited success. The reason is simple. When you connect to the infinite intelligence, awareness expands, perception changes, potentials increase, and your concentration becomes like a powerful laser beam.

With this simple formula for success, you can tap into your genius and be able to achieve your highest objectives. There are so many benefits of meditation and yet the world can distract you from meditating, right!

In order to avoid this, I encourage you to set up some meditation goals and commit to making meditation a consistent practice. Start with ten minutes in the morning and ten minutes in the evening. Affirmations work well with meditation. One I suggest is: "I have no where to go and nothing to do, but be here now."

Today ask

"What can I do to consistently connect with my source and generate wealth?"

"What am I not getting about the brilliance of my spirit?"

"What three steps can I take to to bring in more personal power?"

Actions

Spend some time thinking about what it means to be an infinite being. Where were you before you were born? Where will you be when you leave here? What is most important to you while you are here? Also, If you need help with finding the right teachers for meditation, get Ken D Foster's The Science of Meditation Guide for FREE. www.kendfoster.com/resources

Day 203

"Wisdom and courage combined are unlimited forces which enliven the spirit and bend the natural laws into perfecting dreams."

KEN D FOSTER

Many people are challenged with debt today. Debt in most cases is just a sign that you have too many desires which result in overspending or purchasing things that are not necessary for ordinary living. It can also be the result of being lethargic or developing your gifts, talents, and abilities.

In any case, debt is not a death sentence; you need not drown in a sea of debt. You have the power within you to create a debt-free life. There is no greater force in nature than the power of a soul committed to evolving upward and finding total freedom from all debt.

Since all mental power, prosperity and dynamic will come from Universal Intelligence of Spirit, doesn't it make sense to connect with that power to live debt-free? Through prayer and meditation, you will realize that you are a divine child of God.

Within you right now is the power to attract what you need. Every opportunity that comes your way has been created by you. It doesn't just mysteriously show up. So, commit to being debt-free and start now by generating new opportunities to pay off the debt now.

Today ask

"What are the three most important steps I can take to pay off my debts?"

"How will I remember that I am a child of God and be debt free?"

"What must I do consistently to live debt free?"

Actions

Make a list of your debts, then prioritize which ones you will pay off first.

Day 204

"Live courageously and become the master of your fate."

KEN D FOSTER

Believe it or not, in this moment you are capable of exponential wealth and happiness. The only thing stopping you, and just about everyone else, is the limited thoughts you believe are real.

You may think, *"I don't choose to be unhappy or stay stuck. This is just the way it is for me right now"*. The truth will set you free; do you want to hear it? Your thoughts, choices, and acts of today will be the plan for tomorrow. So why not do a little experiment and change them?

Sit in a chair with your feet flat on the ground, spine erect, and arms on your lap with palms facing up. Then gently raise your eyes to the spiritual eye, the point between your eyebrows. Concentrate at this point. Then inhale and exhale deeply for seven breaths.

Then affirm five times or more in a mental whisper: *"I am submerged in abundance. It permeates every particle of my soul. I am living in that abundance. The divine Spirit fills me with abundance every moment."*

Now that your thoughts are rooted in the soul, with a sense of peace I encourage you to think of your greatest dream. Then use the full power of your intention and determine the most important steps you will take to realize the dream.

Today ask

"How can I let go of my troubles troubles and connect deeply with my soul's wisdom?"

"How can I tune into the dynamic will of the soul and strengthen my mind to generate my dreams?"

"What can I realize that will continually keep my efforts crowned with success?"

Actions

Take time to ponder your deepest trouble and then choose two steps to overcome it.

Day 205

*"It takes courage to make your life a
magnificent example to others."*

KEN D FOSTER

Beauty is all around us but sometimes we are so focused on obtaining our material desires, we forget to stop, slow down and admire the beauty that is everywhere present.

Focus is a fantastic power, but we can't let it get in the way of our heart. Have you ever been too focused on making money or doing a task to an extreme that you lose your center? Have you noticed when you lose our joy, you lose your energy and enthusiasm?

Don't let the roar of material life sweep you up with its many attractions, because one day you may wake up to find you are brittle, overwhelmed or just worn out.

If you are in this kind of place right now, recognize your mistake and vow to turn things around.

Today ask

"What beauty can I observe today that I have not seen before?"

"How can I increase my will power and strengthen my mind to generate my dreams?"

"How can I open my heart and feel a deeper love for the beauty around me?"

Actions

Take the time you need to uncover your joy and find what enriches your life.

Day 206

"It takes courage to dive deep into the unknown fathoms of our infinite mind. But ultimately we discover who we are and why we are here."

KEN D FOSTER

If you write all the scripts of your life from your heart, you will watch the master artist paint the beauty of a life well lived. But, so many people get caught up making a living instead of creating a masterful life from their heart, in other words doing what they love to do and doing the things that are natural to them.

They believe falsely that life is about pushing hard, trying to fit in and do what everybody else is doing. Or, worse, some think that life is just about getting ahead, but when they wake up and discover getting ahead is an empty path they become disillusioned.

Most people are just getting by, living month to month. This is not the way to be! We were born to bring forth the greatness that lies within us. You can't do that if you are sitting in the darkness of your disempowering thoughts. You must break out of small-minded thinking.

Today ask

"What is likely to happen if I meditate daily?"

"What has to happen for me to carve out quiet time for meditation and reflection?"

"What can I do to deepen my meditations and reach self-realization?"

Actions

Meditate today and then ponder how to bring forth more of your greatness into the world.

Note: (If meditation is new for you, I encourage you to get some meditation instruction. My favorite site to learn how to meditate is http://www.yogananda-srf.org/. Also, check out www.kendfoster.com/resources and get my Scientific Meditation Sampler Pack which will also provide instruction.

Day 207

"Intuition is the foundation of courage. If you choose to live a courageous life, then you must choose to tune into your inner wisdom."

KEN D FOSTER

Most people would agree that the quality of your thinking will determine the quality of your life. But what determines the quality of your thinking? It is determined by your ability to tune into your intuitive wisdom.

The biggest challenge most people have in mastering their mind is letting go of restlessness. They can't image that they can calm their minds, and haven't decisively intended to do it. Instead, they allow their minds to wander focusing on endless desires, moving from one thought to the next.

But, if you want to increase success, you must start with a sense of peace. A peaceful mind that is in harmony with one's nature will ultimately create permanent and lasting success. The reason for this is that when your mind is calm, you can hear the voice of intuition. This is the voice of wisdom, and with that voice come right choices, right actions, and good results.

You can calm your restless thoughts by the daily practice of meditation and many of the practices given in this book. You should include everything that can be helpful in calming your mind.

But, practicing techniques to calm your mind will not work with a weak resolve or not believing that you can master your mind. You will seldom be open to insights because you will not be open to receiving them. So, develop a fervent desire to realize your innate wisdom.

Today ask

"Where can I carve out ten minutes today to still my mind?"

"What has to happen for me to become more conscious of each choice I make?"

"What are the wisest actions to take which will create ongoing success?"

Actions

Choose three actions that will give you access to realize your innate wisdom.

Day 208

*"Man cannot discover new oceans unless he has the
courage to lose sight of the shore."*

ANDRE GIDE[103]

Struggle is a healthy indicator that we need to grow. This is a good thing. There is nothing wrong with struggling. It builds character, strength, endurance, and courage. But if you are consistently struggling with an issue in your business or life, it is time to figure out what is going on.

This reminds me of when I was learning to swim. When I struggled, I sank fast and deep. I wanted to move forward. I tried to reach my destination. However, as I fought, it was next to impossible.

It was only when I relaxed and realized I was the one creating the struggle with my fears of drowning that I allowed the water to support me and make progress. Accepting how you are creating your misery is part of the journey which brings you success.

Growth always takes place because of setting an intention to change, and then, relaxing and merely expanding your consciousness. Sometimes it is what you know that is keeping you stuck. To overcome chronic struggling, open your thinking to looking at things in a new light. If there are one or two choices, look for the third or fourth choice before acting. Otherwise, you will keep doing, being and having the same things showing up repeatedly. If you can't see what is going on, then find someone who can see your blind spots. There is no reason to stay in the struggle unless you enjoy misery.

Today ask

"What am I putting up with?"

"What areas am I struggling with in my life?"

"What am I aware of that I am not taking action on?"

Actions

Set your intention to challenge any area that you are struggling with.
Then write out five steps you can take to move out of struggle permanently.

CHAPTER 11

LIGHT UP
YOUR LIFE

Day 209

"Excessive caution destroys the soul and the heart, because living is an act of courage and an act of courage is always an act of love."

PAULO COELHO

To be successful in life, you must build yourself up mentally, emotionally, physically and spiritually. It is important to feed your mind daily with positive and uplifting thoughts. Then emotionally practice detachment.

This means not getting attached to your point of view when challenging circumstances are showing up. Humility is the courage not to engage in a battle of words, to keep the heart connection.

Calmness is the key here. Physically, provide your body with organic high-nutrition foods and aerobic exercise. And spiritually, take time to quiet your mind and connect deeply with your Creator in meditation. Nothing can take the place of a balanced life when it comes to success.

If you take time for real connection with yourself daily, you will find out who you are and what is possible for you. In fact, when you understand who you are—as a powerful infinite being—no obstacle can stand in the way of your success.

Today Ask

"What are the most important activities I can do that will enliven my spirit, bring wisdom to my mind and increase my physical strength?"

"What are three ways I can bring more of me into the world?"

"How can I live a balanced life while I create wealth?"

Actions

Contemplate the deep essence of yourself, write about it and then live from your authentic self.

Day 210

"To love beyond human love into the states of unconditional love takes courage and sacrifice."

KEN D FOSTER

Would you like to have more love in your life? Most of us don't ask that question very often but it is vital for your spirit to stay in a loving place. *When the mind rests, it is love that takes its place.*

Why is that important to know? Because when you are in a state of love you are more energized, you make better decisions, you are more productive, and it attracts more love into your life. You have heard the saying: "Like attracts like." It is true. What you put out comes back to you. So, if you would like more love in your life, you will have to give your mind a rest, open your heart and put out more loving actions.

Think about this! If you felt more love for your work, your home, your body, your mind, your family and your life in general; wouldn't you be happier and have a better attitude? Of course, you would!

Today Ask

"What has to happen to increase my love in all areas of my life?"

"How can I love deeply even when others don't return my love?"

"When I am in a non-loving state of mind, how can I turn it around quickly?"

Actions

How about trying a little experiment? Make a list of what you love and be determined to expand your love in concrete ways. For example, if you like writing, make a commitment to write more or if you love to fish, go fishing or if you love to exercise go exercise! Set you intention to bring more love into your life and then prioritize your choices as you watch your love expand.

Day 211

"Courage is essential. Like a muscle, it is strengthened by use."

RUTH GORDON[3]

You are so much more brilliant and powerful than you think, and you have so much more to offer to the world than you are currently bringing forth. So, what stops you and just about everyone else, from improving your life? It is the lack of commitment to change and incorrectly thinking.

You must commit to bringing forth your greatness into the world because that is how you were created to be. Become an unstoppable "Magnet" for success if you truly want to accomplish your dreams. Magnets attract, so it isn't about doing more but receiving more.

Ask, "How can I attract more success in my life?" or "Who can I be that will open the doors to success in all areas of my life?". Being persistent in your asking is the key. When you persist in asking, no matter what the obstacles, you will get the answers and realize your dreams.

Today Ask

"What am I committed to making happen today?"

"Where can I change my point of view to have more success?"

"What has to happen for me to open up and receive more by magnetizing myself through affirming the truth of the essence of my being?"

Actions

Commit to letting all your brilliance shine brightly. Note: Don't allow circumstances control your life; you are a powerful infinite spirit who can overcome anything in the way of your success. Become the master of your destiny, starting right now.

Day 212

*"Success is not final; failure is not fatal; it is
the courage to continue that counts."*

WINSTON CHURCHILL[3]

Have you ever wondered what truth is and how it fits in with the reality of your life? According to Paramahansa Yogananda, the great Indian sage: "Truth is that which is in exact correspondence with reality."

When you get in touch with reality by consistently seeking the truth, you will realize that you are not a limited mortal being but an infinite being, an offspring of God. With this knowledge, and daily reflection, you can break through your limitations.

Think of some area in your life that is not working. This should be an area that you have tried to change but haven't been able to up until now. Now, stop for a moment and affirm: "I am an infinite being, I am one with God." Repeat this over and over until you feel a surge of energy pulsating through you. By the way, if the affirmation doesn't work, don't blame the messenger, work on feeling the affirmation until it works for you.

Today Ask

"What force would an infinite being call upon to overcome great challenges?

"Who am I being when I am generating ongoing success?"

"How can I get into the success "Zone" and assure my success?"

Actions

Commit to stretch yourself by overcoming every obstacle in your way to achieve continued success.

Tap into your higher-self and increase your intuition with Ken D Foster's guided meditations on Business, Wealth, Expanding Possibility, Peace, and Health. Yours for free at couragetochange.us/meditation

Day 213

Every trial is an opportunity to improve yourself if you intend to be the best you can be. We are all given good fortune and tough challenges. Based on the values you hold, the choices you make and the actions you take, you will either thrive by learning what you need to learn or fail and repeat your lessons time and time again until you change.

What stops most people from achieving an extraordinary life? It is their disconnection to listening and learning from their intuition. They don't realize that life is a school and the way to get past the most significant challenges in life is to listen to your inner wisdom.

Sometimes this wisdom says "Stop," sometimes "Go," sometimes it wants you to put a team on the problem. When you listen, you always get answers to your greatest challenges. In fact, your inner wisdom is at the very heart of your success.

Today Ask:

"What am I being called to learn or do, differently?"

"If I could show up daily in my power what would happen?"

"What steps will I take now to generate an extraordinary life?"

Actions:

Take a few minutes to journal your answers, without filtering your thoughts, so you can get clear with the steps you should take next. Note: (Look back, compassionately, at some of the poor choices you have made. Then replay the experience again in your mind, this time making a different choice. Journaling enables you to make new choices and play them out in our minds. Having tuned into your inner wisdom, you will face challenges differently if they come).

Day 214

*"The opposite of a courageous person isn't necessarily
a coward, but a person who has lost their way."*

KEN D FOSTER

Inspiration is the path that leads to greatness. It is indeed the wind beneath the wings of your success. Wouldn't you agree that when you are inspired—magic happens? You have more creativity, energy and success!

The opposite of inspiration is desperation; and desperate people sometimes do desperate things, which leads to hurting themselves and others. Remove the tar of desperation from your soul and sow the seeds of inspiration.

It may not be a smooth transition, but this is the only way you will leave the stagnation of past suffering and grow through the sunshine of the spirit.

Today Ask

"What inspires me the most?"

"What can I do to inspire others today?"

"What will get me out of bed with a smile?"

Actions

Come up with three additional questions on your own, that will inspire you to take your life to the next level.

Day 215

"Stand in the flames of difficulties with courage and steadfastness knowing you will overcome all challenges if you persist."

KEN D FOSTER

So long as you question whether you will overcome or lose the battles of life, you will lose. It is with an unruffled mind, that is immersed in awareness of the soulful power within, that you become humble and positive—drawing your victories to you. This may sound counterintuitive, but it is one of life's principles.

Detach your thoughts and emotions from your circumstances because they will not help. Your best and highest "thinking" has brought you where you are today. So, isn't it wise to stop the thinking machine and instead; connect soulfully to your intuitive wisdom?

Problems come and go but it is how you deal with them will determine success or failure. It is better to face challenges with wisdom than rote decisions. Wisdom comes when the mind is calm and open to seeing the world with new eyes.

Today Ask

"Who am I being, when I am calm under fire?"

"How can I remember to be peaceful no matter what the circumstances?"

"How will I strengthen my resolve to have more peace in my life?"

Actions

Set your intention to deal with each circumstance calmly, knowing everything will work out for the highest and best. Then, quiet your mind and give yourself permission to slow down and withdraw from the hectic pace of life. If you need help with this, get Ken D Foster's The Science of Meditation Guide for FREE. www.kendfoster.com/resources.

Day 216

*"Why wait for life to bring you success; instead
find your courage to discover your brilliance."*

KEN D FOSTER

As you live priorities aligned with your highest values, you begin moving the mountains in your life and create success uncommon to most. Setting up an amazing life is a lost art. It has become the norm just to get by and do what is expected without thought of how this kind of living is impacting your spirit.

Most people are focused on just getting by because they don't have any real priorities established for creating an amazing life. They consistently rely on habits that don't support excellence.

If you have identified that you're wandering aimlessly doing the same things over and over without achieving the results you envisioned or want to change but never really get anywhere close to living the life of your greatest dreams, it's time to revisit your priorities.

This doesn't have to be difficult. You can frame it in your mind as a new adventure that will lead you to unprecedented success. Remember, change starts when you make up your mind to change. It is an inside job!

Today Ask

"What are my highest priorities which will bring about my envisioned future?"

"What are the fifteen most important reasons I will live my priorities?"

"As I live my priorities what will my life be like a year from now?"

Actions

Pick one area of business or life to improve, then prioritize your actions and focus on the task until complete.

Day 217

"Courage is not the towering oak that sees storms come and go; it
is the fragile blossom that opens in the snow."

ALICE M. SWAIM[3]

Performing continuous actions without contemplation are like running through a forest trying to find a deer with blinders on. You will never find the deer because you have not contemplated the behaviors and habits of the deer, nor have you taken off the blinders to see the infinite possibilities of finding the deer where you least expect it to be.

It takes understanding and knowledge to create an outstanding business and life. This is accomplished with a peaceful mind, wise forethought and being circumspect in your daily actions.

It is better to go slowly and sensibly than to move hastily or fearfully. If you are stressed when deciding most likely you will make the wrong choice and regret it later. Don't you agree that you will be much happier if you make decisions that lead to harmony and enjoyment along the way?

If you get too caught up in the stressful world of deadlines and completion, you may wake up one day to find yourself in poor health without the ability to enjoy the fruits of your labor. Think about it!

Today Ask

"Where do I feel the most stress in my life?"

"How can I accomplish my most important tasks with a calm mind?"

"What has to happen for me to be calm and stress-free in each moment?"

Actions

Come up with two action steps to permanently live stress free. I will give you a hint. This won't necessarily be something you do, but may be a new thought frequency that you embrace.

Day 218

*"We must build dikes of courage to hold back
the flood of fear."*

MARTIN LUTHER KING, JR.[3]

Initiative will unlock the creative spirit in you to rock your world. It is the creative faculty that transforms the unknown into the known. In other words: It is the generative energy that brings thought forms into material existence. Within that energy is the power to help you change your world in a big way.

The energy and state of mind of "initiative" is available here and now. It isn't something you find somewhere or must develop; it is available to you right now. Your job is to choose to increase the availability of this energy flowing into you, while opening to receive it and allowing it to work in your life.

It isn't that hard. Let me tell you my own experience. A friend of mine noticed that I was not generating success like I had in the past. So, he gave me a formula to increase my initiative. He asked me to meditate on initiative and pray that it be increased three-fold.

I did this for about a week and the results were stunning. My energy and drive increased tremendously. In fact, I started and completed a course I teach called "Soul n Money" in six weeks.

This included recording eight CDs, writing a workbook, putting up a web site, writing copy, designing graphics and much more. Normally this process could have taken a few months but with increased initiative it happened quickly. And I didn't burn the candle at both ends!

Today Ask

"What area of my business or life needs attention?"

"What is my goal with a specific time of completion?"

"What steps can I take today to increase my initiative threefold?"

Actions

Contemplate for ten minutes on what it means to increase your initiative threefold. Then set your intention for it to become your reality.

Day 219

*"It takes great courage to faithfully follow
what we know is true."*

SARA E. ANDERSON[3]

Your intuitive thoughts will bring the solutions you need to succeed. Just thinking about anything that comes into your mind will not bring you closer to fulfillment in life. It is only when you become the master of your mind that you will be able to have the success you have dreamed about.

When you try to focus on the positive aspects of life, you bring in peace and harmony. Don't be satisfied with drops of peace; within you is unending happiness and joy. The way to wisdom is not in finding more things to be critical about. Rather, it is about turning to the mind within and noticing the good.

What is lovable about you? Who are you at the essence of your soul? When you find the answers to these questions, you are headed in the right direction. Because by living from love you will find joy.

Today Ask

"What inspires me to be magnificent?"

"How am I changing the ways of my life?"

"Truth, who am I being when I am deeply connected to Source?"

Actions

Make the commitment to increase your happiness today. Turn your thoughts toward what makes you happy and then allow those thoughts to permeate every particle of your being.

Day 220

> *"Children are curious and are risk-takers. They have lots of courage. They venture out into a world that is immense and dangerous. A child initially trusts life and the processes of life."*

JOHN BRADSHAW[3]

One of the most significant stressors in life is being in an argument of who is right and who is wrong. Many times, people get caught up in these dramas only to find that they are impacting their relationships in negative ways.

When we are even-minded and detached from being "right," relationships tend to be much more harmonious. Why, because you are not attached to the outcome. And when you are detached from being right, it makes room for many more possibilities to show up.

So, make a conscious decision to stop being confrontational and let go of "having to be right." Righteousness is usually ego-based and comes from a past belief or story that you have decided is "the way it is." But truly we live in a world of relativity and possibility. Being "right" all the time; most likely will cause strife, separation from others and chaos.

To stop this pattern, be childlike, open your heart and mind to allow Spirit to work through you. When you can do this on a consistent basis, you will be able to detach from the dramas in your life.

And when you can detach from the made-up dramas, you will have more energy for the things that are truly important to accomplish.

Today Ask

"When I am righteous what can I do to break the "righteous habit?"

"What can I practice that will keep me out of the "right / wrong drama?"

"What steps can I take to transcend the habit of "being right"?

Actions

Think about what it costs you in time, energy, money or friendships to be part of "I am right, and you are wrong dramas." Then, decide how you will show up differently.

Day 221

"It doesn't take any courage to be in denial of poor habits; what takes courage is the ability to introspect and change the negative behaviors permanently."

KEN D FOSTER

I have often noticed that people who consistently worry or focus on what is wrong in the world are unhappy. I have also seen, that most of these unfortunate people don't realize what they are missing.

Here is what I mean. Have you been around people who worry constantly? Worrying is not attractive and repels health souls. But did you know that most people who have this habit don't realize they have it. They are in denial of it because it is as normal to them as driving a car. Unfortunately, worry has been shown to negatively impact health, happiness, friendships, family and wealth.

I often wondered why anyone would remain oblivious to a worry-habit and then it dawned on me, they get something out of worrying. This is true for most harmful habits. And

with all harmful practices, they start out seeming harmless but after a while, they become disempowering and wreak havoc.

Today Ask

"What am I getting out of worrying?"

"What has to happen for me to break the worry-habit?"

"How can I let go of worry forever and bring in the power of faith?"

Actions

Make a list of five things you worry about and then resolve to change this way of thinking. Note: (Worry creates unending conflict that distracts you from living life to the fullest. So, do your best to develop confidence in yourself and faith in your creator. When you do this, you can let go of worries permanently.

Day 222

"Few men are willing to brave the disapproval of their fellows, the censure of their colleagues and the wrath of their society. Moral courage is a rarer commodity than bravery in battle or great intelligence. It is the one essential, vital quality of those who seek to change a world which yields most painfully to change."

ERNEST HEMINGWAY[3]

Most people don't remember much of what others say but they do remember what others do. When people watch you overcoming challenges and living the life of your dreams, it inspires them to do the same, wouldn't you agree?

All of us are shaped by people who inspire us, so why not become an example of how to live an exemplary life? You will be amazed at how many people will be attracted to you and your success. They will want to model the greatness that has come forth in you.

Oh sure, there will be people who will want to criticize you and put you down for being successful, but do you care? There will be many others who are admiring your victories and choosing to bring forth their brilliance because of modeling what you are doing.

Today Ask

"Am I being the example I would like the world to model?"

"What has to happen for me to bring out my greatness every day?"

"Where can I improve to model an exemplary life for others to follow?"

Actions

Think about what you would like to model for the people around you and set up some specific goals to make it happen. A person of influence plans their days and carries out those plans until the goals are accomplished. Be that person today!

Day 223

*"Some say courage is found in the high and mighty; I say courage
dwells in everyone who is willing to discover who they truly are."*

KEN D FOSTER

Have you been looking for answers as to why you haven't created the life of your
dreams yet? You don't have to look too far; the answers are within you, but you will
have to uncover them by aligning with Wisdom-Self.

Most people look to get their answers from other people. They look to find what
is real for others and think that by studying how others have created success that
somehow it will rub off on them. In a limited sense, you can study the success of
others to see what is possible for you; but real progress won't come until you connect to your highest values, set noble goals, speak soulful thoughts and understand
just how powerful you are.

Think about this! Spoken words are thoughts turned into sound vibrations. The
words you speak are a good indication of whether the words are coming from the
ego or the soul. Strive to have every word you speak coming from the highest vibration of your soul.

Today Ask

"Who is the "I" that is reading this?"

"Who is the "I" that is beyond thought, feeling, sight and sound?"

*"If I were to start generating my business and life from soulful thoughts, what
would those thoughts be?"*

Actions

Take some time to reflect on your soul. Reflect on who you are at the highest
level. Reflect on the values that move you and drive you into action.

Day 224

*"Courage comes with action. The minute you step forward,
the minute you declare your decision, the minute you say,
"This is how it's going to go," courage comes. It floods
through you and energizes every single fiber of your being."*

GAIL BLANKE[3]

When a man stops thinking in limited terms, he can start knowing himself in unlimited ways. Many people are black and white thinkers. They look at life in a delusional way and limit their choices.

Decisions are based on a judgment of either good or bad, right or wrong, this way or that way but thinking this way limits your life and creates chaos. It is when you realize how many choices there are in any circumstance that you can stop defining yourself in limited ways.

Have you ever wondered where you are limiting your success? Many times, you cannot see your blind spots; but through daily introspection, you can find them out. You may ask: *"What should I be looking for?"* The answer is *results*. You can see by your results what is working and not.

What if you could change the lie that you can't have what you want? What if you could change the myth that you don't have what it takes? Well, of course, you can, because you're an infinite being and within you are the answers to all your challenges and the power to generate all your dreams. You alone will determine how fantastic or how disempowering your life is.

Today Ask

"By letting go of judging what I can and cannot do, what is possible for me?"

"What can I realize about myself that will change for the better?"

"How can I tap into my courage and permanently throw off the challenges that are limiting my success?"

Actions

Determine two beliefs are stopping your success. Then come up with two new ideas that will propel your success.

Day 225

"Courage comes when you say "Yes"
and face your greatest challenges."

KEN D FOSTER

Physical, mental or emotional pain is a warning sign that it is time to change, develop or improve. When I ask people to tell me where they are feeling pain in their life, they often just look at me with a blank stare. My research shows that most people struggle with weight, health, money, relationships, career or many other issues.

Why is it that most people don't respond to the question about having pain in their life? I sense that a significant part of the population has come to believe that life happens to them rather than being the master of their life. They get locked into thinking "this is just the way it is" because they have lived with their pain for so long it is like an old friend. But of course, it is not a friend!

There is danger in not working on yourself and you should be concerned. I have seen many cases where people are suffering. They have symptoms such as lack of peace, stress, depression, poor relationships, overwhelm, over-eating, insomnia and many more.

They get into poor habits because they didn't realize how important each day and each choice is. But it doesn't have to be that way; everyone can improve themselves and their circumstances for the better.

Today Ask

"What am I committed to changing or healing in my life permanently?"

"What are three steps I can take today to heal my body, mind and spirit?"

"Who do I know that can support me in making the necessary changes in my life?"

Actions

Think of one area where you are feeling mental, emotional or physical pain and decide to get rid of it. Then come up with a plan on how you are going to free yourself from these afflictions permanently.

Day 226

"You will never do anything in this world without courage. It is the greatest quality of the mind, next to honor."

ARISTOTLE[3]

You are an amazing, gifted child of the Most-High but are you realizing this daily? If not, most likely you are struggling in several areas of life. But, ponder this question. How can someone who knows that they are an infinite being be struggling? Honestly, they can't, unless they are choosing it!

Do you realize how much energy it takes to keep yourself struggling? Massive amounts! What if you could free up the energy you are using to struggle, what would your life be like? It would be amazing, right?

Many people live in negative thoughts, feelings and emotions on a consistent basis. They judge people, places and things as good or bad. They gossip, criticize and critique others as doing things right or wrong.

They are swayed by the dualities of life in extreme ways by feeling great love then great sadness, lots of energy and then none or much happiness and then great sorrow. But living like this creates drama and struggle. You must start mastering your mind!

You can choose to be at peace even in the storms that life delivers. It is all an inside job! If you control your thinking you will control your emotions and if you manage your feelings you will control your actions and if you control your steps, you will control your destiny.

Today Ask

"What has to happen for me to be more even-minded?"

"How can I experience more peace and happiness during the tough times?"

"What has to happen for me to let go of struggling forever?"

Actions

Choose to have a positive attitude and then see if you can hold onto it no matter what happens today.

Day 227

*"It takes bravery to recognize where in your life you are your
own poison. . . . It takes courage to do something about it."*

STEVE MARABOLI[3]

Some want to know the truth but only when it fits into their picture of reality. And others miss truth because they deny it, while nearly everyone at some time has been afraid of knowing the truth.

Most people do not see reality clearly because their reality is based on false premises. Their lives reflect a self-serving, ego-consciousness which is not connected to the infinite power within. As a result, they have not learned to master their mind, bodies nor the circumstances.

In fact, if more people connected with their Wisdom-Self there would be more harmony and peace throughout the world. Remember, life is a school and you are here to learn, grow and evolve your consciousness. Who you become will be a direct result of how much effort you put into knowing yourself.

Today Ask

"Would an infinite being limit the possibility of having an amazing life?"

"What can I do daily to realize my infinite capacity to succeed?"

"What will help me grow and expand my consciousness now and in the future?"

Actions

Come up with one new approach to expand your awareness of what is possible for you.

Tap into your higher-self and increase your intuition with Ken D Foster's guided meditations on Business, Wealth, Expanding Possibility, Peace, and Health. Yours for free at couragetochange.us/meditation

CHAPTER 12

UNLOCK YOUR WILL POWER

Day 228

When I was single, I was always looking for someone who was a better match for me. I consistently doubted my relationship choices. In other words, I was not available for a lasting relationship.

As a result, I was never really committed to the relationships. I had one foot in and one foot out, so to speak. Therefore, I never really played full out! I was living in a state of doubt which caused a lot of chaos and drama.

Can you relate? If so, think about areas in your life where you are experiencing doubt? Maybe in your current relationship, career or partnership!

If so, then you may want to do what I did and make a commitment to start living a life of certainty. I am not talking about being certain that I am right about everything. I am talking about living from awareness and realizing what my Wisdom Self knows about relationships.

(By the way, when I started living with certainty, I met my wife within thirty days, and we have been happily married for nineteen years. I also started my coaching business which, at the time of writing this book, has been thriving for over two decades).

Today Ask

"What am I doubting that is creating disharmony?"

"What would my life be like if I lived with a greater sense of certainty?"

"How can I become more certain that my choices are the right ones?"

Actions

Make a list of areas in your life which you are living in doubt, then decide how you are going to break this habit.

Day 229

"With courage, one can honestly look at what is working or not and make lasting changes that impact many generations."

KEN D FOSTER

What is the most potent force on the planet? I have found that it is your willpower when it is filled with intuition, inspiration and commitment!

For many people, dynamic willpower is undeveloped and therefore they falsely believe they can't create what they want, when they want it. But the truth is that willpower is the kick-starter of the soul. It works when you use your will to create that which is aligned with your highest calling. By so doing the magic of the soul kicks in and works for your benefit. This is how seemingly insurmountable challenges in business or life are overcome.

It is important to know that the opposite of willpower is addiction. It is the feeling of powerlessness and terminates in being a victim of life's circumstances. When a person consistently makes commitments to themselves and doesn't follow through, willpower is weakened. It this behavior continues willpower is reduced to the point that a person may want to act differently but it seems impossible to change.

To increase your willpower, start with small goals and complete them no matter what. Also track these goals, so that you know what percentage of your goals you are finishing at any given time. You should shoot for 100 percent. At this level, you are making the right choices, not under-committing and consistently creating your dreams.

Today Ask

"What have I been repeatedly doing and expecting things to change?"

"What will I undertake today, that will increase my willpower?"

"What is the most important goal I can undertake to increase my willpower?"

Actions

Think about what will increase your willpower.

Day 230

"I want to be wise; I want the courage to love. I want the courage to sacrifice. I want the courage to be a non-conformist in the face of injustice."

CORNELL WEST[3]

It is not what you have or have not done that holds you back; it is what you have not acknowledged and changed. As a child, you may have been afraid of the dark, but eventually you overcame it. Now you may be fearful of the light—*your* light, your brilliance. If so, how will you become all you were meant to be?

It is easy! Acknowledge where you are lacking presence and power. Then, commit to overcoming your challenges by bringing in more of your light. What is the light? It is your wisdom and will power. Contemplate what you need to do, then take consistent actions until the task is completed. By doing this daily, your personal power will increase, and your life will get better and better.

Remember, we are all here learning and growing, don't be hard on yourself if things don't change immediately. Just take one step, then another and another and don't stop.

Today Ask

"What will I overcome which will increase the quality of my life?"

"What do I truly know must change for me to be more successful?"

"What new belief can I take on that will substantially improve my life?"

Actions

Decide what changes you are committed to making. Then, ask yourself why you will be making these changes no matter what happens. Now is the time to rise up and be a hero in your own life. Right!

Day 231

"Courage is found in unlikely places."

J.R.R. TOLKIEN[3]

Paramahansa Yogananda once said: "Seclusion is the price of greatness". But just blocking time out for yourself won't result in greatness, unless you use your time well and develop the power of concentration.

Are you caught up in the trap of trying to do too many things at one time? If so, think about this: a dog chasing two rabbits won't catch either one and the same is right for you. If you are focusing your energies on too many goals, you may be distracting yourself from success.

A builder friend of mine, who was just starting out, tried to build two homes at one time. He told me these homes seemed like they would never be done. Eventually he "got it" and focused on one house at a time until completion.

ToDay, ask

"What projects do I have that remain uncompleted?"

"What are the highest priority projects for me to complete?"

"What projects can I release forever?"

Actions

Pick a project to complete, set a completion date and then create a plan for completion. Also, allow yourself to go deeper in meditation than you did yesterday.

Day 232

*"Anyone can overindulge in multitasking but the
courageous indulge in self-control and daily improvement."*

KEN D FOSTER

We live in a fast-paced society, where it appears that the faster you go, the more success you will have. But in reality, the opposite is true. It is those who take time for planning and take disciplined actions toward their goals that are most likely to succeed.

A restless mind focused on multitasking is a prescription for failure. There have been several significant studies on how productivity falls when multitasking begins. The opposite is true also: when you are calm and focused, you increase productivity and make better choices and have increased success.

Success habits are the key to less multi-tasking. Develop the habit of doing one thing at a time. When you go from one task to another try to do it smoothly. An example; make a point to leave each conversation on the phone non-abruptly. Don't get off the phone and go to another task immediately. Allow some space between tasks.

Today Ask

"What can I do to stop multitasking?"

"How can I be wholly focused on the task at hand today?"

"By staying focused, in what way will I create more success?"

Actions

Set your intention to have a fantastic, productive day. Prioritize, delegate and decide what you can do to take your business or life to the next level. Also, take a moment and schedule planning time on a consistent basis; when you do, you will find success in uncommon ways.

Day 233

*"Don't forget to pack your courage for
your journey to greatness."*

DAVE WEINBAUM[3]

Environment is stronger than most people's willpower. So, if you have unsettling or cluttered environment that you walk into every day, most likely the environment will impact you in a negative way. Knowing this will help you set up winning settings for yourself.

There are three environments that are the keys to generating success: your inner environment of mind, body and spirit; plus, your home and office environment.

The way you manage your inner environment is by focusing on positive outcomes. Every day in every way let the vibration of success-thoughts waft through your mind and align with your spirit and body. Then set up your home environment to reflect the success of your mind. Make it clutter-free and let it feel nurturing and inspiring which will glorify the greatness of you.

The last element to environmental success is creating a beautiful office environment which reflects a sense of wealth and abundance. You will most likely be spending much time here so why not make it the most amazing place you have ever visited!

Today Ask

"What environment can I create to increase my productivity and happiness?"

"What three steps I can take to have my environments reflect my greatness?"

"What core value can I reflect to create a fantastic environment?"

Actions

After answering the above questions take five minutes and reflect on who you are becoming.

Day 234

*"Courage isn't a quality of the indecisive; it
dwells in the soul of the decisive."*

KEN D FOSTER

Dedication is a common trait of successful people. Have you ever come across anyone who was successful without being dedicated to their cause? Of course not, because effort is a direct reflection of cause. Dedication is to success is like clouds are to rain. You can't have one without the other.

So how do you become more dedicated? For most it is by connecting with your higher self and using your will power to generate your greatest dreams. If you have big dreams, they are there for a reason.

And most likely you will have to increase your will power and your spiritual acumen if you are to achieve them. In other words, you will have to evolve yourself and connect deeply with the brilliance that is within you.

TODAY ASK

"What is the most important thing to dedicate my time, energy and effort to?"

"Because of my dedication, how will I evolve my gifts, talents and skills?"

"What can I consistently do to increase my dedication?"

ACTIONS

List one causes you are dedicated to and decide how much effort you will give it.

Day 235

"Never forget that life can only be nobly inspired and rightly lived if you take it bravely and gallantly, as a splendid adventure in which you are setting out into an unknown country, to meet many a joy, to find many a comrade, to win and lose many a battle."

ANNIE BESANT[3]

We have all heard that you must be persistent to achieve your goals but where does persistence come from? It is a soulful quality that's connected with your life's purpose.

By identifying your purpose, it produces a driving force which has you moving forward no matter what gets in your way. This deep level of commitment is available to all who ask important questions that are aligned with their heart's calling.

Your calling can be in business or some other area of life. It will be something that expands your deep-seated knowing of yourself or brings out and grows your greatest gifts, talents and skills in such a way that you contribute to the betterment of humankind.

Because you are an infinite being who has chosen your course of action, you will ultimately succeed. But you can quicken your success by finding out what you are being called to be, do or have and move forward with it. This is how finding your calling and then being persistent can evolve you one step at a time into your greatness.

Today Ask

"If I had a calling what would it be?"

"Why is it important for me to accomplish my greatest dreams?"

"What is possible for me if I choose to bring out my best every day?"

Actions

Pick one task and commit to increasing your perseverance until accomplished."

Day 236

"Believe in yourself and combine it with determination and courageous acts. Then watch the illusions of failure fade way."

KEN D FOSTER

Do you have the drive to succeed? If not, you may want to develop your determination. Determination is increased by improving your willpower. It is a skill that is honed by consistent efforts toward accomplishing your goals even when you don't feel like doing them.

We all get in moods that seem to stop our success but when we make up our minds that nothing will get in the way of our success, not negative thoughts, negative people or challenging circumstances then success is only a matter of time.

Since you alone are responsible for your success, it behooves you to make up your mind to do more than you think is possible. And once you do more, once you stretch yourself you will never go back to the way you were! You will be amazed at how much more you have in you. You can do the impossible if you will just try.

Today Ask

"What project or goal seems to be beyond my reach?"

"What will it take to become unstoppable in accomplishing what I set out to do?"

"How can I increase my success no matter what the circumstances?"

Actions

List one project or goal that you will complete, no matter what.

Day 237

*"I do not ask to walk smooth paths nor bear an easy load. I
pray for strength and fortitude to climb the rock-strewn road.
Give me such courage and I can scale the hardest peaks alone
and transform every stumbling block into a stepping stone."*

GALE BROOK BURKET

Strength and determination must be cultivated for lasting success, because in times of adversity, a weak-minded person may give up while the strong-minded will overcome any challenge. Through the testing of time, they know that challenges are only tests that strengthen them.

There is one principal on the road to success that must be learned. What is it? It's the knowing that buried within you is the infinite, immortal power. You are a child of the highest and no matter what happens you are being supported to grow and evolve.

I do not shrink before challenges; they inspire greatness to come forth. When faced with adversity, I affirm the quote given to me from Yogananda: "Danger and I were born together, and I am more dangerous than danger."

This is the attitude to have when facing the twists and turns of life. There is no challenge you cannot overcome. Don't let life beat you down. Commit to beating the odds and beating life. For even a moment in time to believe that any challenge is more powerful than your soulful divinity is a lie. You are never given more than you can bear, so bear more and use every trial to improve yourself.

TODAY ASK

"What has to happen to increase my soulful power to overcome any challenge?"

"How can I increase my determination to overcome my challenges?"

"When challenges come what can I remember that will help me deal with them?"

ACTIONS

Determine which challenge you will overcome first. It is best to do the "worst" first, then the rest of your challenges most likely be easier.

Day 238

"Courage shows up as you move through
"No way out" situations."

KEN D FOSTER

When you are accomplishing large or small goals, difficulties will come. It is a fact that resistance will occur before reaching most of your goals.

We live in a world of duality. Where there is light, there is dark. Where there is a great idea, there is resistance to that idea. The universe is designed that way to strengthen and grow us to fulfill our purpose.

To reach your highest potential start using three magic words that will aid you in overcoming all your challenges. They are: I can, I must, I will. Don't skip over these powerful words, see what happens when you apply them to your problems!

When a seed is planted and starts to sprout, it immediately hits the resistance of the ground surrounding it. But the Universe always provides what is needed. If you were to look at that seed sprouting under an electron microscope, you would notice it attracting toward it the minerals and elements it needs to break through the ground. You also can access this attraction power to bring you to whatever you need to succeed.

Today Ask

"What am I determined to accomplish no matter what obstacles show up?"

"What are the three most important actions I can take to solve my problems?"

"How can I become more courageous because of the actions I take today?"

Actions

Pick one problem you are having. Then choose one gift, talent or ability that you can use to overcome it.

Day 239

*"It is easy to move forward when everything is going your way
but it takes real courage to persevere when things get tough."*

KEN D FOSTER

To accomplish any worthwhile goal, there are usually many obstacles to overcome. But so what! You must be doing something, so why not be putting one foot in front of the other and doing what it takes to succeed? Greatness isn't accomplished in a day; it takes persistence over time to achieve it.

Here is a thought! Someone must succeed, so why not you! Do you realize that someday you will succeed if you are persistent? It is the choices to persist each day that will determine how successful you become.

You can plant any thought you choose in your consciousness right now, how about the idea that you will persist until you thrive. Then your actions will follow that thought. How amazing is that?

Today Ask

"What are the most powerful thoughts I can entertain that will keep me determinedly moving toward my dreams?"

"What has to happen for me to persevere no matter what?"

"What do I need to let go of, so that I can increase my persistence?"

Actions

Notice what you are doing that may be stopping and/or increasing your success.

Tap into your higher-self and increase your intuition with Ken D Foster's guided meditations on Business, Wealth, Expanding Possibility, Peace, and Health. Yours for free at couragetochange.us/meditation

Day 240

*"Courage is reclaiming your life after a devastating event robs
you of your confidence and self-esteem."*

CATHERINE BRITTON[3]

Would you like to have more energy and become more productive? You can start today. Did you know that the more willpower you exercise, the more power that flows through you? And if you stay focused on your tasks the more productive, you become.

At this moment, you are immersed in cosmic energy, just waiting for you to tap into it. And the key to this infinite storehouse of power and creativity is the absolute realization that you can achieve whatever you set out to do.

Do you know that you already know how to create a fantastic life? Or do you pretend that you don't have a direct connection to your soul? Do you believe in yourself, affirm your magnificence and play to win or do you tell yourself that life is too hard, you don't have what it takes, and you will just go along with the flow?

Well, no more, you have the power to turn any misguided thinking around. In your little finger is more power than it takes to light the city of San Diego. Just tap into the source of your brilliance by using your infinite willpower.

Today Ask

"What belief can I embrace to step into my power and generate my greatest dreams?"

"What am I committed to accomplishing today no matter what?"

"What will it take for me to become unstoppable?"

Actions

Determine which actions you will take to become more powerful.

Day 241

*"It doesn't matter if we think we're fearless or if we
do things while quaking. The important thing is to be
true to our own dreams and live authentic lives."*

DIANE CONWAY[3]

Have you ever studied children and watched how they are full of life and joy? Why
is it that adults tend to be full of worries, stress and unhappiness? The truth is simple: they have lost their connection to their spirit.

Life brings challenges to everyone, but those challenges are not there to crush us.
They help us connect deeply to the unending source of power that lies within our
spirit. Think of your spirit as a child. At that age, were you peaceful, enthusiastic,
willing and playful? Sure, you were! Maybe not every moment but you had times
when you were fully present to your spirit.

It is simple to get back to your spirit. First, let go of judging yourself and making
yourself wrong in any way. Then bring in unconditional love for yourself and those
who are dear to you. Hold those thoughts of love in your heart and allow them to
expand.

Call your spirit to come home and become embodied with you right here and
now. Use your willpower to call out right now! Get up out of your chair and make
a soul call to your spirit! Let your spirit know that you are ready to realize your
connection.

Let your spirit know that you are open to receive all the good and whatever challenges are there for your growth.

Today Ask

"How can I realize my connection to spirit each moment?"

"What is the most loving thing I can do for myself today?"

"How can I bring in more love in all areas of my life?"

Actions

Come up with three actions to bring more love in your life.

Day 242

"It is only with courage, persistence and faith that we can realize our true destiny."

KEN D FOSTER

Consistency is an essential piece of the success-puzzle. Have you ever said you would lose weight, never get upset again or set a goal to make more money; only to find that you are not as consistent with your commitment as you planned?

Most people have had this kind of experience. Why is this? It is because most people are trying to use only willpower to achieve their goals. But this is only half the formula for consistent results!

There is a force called dynamic will that will support you in accomplishing any goal. Dynamic will is developed by consistently tuning into stillness and tapping into the superconscious mind. When you allow your insights to flow and then tie them into consistent actions, you will experience new levels of success.

Here is how to use dynamic will. Let's say your goal has been to lose weight. Instead of dropping the weight to look and feel better, which are noble purposes but not enough to propel you to success, try tuning into a higher purpose. This can include ideas such as losing weight to be in harmony with your Wisdom-Self or be an example for your children to follow or breaking a family pattern of obesity. These are higher callings which can propel you to success.

Today Ask

"What is the highest and best way for me to achieve my dreams consistently?"

"How can I remember to tune into a higher calling to accomplish my goals?"

"When I remember to tune into my Wisdom-Self what can I accomplish?"

Actions

Make a list of those areas where you would like to improve your consistency and then commit to being consistent from here on out. Note: (Consistency is in all of us. When you make up your mind to be consistent and combine it with willpower, you become invincible).

Day 243

*"I cannot escape my life but can only use my determination
and courage to make it the best I can."*

KAREN CUSHMAN[3]

It is your responsibility to find the best that life has to offer and to bring it into your life. I am not talking about the ego fulfilling all the desires it has; I am talking about connecting to your infinite spirit and bringing forth all your gifts, talents and abilities.

To find the richness in life, you must awaken your spirit and be ready to do battle with the world. Very little success will come to you without sustained effort and faith in your power to succeed.

You control your destiny, don't become lazy or stagnant, this doesn't bring happiness. There is nothing that can stand in your way unless you allow it.

Look at the results you are getting in your life. If you don't like the results, change them. At any moment, you are either moving forward or backward. When you realize that you have the power to overcome any obstacles to your success, you become unstoppable.

Today Ask

"Who am I at the core of my being?"

"What has to happen for me to realize that I am the unstoppable infinite spirit?"

"What can I do today to bring forth the courageous part of me and realize my greatest dreams?"

Actions

Come up with two action steps to pursue your greatest dream.

CHAPTER 13

QUESTION EVERYTHING

Day 244

"Courage doesn't always roar. Sometimes courage is the little voice at the end of the day that says: I'll try again tomorrow."

MARY ANNE RADMACHER[3]

The only thing that stands between you and your dreams is the force behind your thoughts. Awareness is an art that most people have never perfected. Some people are very smart and have degrees after their name but that does not equate to awareness. And without a state of true success-consciousness, the richness of life will most likely avoid roosting with you.

Awareness comes from living in the question, aligning with the inner self and not limiting the answers with the lower ego mind. Questions expand the possibility of what you can generate, whereas thinking you have the answers will limit you.

Until you can get in touch with the ageless, timeless infinite you and exchange your stinking thinking for awareness, things will remain unchanged. Nothing much happens when you just analyse information, although this is where most people spend their time: just thinking.

You must learn to create by applying your intuitive mind to the problem. As you do, you will become aware of the right choices of action which will foster your brilliance and increase your success.

Today Ask

"What beliefs are blocking the awareness of what is possible?"

"What am I willing to know that will change the course of my life?"

"What is possible for me, if I choose to actualize the genius within?"

Actions

Take some extra time to meditate and tune into your higher-self in the next twelve-hours.

Day 245

*"Through each crisis in my life, with acceptance
and hope, in a single defining moment, I finally
gained the courage to do things differently."*

SHARON E. RAINEY[3]

There is a library, chock-full of solutions to every challenge you have ever had, just waiting for you. But you must choose to open the library door by tapping into your inner wisdom and by asking the right questions.

Understand this: The answer is always in the question that you ask, so make sure you form your questions with a conscious intent on the answer you would like to receive. The question is paramount in determining what you are seeking. It must be phrased correctly.

If you were to ask; "Why do I never succeed?" You will get the answer. You will also get the answer if you ask; "What three steps can I take today that will accelerate my success?" For lasting success, practice forming your questions with more awareness as to the outcome you would like to have. If you have trouble forming questions, you can purchase my book; Ask and You Will Succeed, 1001 Extraordinary Questions to Create Life-Changing Results, at KenDFoster.com

Today Ask

"What are five powerful questions I can ask daily to accelerate success?"

"What steps can I take to assure that I ask myself these questions daily?"

"How will I ensure my success continues to grow?"

Actions

Determine which area of your life is most important to create ongoing success right now. Then, commit to taking three steps that will accelerate your success in one area of your life.

Day 246

*Brave people have limitations and challenges
like everyone else. The only difference is they
muster up the courage to overcome them."*

KEN D FOSTER

Can you have it all? Can you have wealth, power, money, happiness, health and the lifestyle of your dreams? The answer is "Yes" but it comes only to those who choose to overcome their limitations, realize who they are and are willing to bring forth their greatness to the world.

Leonardo da Vinci said; "All who have brought forth their full potential know this well: Isolation is the price of greatness." This means taking time each day to be with your spirit, quiet your mind, tap into the Creative Source and wisely plan what you are choosing to achieve.

We all have the same amount of time each day. You are either spending your time wisely or wasting your time chasing illusions. Are you willing to stop the do, do, do in your life and isolate yourself, spending time in meditation to bring forth your greatness? Are you ready to improve your awareness of what is possible for you every day and generate unlimited success?

If so, keep asking powerful questions and commit to isolating yourself from everyone else's point of view and develop your point of view from the truth of who you are and how things are.

Today Ask

"Who am I becoming as I continue to use this book daily?"

"What has to happen to bring out more of "me" into the world?"

"How can I connect deeply with Spirit today?"

Actions

Take time today to go deeper in meditation than you did yesterday. Also, check out www.kendfoster.com/resources to get Ken D Foster's The Science of Meditation Guide for FREE.

Day 247

"No one is perfect and thank goodness it doesn't take
perfection to generate courageous acts that define our lives."

KEN D FOSTER

Are you destined for greatness or destined for a dismal life? As you know, you make your destiny and only you have the power to let in your light or shut yourself down by focusing on things that distract and disempower you.

By actualizing the infinite power within, you can overcome all difficulties in your life. You can remedy your mistakes or choose to ignore them and let them build up. Nothing is stopping you from having a fantastic life, except yourself, because it takes strong commitment to overcome your imperfections.

You must first become determined not to limit your prosperity by living a life of false conclusions. In other words, you will define your life by what you believe is right. For instance, if you think you can't change yourself and improve, then you will go on losing because this is a false conclusion.

But if you realize that you can change anything you put your mind to, you will have realized the truth and empowered yourself.

Today Ask

"In what ways can I generate an amazing life by asking more questions that open up possibilities?"

"How can I let go of limiting conclusions?"

"In what areas can I refocus my efforts to grow my life?"

Actions

Formulate one compelling question that will challenge you and help you improve yourself, then ask it five times today.

Day 248

*"To look at something as though we had never seen
it before requires great courage."*

HENRI MATISSE[3]

When you ask questions that take you into higher states of consciousness, you can transcend your challenges and increase your wealth. Asking the right questions will propel your success, just as asking wrong questions will stall your progress.

You may ask, what are the "right" questions? They are questions that help you gain insight and create momentum. They are also questions that will inspire, motivate and empower you to be your best.

So, connect deeply with your Wisdom-Self by asking the right questions and find soulful answers that will increase success. I

f freedom from illusions is your goal, then use "right" questions to help you find the guiding voice of truth within.

Today Ask

Morning: "What are the three most important objectives I can accomplish today?"

Midday: "What can I do this afternoon to feel joyful and increase my happiness?"

Evening: "What worked today and where can I improve, change or have more fun tomorrow?"

Actions

Ask the questions above for seven days in a row and see if what happens. Also, if you would like to realize the power of questions, check out Ken D Fosters best-selling book; Ask and You will Succeed, 1001 Extraordinary Questions to Create Life Changing Results. Get it on Amazon or KenDFoster.com

Day 249

"Courageous risks are life-giving, they help you grow, make you brave and better than you think you are."

JOAN L. CURCIO[3]

When is the last time you gave yourself a real pep talk? One where you spent ten minutes talking to yourself about how amazing you are, how many people you have helped, how far you have come or the difference you have made by just being you.

Most people have been taught to self-efface themselves by not taking credit for what they do or where they have contributed. In one sense this is good, since nobody wants an ego-maniac around but that isn't who you are.

You are an amazing infinite being filled with gifts, talents and abilities. You have contributed to the lives of many and been a positive example. Now is the time to quietly acknowledge yourself and remember the bright times in your life.

Why do this? Because the more you let your brilliance shine, the more your example will give others permission to do the same.

Today Ask

"In what ways have I become the change that I want to see in the world?"

"How am I a guiding light of change for others to follow?"

"How will I continue to improve and be a greater light for others to follow?"

Actions

Make a list of your five greatest strengths, then pick one and focus on it today.

Day 250

*"There's only one requirement of any of us and that
is to be courageous. Because courage, as you might
know, defines all other human behavior."*

DAVID LETTERMAN[3]

Have you ever created something that no one else has done? We all can quiet our habitual thoughts, tap into our Wisdom-Self and create something entirely new that hasn't yet been on planet earth.

By asking infinite, compelling, positive, possibility questions like: "How is it be possible for me to generate something new for the planet?" you will get the answers. The universe is poised to answer your questions.

Your job is to ask questions that open possibilities, by doing so you will generate answers that will bring something new into the world. How amazing would that be?

Today Ask

"Pick an object or service and then ask: "What can I do to improve, change or modify it?"

"What new possibilities exist for the object of my focus?"

"What is something different than this object or service can be used for?"

Actions

Look around and find one thing that needs improving. It can be a gadget, a service, furniture, computers or just about anything. Then come up with two ways to improve it. Note: (By doing this you will most likely be amazed how ingenious you).

Day 251

*"A man with outward courage dares to die; a man
with inner courage dares to live."*

LAO TZU[3]

Everyone would like to have more success but only those who manage their lives well create lasting success. As you have probably realized, two of the main ingredients in success is managing time and energy.

We all have the same amount of time. Why is it that some people create great wealth and others struggle? A great deal of the problem lies in seeing time as an enemy rather than an ally and not effectively using time to generate amazing dreams.

Think about time this way: Decide on a dream you are willing to spend your life force to accomplish. Then set up a timeline for obtaining it. After that, block out time in your calendar to make it happen and take consistent actions until your dream is fulfilled. How can it get easier than that?

Today Ask

"What do I want, which will change my life for the better?"

"What goal am I done talking about and ready to accomplish no matter what?"

"What can I do to make my life easier?"

Actions

Determine one positive change you will make today which will generate lasting success, then come up with an empowering belief that will support this.

Tap into your higher-self and increase your intuition with Ken D Foster's guided meditations on Business, Wealth, Expanding Possibility, Peace, and Health. Yours for free at couragetochange.us/meditation

Day 252

"It takes courage to see the unholy and
speak to it with the voice of truth."

KEN D FOSTER

It is just as easy to look for the good in life as the bad. Yet, so many spend much of their time looking at the negative and then wonder why they have a poor attitude which produces dismal results.

Why choose to go down the sewers of life looking for what is wrong? Instead, make up your mind today that you will stop generating this type of misery in your business or life.

We live in a world of duality; there is positive and negative in everything. The reality is that what you focus on will expand. If you focus on the negative, you will find yourself being immersed in negativity. Conversely, if you look at what is positive and uplifting; you will find yourself uplifted.

This isn't advice for you to become some Pollyanna with your head in the sand never addressing issues that need to change; this is about being positive, productive and focusing your attention on the goodness life has to offer. One may criticize even the most celebrated masterpieces in art, relationships, business or nature. Isn't it better to enjoy their beauty than to find fault?

Today Ask

"What is good about my business and life?"

"How can I stay focused on the positive no matter what happens today?"

"What can I do to increase the power of my positive focus?"

Actions

Make a list of what is positive in your life and then keep your mind focused on finding the good in all. If during the day, you find yourself being negative ask: "What is positive or good about the situation?" Then, at the end of the day journal how you most often felt. Note: (If you follow this formula, your day will most likely be pleasant and far more powerful).

Day 253

*"There are moments in our lives when we summon the courage
to make choices that go against reason, against common sense
and the wise
counsel of people we trust."*

HOWARD SCHULTZ[3]

Do you realize that when you are holding on to past harms, resentments, guilt or shame, that you are sabotaging your success? We are all connected and unless you release the past and indeed forgive yourself and others for past mistakes, you will limit your success.

Most every time you are unhappy, you are not in the present moment, actively visualizing your dreams, bringing forth dynamic willpower or taking focused actions until you create your destiny.

Unhappiness paralyzes your willpower and stops you from succeeding. So why be unhappy? It makes no sense! Make up your mind to stay this disempowering habit now.

Today Ask

"Where can I increase my awareness?"

"How will I stay present each moment?"

"Who and What am I?"

Actions

Make a conscious choice to focus your mind on the present. Live moment by moment and be ever watchful of your thoughts and actions. By so doing, you will be aware of your spirit which will propel you forward, mentally, emotionally, physically and spiritually.

Day 254

"Oh, lion of liberation ever send through me
Thy roar or all-conquering courage."

PARAMAHANSA YOGANANDA, "WHISPERS FROM ETERNITY³

What is it going to take to have your highest visions come true? Will it take late nights, heavy stress and doing the things you don't want to be doing? Well, maybe, if you buy into the reality of this world.

But if you choose to follow your intuition and increase your receptivity to new possibilities, you can generate an amazing life with ease, grace and lots of joy-filled work. Sure, it will take effort and doing your best every day. But the alternative is living an unfulfilled, mediocre life.

It all starts by connecting with your source and asking questions that will open up infinite possibilities. Think of questions as a knock on the door. The more you ask, the more you knock. The greater the question, the greater the answer. It is an inside job! The Universe is waiting for you to ask, seek, find and choose as new possibilities are presented to you.

Today Ask

"As an infinite spirit, what is available to me in this moment?"

"What is the most glorious and joyful activity I can do today?"

"How can I live with ease, grace and glory no matter what happens?"

Actions

Try to let go of doing so much. Instead, spend some quiet time using your mind to ask better questions and then contemplate the answers until you receive the right answer. Note: (Through the process of asking infinite, powerful, positive, possibility questions you will be gaining power and developing the ability to receive whatever success you choose to create.

Day 255

*"It takes courage and commitment to master your thoughts,
feelings, choices and actions but this is how wisdom is grown."*

KEN D FOSTER

Peace, balance, wisdom and prosperity await those who seek their true identity. Are you ready to find out who you really are and what you are capable of?

It won't happen if you are constantly looking for answers outside of yourself. Many people try to develop who they are based on what others think of them or what they think they should be like. Have you tried living from other people's points of view? How is it working?

To find out who you are takes quiet time, reflection and asking specific questions so that the universe can give you the answers. One of the great truths in the Christian Bible is "Ask and you will receive." Most people ask questions that limit themselves instead of asking questions that will inspire and empower them to bring forth their greatness.

When you dive deep into yourself and ask questions that reflect answers revealing your true strengths, gifts, talents and abilities, you will start to see what an amazing being you are. When you dive deeper into your soul, you will find everything you have been looking for. As Steve Jobs once said: "Have the courage to follow your heart and intuition. They truly know what you truly want to become. Everything else is secondary."

Today Ask

"What else is possible for me when I connect to spirit?"

"How can I bring into being my genius to fulfill an amazing destiny?"

"Who am I destined to become?"

Actions

Write a paragraph about who you are and what you will accomplish in the next thirty days. If you are having trouble connecting with your creativity, check out www.kendfoster.com/resources to get Ken D Foster's The Science of Meditation Guide for FREE.

Day 256

"Confront the dark parts of yourself and work to banish them with illumination and forgiveness. Your willingness to wrestle with your demons will cause your angels to sing."

AUGUST WILSON[3]

A mind that has the certainty of knowing, "I will succeed," is a mind filled with uncompromising power. But how do you obtain such certainty? It is an age-old question with a simple answer.

The successful person is characterized by certainty of knowing. He has looked at the negative and positive parts of himself and knows himself well. He has realized the power of using his mind to accomplish what he chooses. When he says he will or won't do something, he sticks by his word. The more you stick by your word, the more you program your subconscious mind to believe that what you say will happen.

Break out of the mental limitations that have stopped your success. Train your mind to ask powerful questions, think differently and don't let thoughts of uncertainty weaken your resolve.

Today Ask

"What will it take to live from certainty knowing the course of actions I choose are the correct ones?"

"How will I increase my resolve to accomplish what I choose when I choose it?"

"What do I know, that if I were to live from this knowing, would change my life for the better?"

Actions

Pick a challenge, determine what you are certain about and take constructive actions to resolve it.

Day 257

*"Full courage is realized when you are committed
to be the best you can be mentally, physically,
emotionally, financially and spiritually."*

KEN D FOSTER

Success isn't a destination, it is an ongoing journey that continues to bring out the best in you. Everyone has the potential to be great, but it is only those who are devoted with unswerving focus to bring out their best, that greatness visits.

True success achieves goals that are wholesome and enhances their mental, emotional, physical and spiritual wellbeing. When challenges come, and they will, successful people realize the challenges are there to support their growth and help them become their best.

Knowing what will bring out your best and what will create diversions to your success, is how startling success is founded. It is by using reason and discrimination that each choice can be assessed. Knowing what impulses are good for you and which aren't will also quicken success.

Today Ask

"How will I increase my intuition to get the answers for ongoing success?"

"How will I grow and evolve my thinking when things don't go my way?"

"In what ways can I change my actions and accelerate my success?"

Actions

Take some time to decide what steps you will take to move your dreams forward.

Day 258

*"Most problems are self-generated. It takes courage
to see your part in creating your misery, but when
you do, you can turn things around."*

KEN D FOSTER

Do you think you can outperform your greatest thinking? Don't think about this too long, because you can't. Your brain is limiting you because it is programmed with other people's points of view, restrictive beliefs and your past experiences.

Your brain can process information from the past and figure out logical answers but is this where you want to create your life from? I doubt it! If you stop using the rational mind for anything but processing information and start asking great questions, you will tap into your intuitive awareness.

This is a worthy objective, because your intuitive awareness is unlimited. It is sourced from the superconscious mind which includes everything and excluding nothing. It is where the infinite possibilities exist and where creation starts.

Let me explain. As an infinite being, you are not your thoughts, feelings or body. You have a body, thoughts and emotions by at your core you are *Sat, Chit, Ananda. In* Sanskrit, this means *Sat*—ever existing, *Chit*—ever-conscious, *Ananda*—ever new bliss. As such, you have the potential to connect with Spirit, increase your awareness and generate an amazing life.

Today Ask

"What questions can I ask that will set me up for unlimited success."

"What can I do to hear the answers to my greatest questions?"

"How can I see my challenges clearly and ask the perfect questions for immediate resolution?"

Actions

Decide on an area of your life you would like to improve. Then come up with two action steps you can take today.

Day 259

"Those who know no hardships will know no hardihood.
Those who face no calamity will need no courage. Mysterious
though it is, the human characteristics we admire most
grow in a soil with a strong mixture of trouble."

DALE TURNER [3]

Failure and success are two sides of the same coin. They both help us to develop, evolve and grow if we are determined to learn from both sides.

The Great Depression gave birth to a better America. As a nation, we developed a sense of strength, innovation, compassion and generosity. We are known to the world as one of the most generous nations on the planet and the home of the American Dream.

What are you learning from your life-challenges in today's economy? Think about this for a while. Do you believe you are meant to live in drudgery having the same or greater problems showing up time and time again? I hope you answered *"No."* Either way, choose to ask a new question to open new possibilities and change what is happening!

Today Ask

"What can I do today to innovate and overcome my greatest challenges forever?"

"How can get free of every limitation that I have?"

"How can I increase my initiative and strengthen my resolution to succeed?"

Actions

Make time to assess whether you are repeating your failures or paving new paths toward success.

Day 260

*"Many beliefs which we deem as "truth," shut out
our courage and block abundance from flowing into
our lives. Think about what your willing to doubt,
which may create greater happiness for you?"*

KEN D FOSTER

You have the power to accomplish your dreams, but will you do what it takes to tap into your intuition and succeed no matter what comes along? Many people stop just short of success, but it doesn't have to be that way for you.

Even if you have given up on an important dream, you can reignite the flame of your initiative and tune into your intuition to overcome any challenge by asking questions like: "What else is possible?" or "What can I do to reignite my dream and generate success beyond measure?".

These kinds of questions will ignite your initiative and help you put the superconscious mind to work helping you. The answers provided by the superconscious mind are always there waiting to be retrieved by you.

Your job is to ask, be open to receive new possibilities and then choose the best course of action using your intuition. If you do, most likely much success will be yours. If not, you will most likely live an unfulfilled, mediocre existence.

Today Ask

"What are three questions I can ask to rekindle my dreams?"

"How can I increase my initiative threefold?"

"What has to happen for me to redouble my efforts to succeed?"

Actions

Set aside some time to ignite your passion and personal power.

Day 261

It isn't what you have accomplished, who you know or your failures that hold you back; it is what you believe about yourself and what you think is possible that will either foster future success or leave you stuck in the muck.

Many people try to change their jobs, careers, their relationships or circumstances only to find that things have not improved, and many times have gotten worse.

They wonder why things are showing up for them the way they do. They don't realize that the common denominator that shows up in every circumstance that stops their success is themselves. To receive the prosperity and abundance that awaits you, all thoughts of poverty, lack, fear and limitation must be drained from your mind.

To reach the never-ending supply of wealth that is available, you must still your doubting, critical thoughts and tune into the infinite mind which is always conscious of abundance.

Even when you don't know when things will turn around or where your next dollar is coming from, you should refuse to be apprehensive.

Today Ask

"What would someone have to believe to be in my circumstances?"

"What is an empowering belief that can chance my circumstances around?"

"As I hold this new empowering belief in mind, what actions should I take now?"

Actions

Spend some quiet time with yourself and tune into your soulful calling. Afterward, visualize yourself accomplishing your goals. Also, allow yourself to go deeper in meditation than you did yesterday. If you need help with this, get Ken D Foster's The Science of Meditation Guide for FREE. www.kendfoster.com/resources.

Day 262

*"A life of freedom and happiness awaits you if you have the
courage to still your thoughts and connect to your Wisdom-Self."*

KEN D FOSTER

You can expand your success by using the power of your superconscious mind
which is beyond the conscious or subconscious mind. The superconscious
part of yourself is the part that has all the answers to any challenge you may
have. It is accessed by quieting your thoughts and then by asking open-minded,
possibility-questions.

I have found that the best quests in life will answer questions that you didn't even
know to ask in the beginning. Use the power of questions to kick your superconscious mind into high gear. It will change the course of your life when you ask
powerful questions about subjects unclear to you and stay in the questions until
you receive the answer.

For instance, if you ask; "What can I create that will enhance people's lives and
bring out my greatest gifts, talents and abilities?" You will get the answer!

The superconscious mind can always be accessed. It is a part of your soul, therefore, a part of you. So, pay attention to the questions you ask because they will
determine the answers you receive.

Today Ask

"What am I committed to accomplishing?"

"What action steps will I take to tap into the superconscious mind?"

"What are the most important questions I need answers to?"

Actions

Choose two action steps that will increase your success today.

Authors Note: For those of you who need examples of empowering questions to
ask, I encourage you to get my best-selling book; *Ask and You Will Succeed*, 1001
Extraordinary Questions to Create Life-Changing Results. It will expand your
consciousness and show you how to tap into your genius. You can find it on
KenDFoster.com or Amazon.

Day 263

*"It takes Courage to shine when the storms
of delusion are pounding at your door."*

KEN D FOSTER

Have you ever wondered why you aren't making a bigger difference in the world or why you are not making more money or why you don't have the peace of mind you are longing for?

Well, as you know, life is a journey to perfect your relationship with God and in the process, you must get to know who you are at your core. As you do, you learn the presence and power of the infinite being that you are and how to manifest your greatness in the world. This leads to living a life of excellence. It is a path that comes from the spark of the divine within.

Excellence does not mean you won't make a mistake. It means you look at your mistakes from a dispassionate point of view and learn from them. It says you take time to see what areas you can improve in and then take daily actions towards bettering yourself. It means we don't just move on from our mistakes carelessly but instead, learn and avoid the errors in the future.

Excellence comes to those who use every opportunity to reach the forefront of their personal and professional lives. When you strive for excellence, you become an inspiring uplifting and radiant light for others to follow!

Today Ask

"Who am I at the core of my being?"

"What is the purpose of this lifetime?"

"How can I evolve my life purpose?"

Actions

Although you may have answered the above questions before, contemplate what they mean to you now that you have evolved over the last year.

CHAPTER 14

SUPERSIZE SUCCESS

Day 264

"Because of great love, one is courageous."

LAO TZU[3]

What is the best way to measure success? Results! Few people understand the expanded consciousness it takes to get outstanding results. Most people live without scientifically trying to understand the effects that are showing up.

They don't realize that if they continually adjust along the way, they life will get better and better. But this can change right now!

Take a quick snapshot of your life and rate yourself, dispassionately, on a scale of one to ten, with one representing "dismal" and ten representing "outstanding," in the following areas; (finance, health, fitness, spirituality, life-purpose, social, friendships, relationship with significant other and career).

How did you do? If you are like most, all areas were not a ten! So, what do you need to make all areas a ten? More Love! Think about it. Great love comes with unshakable faith. It is a power that builds with repeated right actions.

Go back to the areas that you rated and find out what it will take to bring more love into each area. When you do, your life will expand.

Today Ask

"What has to happen to take the areas I have chosen to a ten?"

"What could stop me from achieving a ten?"

"What success habit could I put in place to assure my success?"

Actions

Decide which area of your life is most important for you to improve. Then take immediate actions around improving yourself today.

Day 265

*"It takes courage to change from being right to being open
but every time we do, we make the world a better place."*

KEN D FOSTER

If you look for what's wrong, you will find it. If you look for what's right, you will also find it. So why not focus on what is whole, complete and perfect in this moment?

Most people have been taught from childhood to be critical thinkers. But is this really the way to go through life: looking at what is wrong and being critical when you find faults? Criticism condemns the neighbor and damages our own mind.

We must seek to raise others, to raise ourselves. That is the paradox and the key to all life. Your thoughts make a difference. That is why Mahatma Ghandi said "Be the change you wish to see in the world."

Instead of being a critical thinker, what if you were aware of all possibilities by asking questions to reveal the upside and the downside, the positive and the negative, the good and the bad, the right and the wrong; without judging any of it? What if you were aware of the next step to take, by using your intuition and tapping into a bigger consciousness than just using your logical mind?

What would you have to let go of to become aware of everything? Yes, *everything!* What would you have to embrace to expand the awareness of that which you are? Would you let go of generating your life from the rightness and wrongness of anything and everything?

This is a large conversation but a most important one because when you can embrace all of you and become aware of everything that is happening to you, from you and through you, you open the doors to perceiving what will propel your success.

Today Ask

"As an infinite being, am I making choices that will propel my success?"

"What is right about all situations I come across?"

"How can I increase my awareness even more?"

Actions

Increase your awareness by noticing the good, bad and the ugly in all situations without judging it. See reality clearly from all points of view.

Day 266

"I nodded, pretending to be a hundred times more courageous than I felt. But that was the thing about courage. Sometimes you had to fake it to feel it."

LISA TAWN BERGREN[3]

It is good to read about the truth, but it is better to realize it and live by it. How many books, classes or workshops have you taken which inspired you? Many people put down a book or leave a workshop with intentions to do things differently but then forget or put their intentions on the backburner.

To be successful, making and keeping commitments to yourself will help you differentiate between over-committing, making commitments you wish you could change and making the commitments that propel you toward success.

It is important to affirm and believe that you will do what you set out to accomplish because if you don't keep commitments with yourself eventually, you will stop believing in yourself.

Most people have good intentions about wanting to change and improve but intentions alone will not create success. It takes awareness of what is possible for you, a firm bond of commitment and focused actions, to achieve success.

Today Ask

"What is the most important commitment I will keep to accelerate my success?"

"How can I keep this commitment no matter what?"

"By keeping my commitments, what else is possible for me?"

Actions

Look at areas where you have incomplete tasks or broken commitments. Then either recommit and complete these tasks or let go of them permanently.

Day 267

"Courage and Grace walk hand in hand with strength and faith. Every day confirm: "I can, I will, I must accomplish my dreams."

KEN D FOSTER

Have you ever felt stuck or been in a place where it feels hopeless with no way out? It doesn't have to be that way again. The biggest mistake a person can make is to lose hope. Without hope, nothing can change, because without it you have lost the connection to your Wisdom-Self.

When you remember that you are an infinite being endowed with access to answers for every challenge, then it becomes a matter of asking the right questions, opening to receive new possibilities and choosing to take inspired actions.

You would not substitute watching an exercise video for a physical work-out, but many people fall into the pit of regurgitating what they have read, rather than putting the principles into practice.

It is with awareness and actions that you can connect with your inner wisdom and transcend your troubles. You are the creator of your life. You make the choices that lead you toward success or failure. Therefore, there is no challenge you cannot overcome with the infinite power behind your mind.

Today Ask

"When I am sourcing the power that is within me, what can I overcome?"

"What must I believe and apply to overcome the challenges I am facing?"

"How can I increase my resolve to blast through every challenge I have?"

Actions

Think of an area in your business or life that seems hopeless to change. Then come up with five solutions that you have not thought of before.

Day 268

"Courage is always there, waiting for you to invite it in."

KEN D FOSTER

Most people don't sit around and consciously think about what they fear. But if you ask them what they are worried about, they will give you a list of what may happen in the future. If you doubt this, ask yourself: "What am I concerned or worried about?" You may soon see a list of things that could happen!

Did you know that fear is one of the greatest success-stoppers? And fear's closest cousins are doubt and uncertainty. Don't waste your time on unnecessary worrying about things you have no control over in the future. Problems are finite; solutions are infinite.

Since clarity is power, waste no more time in doubt, tune into your intuition and make sure the direction you will take today to increase your success. You have the power to overcome all fears, doubt and uncertainty by using your mind and spirit to find the answers to all your challenges right now.

Today Ask

"What can I do consistently to let go of my fears and focus on solutions?"

"How can I increase my certainty that I have what it takes?"

"What would I have to believe, to move through challenges with ease?"

Actions

Take time today to become aware of how you will overcome the obstacles that are standing in the way of your incredible dreams.

Day 269

*"Be courageous and ask others to help you when
you are stuck. No one has all the answers but
together we can find lasting solutions."*

KEN D FOSTER

We all need positive role models and mentors in our life. We cannot become our very best without them. They show us what is possible and help us reflect our greatest gifts to the world.

I have found in my own life that greater success comes with finding the right role model; one who can be there with me in the good and bad times. Most of my most significant teachers have long since passed from Earth but their teachings live on in organizations, books and most importantly in the hearts and minds of those who apply their lessons.

I found my role models by prayer, commitment to better myself and an undaunted determination to know the truth about life. I asked specific questions until I found the Master Teacher to move me to the next level.

I encourage you to do the work it takes to find the right models also. I encourage you to make a list of your highest values and know precisely the qualities you would like to have your role model help you bring out in your own life.

Today Ask

"How can I find the right mentor for me?"

"What are the most important qualities I am choosing to have a mentor?"

"What are three action steps I can take today to find a mentor?"

Actions

Decide in what areas of your life a mentor would be of great benefit. It can be in the areas of finance, health, fitness, nutrition, relationships, spirituality or whatever you choose.

Day 270

"Courage is going from failure to failure
without losing enthusiasm."

WINSTON CHURCHILL[3]

Focus is the key to success and what you focus on will determine whether you have short or long-term success. Most people focus their attention on outside circumstances to decide what they will do to succeed. This only generates limited success.

When you look inward, all your outer energy focused activities go away. This book is about harnessing your power, so you can choose where to focus on achieving success. As you commune with the immortal part of yourself, all bonds that limit you are revealed and can then be overcome.

Stop / Start patterns of success are typical symptoms of people who live from the outside in, rather than the inside out. This means that they are looking outside of themselves for the answers rather than from the inside out where all your answers genuinely reside. As you continue to realize your divine nature and tap into the unstoppable part of yourself, you will achieve success in any area that you focus your attention on.

Today Ask

"What could happen if I tap into the infinite part of me consistently?"

"How can I achieve even greater success?"

"What is the greatness I am committed to bringing into this world?"

Actions

Take some time to quiet your mind and give yourself permission to slow down and withdraw from the hectic pace of life. Also, are you open to going deeper in meditation today than you did yesterday? If you need help with this, get Ken D Foster's The Science of Meditation Guide for FREE. www.kendfoster.com/resources.

Day 271

*"Courage and teamwork go hand in hand. Do
you have the courage to fit in and do what it
takes for the team to be successful?"*

KEN D FOSTER

Teamwork is the sign of not only a successful entrepreneur, but a successful leader in their home life also. A highly efficient team is a sign that the leader has built positive relationships and has a positive attitude. Believe it or not, a powerful team starts in the leader's mind.

Have you ever noticed how others seem to take on your mood? If you are having a crummy day, it may look that others are having a crummy day too. If you talk about how bad your day is, you may find others commiserate with you. And since you now have social proof that this is a bad day, you may spend the rest of your day feeling down or stressed out.

Research has shown that whoever is most certain about their state of mind will move others into that state. In other words, if you make up your mind that no one and nothing will upset you, this attitude can sway others to move toward your attitude.

In the same way that a super-computer will outperform a system running MS DOS. As you progress through this book, you will watch your power unfold.

Today Ask

"Who will I become to take my team to a completely new level of excellence?"

"What can I improve upon that will fully empower my team members?"

"How can my team and I get better and better?"

Actions

Take some time to contemplate how you are showing up for your team. Are you showing up with a positive attitude? Are you empowering your teammates by asking powerful questions or jumping to conclusions and being a know-it-all with a poor attitude?

Day 272

"Courage is stepping forward when all you can see is darkness."

TONI SORENSON[3]

How much faith do you have? It has been said that faith is founded on beliefs that have been tested. It is *the rock of knowing*, that with success of past actions, you have success in your future. It is built in steps. You have had many successes in your life. Make a list of your top ten for any doubters.

Now, think of one area you have been working on in your business or life that has eluded success so far. Do you ever doubt your abilities and believe that success may never really happen to you? If so, then stop that way of thinking now!

Imagine having one hundred percent faith in the fact that you will succeed. What does that feel like to you? This isn't a mental exercise; go ahead and feel what that would be like for you. Now, imagine living with that faith every day until it happens to you!

The power of faith combined with one hundred percent certainty that you will achieve your dreams is an unstoppable combination. In fact, it is so powerful that any obstacles to your success are removed without much effort.

Today Ask

"How will I consistently generate unstoppable faith to have certainty of success?"

"What step can I take daily to increase my faith?"

"What will have me increasing my faith no matter what?"

Actions

Come up with three practice ways to increase your faith.

Tap into your higher-self and increase your intuition with Ken D Foster's guided meditations on Business, Wealth, Expanding Possibility, Peace, and Health. Yours for free at couragetochange.us/meditation

Day 273

*"Hurricanes, earthquakes, tsunamis and all other
natural calamities cannot stop an infinite being from
taking courageous actions and remaking their life."*

KEN D FOSTER

The Sages tell us that the mind is the cause of our bondage and that the mind is also the cause of our liberation.

Thoughts are like birds flying overhead; they have no real power to harm you. But, if a bird lands on your head; and you let it nest there because you don't think you can make it move, then you are in trouble. Thoughts have no real power unless we give them power. They vibrate in the ether and we tend to magnetize them with views we carry within ourselves.

Everyone has thoughts floating across their minds all the time. When you pick a thought, choose wisely! The nature of your thoughts will impact you for good or for ill. Right now, notice your state. Are you feeling calm, happy, sad or neutral? Now, just think of one great success you have had in the past.

Think of two more, then three more. I want you to dwell on your successes for a minimum of 10 minutes. Then notice how you feel. If you want, you can also do this with negative experiences that have happened to you. But, why would you?

Today Ask

"As an infinite being who is acutely aware of how to create success, what successes would I like to generate today?"

"When this day is over, what will be my greatest success?"

Who am I becoming as a result of consistently tuning into empowering thoughts?"

Actions

Make a list of three beliefs you would like to own which will generate unlimited success?

Day 274

"Courageous are those who are not afraid to look past material forms and connect with formless infinite possibilities."

KEN D FOSTER

There is a guiding voice of truth within every person. This truth is unshakable and connects us to our very essence of self as the soul. When we tap into this conscious voice, we are connected to the wisdom that naturally guides our success.

The type of success I am talking about here is unending, bountiful success. This success is determined not so much by what is happening on the outside but by every poor habit that is overcome and every good habit that is formed through consistent effort on the inside.

Why would an infinite being have habits that disempower them? It would make no sense unless the infinite being was stuck in a story of "how things are" and has limited its choices. Things are how you have defined them, whether you are aware of this or not. If you define life as hard, it is hard for you. If you believe life as a struggle, it will be for you.

The more you can let go of the tribal beliefs you have come to admire and start connecting with your infinite spirit, the more you will realize your inner nature, be happier and much more successful.

Today Ask

"What poor habit will I overcome with commitment, ease and grace?"

"What productive habit will I replace my poor habit with?"

"What are two choices I can make today that will positively impact my life?"

Actions

Take two action steps to impact your life in a positive way.

Day 275

"Courage is the most important of all the virtues because without courage you can't practice any other virtue consistently."

MAYA ANGELOU[3]

All truly successful people spend time meditating, introspecting and contemplating their business and life. Enlightened individuals withdraw from the distractions of the world and go within to find the solutions to their most significant challenges. In meditation, concentration is used to know God and realize a much broader perspective which eventually encompasses everything.

These curators of success have used these principles first to master themselves and then mastered their lives. They have learned to be authentically themselves by fertilizing the good and weeding out the bad points.

In fact, success curators have developed their minds to the point that they are like a white-hot fire—when stoked they overcome any obstacle standing in their way.

Today Ask

"What can I do today to remove any negative thinking in my life?"

"How can I overcome my self-imposed poor habits?"

"What has to happen to bring more of my spirit into the world?"

Actions

Today only focus on positive thoughts. Do not let any disempowering thoughts into your mind. Also, visit KenDFoster.com/Resources and pick up your free copy of Ken D Foster's The Science of Meditation Guide: www.kendfoster.com/resources.

Day 276

*"If your dreams are as large as mountains, make
sure you summon the courage to climb them."*

KEN D FOSTER

Success is a concept that can either bind us or free us. It binds us if we define it in limited ways that result in stress, overwhelm or overwork. It frees us when we define success in unlimited ways that bring out the best in us and support us in generating a happy and joyful life.

Analyse your life and determine if you feel successful or not. If you feel like a failure in some area, it is because you have not created the success you have longed for yet. Think about your childhood dreams. Is there one you would still like to accomplish? If so, then it is time to reenergize your dream! Does that scare you? It may, but I encourage you to take the first step and visualize what it would be for that dream to come true.

You can do this! Within you is the power to overcome all obstacles to manifest your dream, so what are you waiting for?

Today Ask

"What dreams remain undone that I will generate now?"

"How can I define success in such a way that my life is consistently improved?"

"In what ways have I been limiting my success?"

Actions

Make a list of ways you have been limiting your success, then eliminate one of them.

Day 277

"When faced with challenging decisions some say, "I am waiting for God's decision". But those who know courage say, "God is waiting for my decision".

KEN D FOSTER

Are you ready to accelerate the pace of your success? If so, contemplate the following questions. "What is your ultimate vision of your work and where is your business leading you?"

Next, think about what you stand for and what lifestyle you would genuinely like to live. Then determine how your business will develop to support your ideal lifestyle. And finally ask, "What adjustments can I make to attain the life of my dreams?".

When you contemplate questions such as these you get in tune with the essence of what your business and life will be all about. These types of questions will help you align with the spirit of you, why you are here and what you are choosing to be, do and have.

It makes sense to take some time to contemplate these questions. Laziness will not create happiness but if you make the effort to tune into the essence of yourself, you will eventually find happiness beyond measure and unending success.

Today Ask

"What can I do to increase my power and drive?"

"What beliefs, choices or actions can I change to assure my success?"

"What is the most important actions I can take which will propel my life forward?"

Actions

After answering the above questions take two action steps toward your new goals.

Day 278

"It takes much courage to follow your intuition no matter how many illusions to the contrary appear."

KEN D FOSTER

The mind is the "magic factory" where everything is created. Notice I said "mind" not the brain. The mind which is found within and outside the body is the source of infinite possibilities; the brain is a processing vehicle for information. It is excellent for logical sequencing of information but very limited when trying to create an amazing life.

The truth is you are a divine being with the power to light up New York in your fingertips. You have the potential to overcome all disease and any form of limitation. You are the master of your destiny and you alone will determine whether you are successful or not.

It is important to realize that you are not broken, nor do you need fixing. You are an amazing, brilliant gift from God. All you need to do is bring forth your greatness by improving your knowledge.

Today Ask

"What do I know for sure?"

"How can I open to receive everything the universe has in store for me?"

"How can I improve my knowledge?"

Actions

Meditate, be still and know your essence. Who are you? What is your purpose for being here?

Day 279

"It takes courage to hold on to our own suffering and bear it without spreading it to others.

KEN D FOSTER

Understanding your pain and suffering is the door to happiness. There is no way to live a happy life if you cannot acknowledge areas that are blocking that happiness. Whether it is something from the past where you have been wounded or some situation that you are not addressing in the moment. You will not achieve lasting success and happiness until you acknowledge and change what needs to modification.

I encourage you to notice what is working and what is not working in your life. Then decide where you need to perceive differently, grow, improve or change to better the situation. Notice I said, *"where you need to change"*, not someone or something else! Success is an "inside job". As you change on the inside, life gets better on the outside.

As you may have noticed, most people don't take the time to become the observer of their life. They go through life with programmed points of view and never really change from birth to death. They waste lifetime after lifetime and are unaware of what life is about, which is to realize their divinity and share it with the world.

But this cycle can be broken as soon as there is a commitment to acknowledging and feeling the pain and making the changes necessary through daily actions.

Today Ask

"What have I not acknowledged that is blocking my success?"

"Where can I improve, develop, change or perceive differently?"

"What has to happen for me to take more time to meditate and connect to my source daily?"

Actions

Come up with two areas in your life that you are experiencing suffering and make the commitment to resolve them.

Day 280

*"Forget the past, focus on courageous acts
daily and the future will take care of itself."*

KEN D FOSTER

You can do anything that you put your full attention on completing. If you haven't succeeded yet, it doesn't mean that success isn't in your future. Whatever has been stopping you from succeeding at the level you choose must be removed.

When you realize that you are an infinite being filled with unlimited power, you begin the journey toward success. All bonds that have limited you in the past can be broken if you make a spiritual effort now. There is no such thing as fate; you create your destiny.

Apparently, you have tried to think through your problems in the past, but your greatest thinking has gotten you exactly where you are today. Thinking alone will not solve your challenges. If you could have solved all your problems with your mind, you would have done so long ago.

It takes more than an imaginative mind to create ongoing success; it takes intuition. It is important to quiet your thoughts, meditate deeply and tap into the creative source of your supply. When you do this consistently, you will see that where once there was a failure, now success starts to become the norm of your day.

Today Ask

"When will I choose to become the success, I have longed to be?"

"What thoughts must I focus my mind on to become more receptive to ongoing success?"

"Honestly, what can I do to assure my success?"

Actions

Meditate on the highest and best choice to create success today.

Day 281

*"Being unstoppable is a soul quality
that is ignited by a courageous heart."*

KEN D FOSTER

Are you leading your life toward health, wealth, success and joy -- or somewhere else? If you don't like the direction of your life, then what are you going to do about it? As you know, no one will lead you toward real success in life other than yourself.

A good leader is disciplined and knows the direction they are going. They are committed to accomplishing their goals and dreams. They are willing to do what it takes to succeed.

As the leader of your life, what are you willing to do differently to accomplish greater results? If you choose success, then have it. There is nothing stopping you when you decide to generate it.

Success really doesn't rely on external conditions but on the thoughts, you dwell upon and the actions you take. When you can reflect on your attitude and embody a state of being unstoppable, circumstances become neither good nor bad. You have a knowing that you can overcome them with each effort you make.

Today Ask

"How can I reestablish my confidence and become unstoppable?"

"With an unrelenting attitude what can I accomplish today?"

"Why am I passionate about generating greater success?"

Actions

Think about what it means to be unstoppable for you. Then embrace it. In the evening, reflect upon how things went for the day. If there is anything you can do better, then make a promise to yourself that you will do it tomorrow.

Day 282

*"It takes courage for people to listen to their
own goodness and act on it."*

PABLO CASALS[3]

Successful people are characterized by wisdom and awareness. Those who lack this awareness float through life on the rough seas of seemingly uncontrollable circumstances. They rarely succeed in any lasting way.

This ability, which we all have, is there to expand our awareness. It is developed through meditation, introspection and asking powerful questions many of which can't be answered with the logical mind.

Freedom is the goal. It is being free from negative habits and unconscious behaviors that keep a person stuck in karmic patterns of failure, lack and ongoing difficulties.

Wouldn't you like to have great power over yourself to be, perceive, know and do what will boost your success? Why settle for spurious imitations of success? One day, you have money, the next day you are broke.

One day, you have a happy relationship, then it disappears. One day, friendship; the next day, dramas. This is no way to live! You can learn to hold onto success no matter what happens.

Today Ask

"What am I committed to doing differently to burst out of my self-imposed limitations?"

"How is it possible for me to generate ongoing success beyond my thinking?"

"What are three steps I can do today to bring more awareness about how to personally succeed in all areas of life?

Actions

Take time to introspect on what you know for sure about creating success. Then, surrender to Spirit the timing, struggling and judgement of how success should show up. This will allow the space for your Wisdom-Self to provide what is impossible for you to accomplish alone.

Day 283

"Dig deep, find your courage and go forth like a blazing light, consuming every obstacle of darkness in your way."

KEN D FOSTER

Some people chase success, but success cannot be caught; it can only be experienced moment by moment and is determined by the journey you are on.

So, what about success is important to you? And what does it even mean to be successful? Is it something you can be, do or have? Where does it come from? How do you know when you are successful? It is imperative to answer these questions and to define what success means to you. Otherwise, you may be chasing air rather than defining a meaningful life.

The real measure of success is how much happiness you feel in your heart. Money, friends, possessions and even family members come and go. Today, you have them; tomorrow they are gone.

If your success is based on outer things, you may find yourself waking up to an empty vessel feeling unfulfilled and wondering what happened. Finding inner contentment by defining what true success means to you is the way to unlock unending happiness and ultimate success.

Today Ask

"Where am I being called to bring in more awareness and greater abundance?"

"How will I be the success that I truly am?"

"How can I increase my fulfillment and happiness in the coming days?"

Actions

Contemplate what true success means to you and then take three action steps to increase your success.

Day 284

"Courage is the catalyst that takes love to the next level."

REVEREND CHRISTIAN SORENSON[3]

Trying to solve the problems in life with only the logical mind is like trying to chop down a tree with a dull hatchet, you might be able to do it, but it will take a long time. Have you gone through enough challenges in life that you are willing to cease resisting and open to the possibility that there is more to creating success than just using your logical mind?

Have you ever wondered what you could do to solve your greatest problems permanently? I have found that one of the keys to lasting success is the ability to tap into your intuition and make wise choices consistently. Why? Because the intuition is one-hundred-percent accurate, so wouldn't you like to make decisions from this point of view? Of course, you would!

All of us can tap into our inner wisdom but many don't make an effort. That can change for you today! It only takes a few minutes of your day to start a meditation practice. I recommend ten minutes in the morning and evening to begin.

What you will find is that consistent practice will make the difference between discouragement and joy. The choice is yours, but doesn't it make sense to have more love in your life starting today?

Today Ask

"In what areas of my life do I need a big breakthrough?"

"If there was something I need to know to be more successful, what would it be?"

"How can I make sure I connect soulfully each day?"

Actions

Commit to spending time in the morning and evening quieting your mind and connecting deeply with your intuitive self.

CHAPTER 15

MASTERING
THE MIND

Day 285

*"Courage dwells in the soul and is released
with daily actions towards noble goals."*

KEN D FOSTER

Only you can predict what heights you can soar to, but you won't know how high you can soar until you tap into the super-conscious mind and align your thinking with inspired actions.

Why would you try to make your life work by using the same thoughts that have successfully stopped you from having what you want? It makes no sense! Wouldn't you rather tap into a source of answers that is greater than what you have been getting?

I mentioned in the introduction that "The mind is the cause of your bondage and the mind is the cause of your liberation." Did you know we have two minds? There is the lower sense-mind which is supporting the ego and limited self and the higher or super-conscious mind which works with the soul.

Most people only work with the lower mind. The proof of this is that they are just asking basic questions which keep them limited and stuck in their thoughts and behaviour patterns, which only fulfils the needs of the senses.

But the person who is evolving mentally, emotionally and spiritually has reached an awareness or state of consciousness where they are identifying with the inner self and are asking questions which will put Spirit to work for and with them. This works by tapping into the infinite mind, by asking questions that will boost your success, opening possibilities that you have never thought of before.

Today Ask

"What are the most important questions I can ask to increase my prosperity?"

"How will I increase my magnetism and accomplish my greatest dreams?"

"If I were to let go of my limited thinking, what would be possible for me?"

Actions

Ruminate on the fact that you can't out-think your own thinking, but you can free yourself from disempowering thoughts by tuning into your Wisdom-Self.

Day 286

"If you don't find the courage to change your beliefs, choices, and actions, your life will be the way it is forever; and for some, this isn't good news!"

KEN D FOSTER

Health, wealth, peace and happiness start with your thoughts because no one experiences anything that they don't hold first in their mind. So, what ideas are you buying into that are stopping you from having what you want in life? Think about this question for a while!

Awareness is the key to changing thought-habits. In fact, change can't happen unless consciousness expands, so become the observer of your mind and notice if the thoughts you are choosing are empowering you or disempowering you. If you are having thoughts such as: *"I don't have enough money to _____ (fill in the blank)"*; or *"I don't have enough time to _____ (fill in the blank)"*; or *"I do this or that, because this is just who I am"*, these thoughts need to be reversed to charge the mind with positive focus.

Today Ask

"What thoughts can I focus on to create an amazing life?"

"If I let go of failure-thinking, what could I accomplish?"

"What are the most powerful thoughts I can hold in consciousness today?"

Actions

As thoughts cross your mind try saying: "Interesting that I have this thought" or just "Interesting." As you do, notice that you instantly get some distance between the thoughts floating across your mind and you the infinite being who is the observer of these thoughts.

Day 287

*"It's with courage that we must delve into the unknown parts of
ourselves and realize the truth of who
we are and what is possible."*

KEN D FOSTER

Truth told; everyone has what it takes to create an amazing life. Problems come when you circumscribe your power by tuning into thoughts such as: "This project is too large for me," "I don't have enough time or money to ...", "I'll never get ahead," "I am too old," "I am too young," etc.

There are many thoughts we can focus in on to limit our success, but it has been said many times that the truth will set you free. When you consistently talk to yourself in an empowering way, you will be amazed at how fast you can turn things around.

Why affirm negatives to yourself? This will only hurt you. Affirm the goodness in you. Tune into your greatness and you will be miles ahead of the pack.

Today Ask

"What are the three steps necessary for me to generate unending success?"

"What has to happen for me to create the life of my greatest dreams?"

"What will I affirm about myself daily until the desired changes take place?"

Actions

Be the powerful being that you are and come up with ten empowering things that are true about yourself. Then, pick one and say it repeatedly until you feel it permeating throughout your being.

Day 288

"We have to be braver than we think we can be, because God is constantly calling us to be more than we are."

MADELEINE L'ENGLE[3]

After the storms, when water flows down a mountain it converges and forms streams. Some of the streams find their way into larger bodies of water and some do not. The ones that find the rivers are assured success and reconnect with the sea, but the ones that don't eventually dry up and evaporate.

The same goes with us. If you are not connecting with your inner wisdom after the storms of life hit you, you have stopped connecting with the flow of life. When this happens, challenges seem magnified and you will struggle.

But it only takes a moment to reconnect with the infinite power and wisdom that is right within you. If things have been challenging today, take some time to nurture yourself. Start you day over, then calm you mind and know everything is unfolding for your highest good. Even if it doesn't seem like it at the time, it is true.

Today Ask

"What tools do I have at my disposal to reconnect with my spirit quickly?"

"How fast can I let go of upsets in the past and "Be Here Now"?"

"How can I use my strengths to quickly calm my mind?"

Actions

Try setting the intention to let go of any stressors within ten minutes. Become present by saying: "I am here", I am here", I am here". Practice this for a couple weeks until you get good at it, then try lowering how fast you can recover from stressors.

Day 289

*"Courage is resistance to fear, mastery
of fear—not absence of fear."*

MARK TWAIN[3]

Are the choices you are making freeing you or enslaving you? Is your life getting a little better each day or not? These are the questions we need to ask consistently to make sure we are on the success path.

Before making any decision, meditate and connect with the infinite. This will free your mind from focusing on mundane challenges and open possibilities to create a compelling future.

After meditating, look at the positive aspects of making the decision and the negative. Then ask: "What else is possible?" or "What other choices can I make?". Don't lock yourself into one course of action until you have explored all possibilities with a clear mind.

Making decisions from impulse, whims or emotions may lead to temporary feelings of happiness but in the long-term, results may be dissatisfying, so calm your mind before making crucial decisions.

Today Ask

"What are the infinite possibilities available to me?"

"How can I increase my success by opening up more opportunities?"

"How can I remember to meditate and calm my mind before making important decisions?"

Actions

Take time to be aware of your choices and contemplate the results of your decisions. Then when you are sure you are making the right choice, proceed with conviction.

Day 290

"Soulful wisdom causes courage to arise gloriously in your life."

KEN D FOSTER

Good judgment comes from experience and wisdom. It is a synthesis of the two. So, if you lack experience, you will have to develop your wisdom. And just like experience, wisdom is grown in the soil of daily actions to improve.

You will not become wise by trying to think yourself into wisdom. Many educated people have very little common sense. Wisdom comes from freeing yourself from the confines of duality by increasing awareness through soulful actions such as meditation, self-inquiry, contemplation and serviceful activities.

These practices escalate the ability to see reality clearly and thus build up the desired muscle to exercise good judgment.

Today Ask

"What has to happen for me to grow my wisdom?"

"How can I harmonize with my deep intuitive self?"

"What is the outcome when I consistently exercise good judgment?"

Actions

Make a point of taking time throughout the day to be the observer of your life. Notice how you are feeling, observe the roles you are playing and how correctly everything is showing up to help you take your life to the next level.

Day 291

"I am not a courageous person by nature. I have simply discovered that, at certain key moments in this life, you must find courage in yourself, to move forward and live."

JOHN PATRICK SHANLEY[3]

What do you do when you are stuck? Do you ask for help? Do you pray? Do you distract yourself? Do you give up? Whatever is going on in your life, it is "you" who put yourself there. How much awareness you bring to your life and how you use your mind will determine how much happiness or misery you will have.

By misguided thinking or misunderstanding, you will get nothing but troubles. When you tap into your Wisdom-Self and become aware of what is possible for you, you can overcome all obstacles to success. The cycling of negative thoughts will disempower you and lead to failure. But when you can start generating your life from your inner knowing or intuition, you will become an unstoppable force.

When you're able to control your thoughts, you will become the master of your destiny. You can do this by asking questions, expanding choices and contemplating how to improve your world daily.

Today Ask

"What can I do to expand my awareness and make choices that will create unlimited success?"

"How can I consistently focus on success-thoughts?"

"What has to happen for me to quit my mind and tap into the infinite source of my wisdom today?"

Actions

Come up with a written success plan with specific dates of completion.

Day 292

"It takes courage . . . to endure the sharp pains of self-discovery."

MARIANNE WILLIAMSON[3]

Unhappiness, failure and illness are natural results of transgressions of universal laws. How do you avoid these calamities? Going within and tapping into your inner wisdom is the key.

When you can find gratitude, happiness and peace within yourself, your life will be very different. There is nothing that shuts down the creative powers more than overwhelm, stress and ignorance of universal laws.

If you put rotten foods into your body, your body will get sick. If you put rotten thoughts into your mind, your mind will get sick. If you put rotten people in your business, your business will get sick. So, feed your mind, body and business with success thinking to attract what you truly want.

It is all an "inside job." If you want more success, focus on thoughts of success. Like; "I am getting better and better every day in every way," or "I love life and life loves me," or "The perfumes of success-thoughts are flowing through me."

Today Ask

"Where am I choosing to have greater success in my life?"

"What thoughts can I focus on change my brain into unending success mode?"

"What will empower me to take immediate actions and propel my success?"

Actions:

Don't be satisfied with a small amount of wisdom from others. Tap into the inner source of truth within you by meditation, asking questions and seeking wisdom that is all-bountiful and ever flowing.

Day 293

"There is nothing that says you will live a life of great difficulties or have everything go your way; but either way, it will take courage to become all you are meant to be."

KEN D FOSTER

It is not so much what you do but how you do it, that determines how much success you have. Some people do tasks with resentment in their hearts, while others accept what life is asking them to do and do it with an attitude of love. Which approach do you think brings more success?

It does seem obvious, so why not increase your efforts to bring more love into everything you are doing? Love is an action word which requires willpower to bring it into existence.

You cannot bring more love in unless you set your intention to express it more often. If you want more love in your life, be more loving. It is simple to say but sometimes difficult to accomplish.

Today Ask

"What can I do to fill my work with love?"

"How can I infuse a loving attitude into everything I do?"

"In what areas of my life can I increase my love?"

Actions

Notice with a sense of awe and wonder how perfectly your life falls into place. Imagine doing this every day!

Day 294

"Courage is knowing what not to fear."

PLATO[3]

Have you ever wondered why you are going through the experiences and conditions you are going through? Well, since your thoughts, choices and actions are the cause of your success or failure, to change anything you must first change your thinking.

The thoughts you are focusing on will either cause you to be limited and small or cause you to expand your possibilities and increase your happiness. You may have heard this many time before, but don't you think now is a good time to stop allowing disempowering thoughts to limit your life?

I recommend you focus on courageous thoughts and stay empowered. Try to have one day where you don't allow anything to upset you. Stay power filled the whole day and see what happens.

Today Ask

"What will I focus on to stay empowered throughout the day?"

"How can I remember to still my mind before all major decisions?"

"What do I know will happen as I make all my decisions while feeling empowered?"

Actions

Make a list of what you know for sure and then test it to make sure it's true.

Tap into your higher-self and increase your intuition with Ken D Foster's guided meditations on Business, Wealth, Expanding Possibility, Peace, and Health. Yours for free at couragetochange.us/meditation

Day 295

"It takes a lot of courage to show your dreams to someone else."

ERMA BOMBECK[3]

Success comes to those who apply the power of their imagination to generate indelible mental blueprints in their mind of the ventures, projects or goals they want to achieve.

Start with little things and imagine yourself completing them in your mind. Do this repeatedly, until you develop the conviction and a sense that you have the capacity to achieve your goals or projects no matter what. Then apply the same mental power to larger and larger dreams until you start to generate whatever you imagine.

By using your imagination repeatedly until it is converted into indomitable willpower, there is no doubt that you will prosper, because whatever your vividly image your brain will experience as reality.

Remember, your imagination must be developed to the point that you are stronger than the thoughts and suggestions that you pick up from others. This is the way to be victorious in your life.

Today Ask

"How can I intensify my dreams to become so vivid that they will inspire me?"

"What is possible when I remember that I am a dream fulfilling infinite being?"

"What are the most important steps I can take after I visualize my dreams?"

Actions

Spend five minutes or more visualizing your greatest dreams coming into manifestation.

Day 296

> *"The courage to change lies in moment by moment*
> *decisions, and those decisions will determine your destiny."*

KEN D FOSTER

Good judgment is the key to tremendous success. But where does good sense start? For many, it may come from experience. For some, it comes from studying wise choices others have made and for a few disciplined souls, it comes from intuition.

If you don't have the experience, you will have to depend on others to help you. If you don't have enough wisdom, you will also have to find people that possess knowledge to help you make good choices.

But everyone has the power to tap into their intuition and guess what? Intuition is one hundred percent accurate. Wouldn't you like to have more insight? If so, then make the effort to check in with your inner wisdom before making important decisions.

Each time notice if you are making choices that are aligned with right decisions that lead to success. If not, notice when you make poor decisions and if these choices were because you didn't check in with your inner wisdom. Most likely you will find that it is.

Today Ask

"What has to happen for me to allow my intuition to come forth in greater ways?"

"How will I know when my intuition is speaking to me?"

"How can I expand my awareness to increase my insights?"

Actions

Notice two times today when your intuition is guiding you.

Day 297

*"If you have a dream, don't just sit there. Gather
courage to believe that you can succeed and leave
no stone unturned to make it a reality."*

ROOPLEEN[3]

Success or failure is determined by the amount of awareness you have and your ability to use your mind by focusing on empowering thoughts. If you believe you cannot find the solutions to your most challenging situations this will become your reality and you will be stuck in your story.

The way to break out of stories is to realize that life is like a movie and you are the writer, producer and actor in this life-movie. The only thing holding you back from producing the movie of your dreams is your belief that you can't.

Step into your power and realize that you can have a fantastic day if you choose. In fact, this could be the most memorable day of your life, if you decide to have it that way.

Today Ask

"What stories am I telling myself that stop me from achieving my dreams?"

"If I were to let go of all the stories and other points of view of how my business should be, what would I like it to be like?"

"How can I permanently let go of disempowering stories I have been telling myself?"

Actions

Make a list of disempowering stories you have been telling yourself and then do what it takes to let them go. Note: (By letting go of your disempowering stories, new possibilities will come into focus for more considerable success).

Day 298

*"There is nothing more courageous than a soul
connected with the unlimited mind of God."*

KEN D FOSTER

Is your consciousness running at ten volts or ten thousand volts? Most people are doing the same things repeatedly, trying to stay in their comfort zones. They may be living their lives in a ten-mile radius or running on unconscious fears of trying new things.

Either way, their minds are ten-volt minds instead of powerful, creative, ten-thousand-volt minds. This doesn't have to be. The way out is to have a quantum breakthrough in consciousness by asking questions that will break through the ruts.

Think about this. There are millions of inventions that have not been seen yet but soon someone will tap into their unlimited awareness and generate it for the world. Why not have it be you?

Look around and study objects and situations in your immediate path, then think about ways you can improve each object or situation. By so doing, you will start to open your awareness to new possibilities and soon you will be on your way to creating something new.

Today Ask

"What can I invent or do that has not been done before?"

"What new possibilities can I imagine for each object I come across?"

"Where can I have a quantum breakthrough in my awareness that will allow me to see with the eyes of a creative inventor?"

Actions

Make a list of three new products you could invent.

Day 299

*"No matter how many times your business or life has
beat you down, find the courage to connect to your
unstoppable self and accomplish your dreams."*

KEN D FOSTER

How will you ensure that next year is better than the last? It starts by looking past the surface appearances of this world. Going deeper into the silence within until you have risen above any failure-thinking and touched the creative factory of the universe.

New and more significant opportunities are ever present when you choose to look beyond the limits of the human mind. The way to start this process is to still the mind in meditation and become the observer of your thoughts.

As you start to bring more awareness to your thoughts, you may notice your thoughts can come from several places. For instance, you may pick up on the thoughts of others or tune into past experiences from your subconscious mind. You could also pick up astral thoughts of angelic beings or possibly tune into thoughts of animals or Nature.

Think of your thoughts this way: If birds are flying over your head you have no control over them but if one lands on your head and tries to nest there, you have the choice to let it nest or shoo it away.

Many people believe they have no control over their thoughts and therefore their fate is sealed. But thoughts are just passing through, so why not choose powerful thoughts that will ensure happiness, success and joy?

Today Ask

"Are the thoughts that I am consistently choosing, assuring a better life?"

"Are the thoughts I am dwelling on bringing me happiness and success?"

"What thoughts can I choose to focus on that will help me bring forth my brilliance into the world?"

Actions

Come up with two enlightening beliefs you know will move you closer to your soulful calling.

Day 300

"Courage empowers us to write new scripts in our lives and join the forces of good to make unfathomable changes benefiting all."

KEN D FOSTER

Failure leaves clues. Things like: not having enough money, being unorganized, relying on others to accomplish what you need to do, being unmotivated, being complacent, not taking care of business. If you have symptoms of failure, you are most likely playing by rules that don't work.

We all set up rules in our lives. We have rules for just about everything we do from driving a car to how you behave in the workplace. But rules are not meant to be our masters; they are servants intended to improve our life not restrict. You are the master of your fate since you alone set up the rules. Why not set up standards that will accelerate your success?

You can tell the rules that you are living by when you examine your habits. If you have the habit of staying up late, you may have a rule that says you get more done when you stay up late.

If that rule is working for you then fine, keep it. But if you wake up in the mornings depleted, it is in your best interest to change that rule. Remember, it isn't your brilliant ideas that will create your success but the everyday mental habits you form.

Today Ask

"What are the three most disempowering habits I have formed?" Then, make a list of the underlying thoughts or rules that keep these habits in place.

"What is the most important rule I can set and live by each day?"

"What new success habit will I commit to setting and doing each day?"

Actions

After determining your new habit, find a book or article that supports your new habit.

Day 301

If you believe that you will be wildly successful, chances are you will be, because what you habitually think about will determine your psychology, skills and actions.

If you don't like what is showing up for you, then the first step is to open your mind to be receptive to change. And change is all about first a shift in being that then shifts you to respond and do something different.

Let me ask you a question when things are going well for you who are you being? Are you courageous, confident, clear and focused? How about when things are not going well for you who are you being then?

Simply changing who you are being will change the direction of your life permanently. A simple change in focus will transform failure to success, from unhappiness to happiness, from stagnation to inspiration.

It is only when a person has fixed thinking, believing, "It will always be this way for me" or, "I am the way I am," that he or she will become permanently stuck. Honestly, this type of thinking is mental laziness. You are more powerful than these thoughts.

Today Ask

"How will I show up today and be powerful?"

"What is the most amazing thing I can accomplish today if I were to let go of defining myself as limited?"

"How can I reimagine myself today?"

Actions

Change starts first in mind with a willingness to see things differently. Determine what you would like to see different.

Day 302

"Anyone can get upset or outraged when things don't go their way. It takes great courage to remain dispassionate and calm during storms and trials."

KEN D FOSTER

Success isn't achieved by only hearing the good news. You must be able to hear and receive the negative news without retreating. You must learn to listen to problems with a dispassionate mindset.

If you are oversensitive to bad news or if you get emotional when things don't go the way you hoped, you may very well limit your success.

In fact, most likely if you are making decisions when you are upset, they won't be good ones. However, when you can honestly look at what has gone awry, without judging it as right, wrong, good or bad, just see the root cause and learn, you can consistently improve and your whole life will become a thing of magic.

Today Ask

"What are the most important challenges I am facing that need to be solved?"

"What is the easiest and most fun way I can solve these challenges?"

"As I solve these challenges, what is the mindset I am choosing to maintain?"

Actions

Come up with five solutions to your most significant challenge.

Day 303

*"Self-control is the chief element in self-respect and
self-respect is the chief element in courage."*

THUCYDIDES[3]

An occasional positive thought will not assure success. It takes a powerful mind
that is focused on positive outcomes to create ongoing success. Wishing or hoping
things will work out is magical thinking in the worst sense of the word. It's not a
mindset that brings about a transformed life.

Take control of your mind! Thoughts are consistently flowing past your mind, but
you are the one who chooses which thoughts you allow in and which ones you
don't, which ones you act upon and which ones you don't. So why not only allow
thoughts in your mind which empower you?

Remember this: Just behind your mind is infinite wisdom. And just behind your will
is a power beyond measure. But you must tap into these strengths daily to overcome any obstacles that will keep you stuck in mediocrity. This is done by quieting
the mind by daily meditation, asking compelling questions and by taking focused
actions.

Today Ask

"What astonishing and wonderful thoughts will I allow in my mind today?"

"How can I focus on more loving and courageous thoughts in all I do?"

"What can I do consistently to remind me that I am the master of my mind?"

Actions

Stay positive and focused on your road to success. Read a book that inspires you,
invite a positive mentor to lunch and remove mental limitations by deepening
your meditation each morning and evening.

Day 304

*"The courage to change is developed moment-by-moment by the
decisions you make, which will ultimately
determine your destiny."*

KEN D FOSTER

Are you really playing full-out in your life or are you just tolerating things? Complacency is easy to fall into but many times there is a lull before the storm. In other words, by living in your comfort zone, it can seem that everything is going well until you notice that things are starting to fall apart.

If you are living in complacency, there are decisions being made that are slowly and surely diluting who you are as an infinite being and the power at your command.

As a result, you may wake up one day with a sense of loss or worse. What you lost was your spirit. Every time you decide to do what is easy instead of what you know is the right choice, you lose connection with yourself.

For instance, let's say you have the value of keeping a clean home, but you become complacent and a year goes by where you find yourself living in clutter. You wonder, "How did I get so overwhelmed?"

The answer: This situation has its root cause in your mind. The mind will tell you: "Don't worry about the clutter. ... I will get to it tomorrow." But if you ask, "What is the highest and best choice for me today?" you will get the answers that will continually move you forward in life.

Today Ask

"How can I let go of my disempowering thinking forever?"

"What are the three steps I can take today to free myself from _____?"

"Who am I being when I have tireless energy to accomplish what I choose?"

Actions

Make a new decision. Choose to play full out on one area that you have been wavering on. Note: (If you don't like your past beliefs, choices and actions you can change them in this moment)

Day 305

Master your mind and you will master your life. Successful men and women have recognized this adage for eons. But how do you master your mind and what mind will you master—your conscious, subconscious or superconscious mind?

You will need to master all three. But in a real sense the mind is another name for consciousness, so you don't have to master any mind, all you need do is learn how to use awareness to generate your life.

The brain is there to store data and process information, but awareness includes everything and excludes nothing therefore awareness includes the brain and mind but is not limited by either.

Your awareness is connected to the universe and everyone and everything in it. So, doesn't it make sense to remember your presence as an infinite being and increase your awareness to master your business and life?

Today Ask

"What have I not been aware of, that when I am aware of it, will substantially increase my wisdom?"

"As an infinite being of pure light, what else can I bring into existence?"

"What has to happen for me to create different choices which will support me to realize success beyond measure?"

Actions

Today practice visualizing your greatest dreams manifesting until you feel a sense of inspiration flowing through your mind.

Day 306

*"The most powerful vision is one that seems impossible
but becomes inevitable through courageous acts."*

KEN D FOSTER

Adapt, innovate and change if you want to succeed. Being rigid can cause stagnation to creep into your life and create havoc. Rigidity leaves clues such as others not wanting to be around you or a trail of upset people who are complaining about you.

People who are too rigid live by disempowering rules. Their minds are filled with *'shoulds,* *'have to'*s, *'must'*s, fears and continual judgment. But this will not create success! It is important to stay flexible in an ever-changing world. Free your mind from thinking you must do things a certain way or, worse, that others must do things a certain way.

This type of thinking creates a sense of false control! The more rigid you are, the more you shut down possibilities and choices. As Einstein said: "A man should look for what is and not for what he thinks should be."

Creative thinking is the best antidote for a rigid mind. What if you were to let go of the right, wrong, good and bad of whatever you are doing and just ask a new question! Wouldn't this be a more natural way to live? Wouldn't you have more peace and harmony in your life?

Today Ask

"What are the infinite possibilities that are available to me at this moment?"

"Where can I find the courage to let go of black and white thinking?"

"What has to happen for me to focus on what is possible and become a possibility thinker?

Actions

Get real with yourself and think about where you have been rigid in your thinking. Come up with one belief that you believe to be true and then question it.

CHAPTER 16

LIVE BY NOBLE CHOICES

Day 307

*"If we never had the courage to take a leap of faith,
we'd be cheating God out of a chance to mount us
up with wings like eagles and watch us soar."*

JEN STEPHENS[3]

There is no such thing as fate. You create your own destiny; and your destiny is determined by your choices. If you choose indiscriminately most likely you will experience lack in your business and life. But if you use the power of discernment then success will soon be yours.

Discernment is a soulful power; therefore, doesn't it make sense to tune into your soul if you want to make wiser choices? I recommend you do this by being still, quieting your thoughts and asking soulful questions to find the right answers for any situation.

Through this practice, you will realize when not to make unimportant things important, nor make important things unimportant. This alone will increase your success but to develop discernment it is also important to ask what is the highest and best for all concerned.

I encourage you to spend the first part of your day planning to succeed by asking discerning questions to clarify your priorities and direction for the day. By doing this you will create a success habit that will propel your business and life forward.

Today Ask

"As I start my day, what are the best actions I can take to increase success?"

"What are the wisest choices I can make to overcome any obstacles in my path?"

"How can I become more discerning in each choice I make?"

Actions

Make a list of your projects and tasks and prioritize them.

Day 308

"The most courageous people I know are those who listen to their inner compass instead of the opinions of others."

KEN D FOSTER

Have you ever wondered if you are making the right choices? We have all made the right decisions and the wrong decisions at some point in time but how do you know the right direction to take on a consistent basis?

What I have found is that taking some "time out" for quiet reflection before making critical decisions is the best way to assure success. During that quiet time, I like to ask: "Is the choice I am about to make in the highest good for all concerned?"

If so, it is usually a natural choice to make but if the answer is unclear, then I recommend you wait until you have clarity before proceeding. There is an old says; "when in doubt don't". In other words, don't' move forward until you have certainty of the best direction to go.

Today Ask

"What are three questions I can consistently ask myself when I need clarity?"

"What is the indicator that I am making the right choice?"

"How can I know when I am not making the right choices?"

Actions

Commit to quiet your mind before making critical decisions and move forward only when you are sure it is the right choice. As you do this, notice if the right opportunity becomes more evident to you!

Tap into your higher-self and increase your intuition with Ken D Foster's guided meditations on Business, Wealth, Expanding Possibility, Peace, and Health. Yours for free at couragetochange.us/meditation

Day 309

You have heard it said many times before: "Watch your motives". But how important are your motives really? Well, let me put it this way. . . . They determine whether your success is lasting or just "flash in the pan".

The greedy person goes into business to make a profit for himself; the wise man goes into business to be of service to others while making a profit. It is essential to check your motives when making decisions.

When your purposes are aligned with your values, then you will be making good choices that will further your success. When they are not, most likely these choices will fall short.

Today Ask

"What are my most important motivations?"

"How will I align with my values in my business to create unending success?"

"Who can I motivate today that will be helped to increase their success?"

Actions

Align your motives with your highest values and watch your personal and professional life flourish!

Day 310

"It takes courage to set your sails and navigate life's storms until you find the safe harbor of wisdom and abundance."

KEN D FOSTER

Lack of money is a symptom that you may not be applying business or spiritual principles correctly. The universe runs on exact laws and so does business and life. It is up to you to discover where and how to apply the principles to create ongoing success.

These principles include taking time daily for meditation to raise your vibrational frequency, introspection, contemplation and taking inspired actions.

Imagine every day in every way, your life is getting better and better. It will, if you have the discipline to practice spiritual and life principles. Also, it doesn't hurt to believe in yourself.

Today Ask

"What am I doing that is blinding me from seeing my brilliance?"

"How can my business and life grow exponentially?"

"What is the next positive step I can take to evolve myself?"

Actions

Make a list of at least five things you know will create success in your life if you apply them.

Day 311

*"It's with courage that we save ourselves, heal our
past mistakes and move to a bigger and brighter future."*

KEN D FOSTER

The fastest way to success in the money game isn't just modeling and learning from other wealthy mentors. It's clearing a path past secondhand, rubbish-thinking around money and reprogramming your mind to be a magnet to money.

It is important that you open to receive abundance and realize that you deserve to be rich. Not because you were born with privilege or that you are so great; but because you are an infinite being who can generate wealth and live an amazing life. You were given the power of choice not to blunder around merely surviving but to make wise choices that empower you.

Start today and know that every day in every way you are a magnet to money. Say to yourself repeatedly until it happens for you: "Money is easy for me to make" and "Every day in every way I am generating more and more money." Your capacity to earn, hold and grow money is expanding as you read this. Start to visualize and feel what it is like to have a lot of money.

Today Ask

"How can I make money today?"

"How can I expand my capacity to receive more money?"

"What will it take to bring in more money every moment of every day?"

Actions

Resolve to increase your self-worth and have more money flowing into your life. Today take ten-minutes to visualize what it will be like for you to be financially free.

Day 312

"Anyone can spew out their emotions onto others.
But the courageous learn to master their minds
and remain calm through the storms of life."

KEN D FOSTER

If you are making choices from emotional states, chances of success diminish. It only makes sense! Imagine making decisions from a state of anger, sadness, fear or over-optimism. Most likely you will not make the right decisions, because emotions blind the mind with lack of discernment and absence of awareness.

It is with even-mindedness that wisdom flows into a calm mind. The Biblical teachings say: "Be still and know that I am God". Indian scriptures teach: "I am that stillness beyond all motion, beyond all vibration, beyond all form".

When you meditate and concentrate fully on God, you enter these states of consciousness. In that state, God's first expression to us is usually peace; and many times, it is followed by insights which can change the course of your life if you act on them.

As Minister Robert H. Schuller wrote: "Never cut a tree down in the wintertime. Never make a negative decision in the low times. Never make your most important decisions when you are in your worst moods. Wait. Be patient. The storm will pass. The spring will come." This advice applies to the daily moments of our lives.

Today Ask

"What can I do today that will cause me to be more even minded?

"What am I not aware of that could possibly block my success?"

"How can I ensure that when I make decisions I am in a calm state?"

Actions

During your day, I encourage you to stop and calm the mind. Take in five deep breaths and as you exhale let the stress of the day be exhaled. Then feel your body and mind relax.

Day 313

*"It doesn't take much courage to follow the pack, but it takes
lots of courage to carve your own unique way through the maze
of life and create a beautiful sculpture of a life well lived."*

KEN D FOSTER

Rushing through life and taking on more and more is no way to live. Take some time for yourself and ask: *"Why am I doing what I am about to be doing?"*. If you don't have a good reason, then don't do it.

To have success, you must make your dreams a priority and not get distracted. If you are not living your dreams, then they are not your priorities. Think about this for a moment. How can something be your priority if you are not focusing on it?

Many times, you may have good intentions to get something done but you make other things a priority, so your dreams get put on hold. Why keep doing this? Aren't your dreams vital to you!

ToDay as

"How can I become more successful?"

"How can I increase my faith and accelerate my will to accomplish my goals?"

"What has to happen to increase my determination to overcome all difficulties?"

Actions

Take some time to quiet your mind and give yourself permission to slow down and withdraw from the hectic pace of life. Also, are you open to going deeper in meditation today than you did yesterday? If you need help with this, get Ken D Foster's The Science of Meditation Guide for FREE. www.kendfoster.com/resources.

Day 314

"There are always difficulties arising which tempt you to believe that your critics are right. To map out a course of action and follow it to an end requires courage."

RALPH WALDO EMERSON[3]

Your destiny is not determined by chance but by every choice that you alone set in motion. Yes, you are the source of your success and you are the source of your misery. You are either a host for the ego or a host for the divinity of your soul.

When you realize that you have the power to change the course of your life, it will get better. But how do you recognize this? By asking questions that will inspire greatness in you.

Rather than looking for what is wrong in your life, start asking questions that will empower you, like: "How can I shift my thinking and let wisdom flow into my mind consistently?" Since there is no such thing as fate or destiny; you have as your birthright the courage to create a fantastic business and life.

Today Ask

"How can I remember to align with my highest thinking and divinity of my soul?"

"What can I transcend in my life that will accelerate my happiness?"

"What opportunities are available to me that will bring out the best in me?"

Actions

Make up your mind to become the person you most admire in the world. Write out the values and noble goals you are choosing to have in your life, then start living from the values, thoughts and actions that you admire.

Day 315

"He who seeks wisdom combined with a courageous heart evolves and becomes a magnet for success."

KEN D FOSTER

When you live from Spirit and are in harmony with Nature, life becomes joyful. I am not talking about something that is outside of yourself but the Spirit that dwells within you and the Nature of who you are.

When you are completely immersed in the material world, making no time for Spirit, your world becomes brittle and out of balance. When this happens, symptoms such as overwhelm, stress, depression or over-indulgence appear.

The same is true if you over-emphasize the spiritual aspects of life. In this case, symptoms like disconnection from the world, lethargy, lack of vision and weak will-power may appear. In either case, you will fail to achieve harmonious development and therefore not live up to your highest potential.

I have coached many spiritual clients that have created material wealth as soon as they started to pay more attention to the material side of their lives. And I have coached many wealthy people who were unhappy until they decided to bring the spiritual side of life into focus. To have joyful experiences in life, both Spirit and Nature must be in harmony.

Today Ask

"What is a noble goal I can set to balance my life?"

"How can I bring more joy and fulfillment into my life?"

"What is true about my life, that when I see it, I will manifest more joy, success and fulfillment?"

Actions

Decide where you need to put more focus, either on your material or your spiritual side then take immediate steps toward that decision.

Day 316

> *"Because a fellow has failed once or twice or a dozen times, you don't want to set him down as a failure till he's dead or loses his courage and that's the same thing."*
>
> GEORGE LORIMER[3]

When your wants are boiled down to your real needs, life becomes very simple. And by simple living, you can become more playful, joyful and healthy.

I am talking about expanding your awareness of what is possible for you by being able to enjoy life with the necessities, instead of living on the edge, keeping up with the latest fads or chasing money every month to pay the bills, these types of behaviors are detrimental to your health and happiness.

If you are on the *"get more and more* treadmill," then you may want to stop and examine what is important in your life and start letting go of impulse-buying and excess spending. Isn't it more important to you to have money instead of chasing money every month to accommodate your spending habits?

Most of the time impulse-buying is related to filling up a gap in the psyche or generating your life from cultural points of view. Next time you go to buy something, notice if you are non-attached to getting it or in a mindset of *"I have to have it."* If you are in the mindset of *"I must have it,"* then stop and ask: *"Is this something I truly need or just want?"* If you don't need it, don't buy it.

Today Ask

"What can I do to spend less and save more?"

"What has to happen for me to let go of impulse-buying forever?"

"How can I simplify my spending habits and have more peace of mind?"

Actions

Commit to letting go of impulse-buying. Take on the mindset that: "If it is meant to be, it will be there in a day, week or month." In other words, practice non-attachment to things.

Day 317

"Don't let dogma or disempowering social beliefs stop you from being all you were meant to be! It takes courage to break through the opinions of others."

KEN D FOSTER

The laws of success are simple to understand but often hard to follow. One of the laws I came across is to: "Live your life as a contribution to others." In other words, find your gifts, talents and skills and empower others by sharing these with them.

Did you feel resistance to this when you read it? I did, so I asked myself, "What is my resistance to helping others?" The answer was; "I would rather think of myself first," and if I give away what I have I will starve! Ouch! That was the unreality I was dealing with, lack and self-centered thinking, so I chose to change myself and I did!

Today, I serve God and I am here to empower others along with myself. By making this shift in consciousness my business increased, my health became more vibrant and I attracted more successful people into my life. So, if you find yourself having any resistance to helping others, it may be stopping success in many other areas of your business and life.

Today Ask

"What beliefs do I have around serving which may be blocking my success?"

"What can I do to be of greater service in this world?"

"What are my greatest skills that I can empower others with?"

Actions

Take two action steps to contribute to someone you love.

Day 318

"The bravest thing you can do when you are not brave is to profess courage and act accordingly."

CORRA HARRIS[3]

Do you know anyone who has not had disappointments in their business or life? Of course not; disappointments are part of life. But the point that many don't understand, or embrace is that disappointments are there to teach you and strengthen you.

When disappointments hit, how do you handle them? Do you get upset and fearful or are you calm, taking things in your stride? The latter is the result of a well-disciplined mind that has been trained to be calm under all circumstances.

When you can get yourself to the point that you know there is always a gift waiting for you under the disappointment, you will start looking for the gift and not spend your time on what "could have," "would have "or "what may have been."

Since the thoughts you choose are creating your reality, if you focus on your disappointments you will end up feeling disappointed but when you focus on what you can learn from the circumstances, you will be empowered.

Today Ask

"The next time I am disappointed, how can I stay calm?"

"What are three things I can choose to do when I am disappointed?"

"What do I need to put in place to have my disappointments serve as learning?"

Actions

Take some time and assess areas in your life where you have felt disappointed and find the gift in them. Note: (By so doing, you will establish a pattern of learning. Then, the next time circumstances disappoint you, just stop, learn, grow and be empowered).

Day 319

*"If you haven't found the key to unlock the door of success,
gather the keys of wisdom and courage to open new doors."*

KEN D FOSTER

Awaken yourself from any thoughts of failure. Everyone has had many failures but so what! Behind every failure is a brilliant empowering idea waiting to be born which will lead you to victory.

Do you realize that you have all the gifts, talent and power within you to free yourself from any challenges that you are facing? I know sometimes you forget but honestly you are a child of God, filled with courage and power to overcome all obstacles.

When you calm the storms of delusion by quieting your mind and connecting deeply with your source, you will find the answers to your greatest challenges. How do I know this? Because I have been practicing this for twenty-six years and it works every time. Remember, just a little success will not do, you can succeed in all areas of life when you realize how much power is within you.

Today Ask

"Where have I let failures stop my success?"

"What can I do today that will assure much more success in my life?"

"How can I make brilliant choices daily that will lead to balance and fulfillment?"

Actions

Take some time and examine any thoughts you may have that are limiting your success. Note: (Sometimes your dreams don't generate physical reality immediately but by faith, intuition and persistence your dreams will come to pass.

Day 320

"The courage to ask for help may be the highest gift you can give yourself. Greatness in life comes from seeking wise counsel."

KEN D FOSTER

The saddest summary of a life is looking back and wondering, "If I only would have, could have, might have or should have." I cannot imagine how painful this would be and yet, I work with people all the time that don't dare to accomplish their greatest dreams. If this is you, then stop and pay close attention to this message.

The future is yours for the asking and nothing is holding you back but your misguided mind. There is no such thing as fate; you create your destiny so make up your mind today to change the course of your life. Are you in? If so, then here is the formula for success. "Change your thinking and change your life."

The quickest way to change your thinking is to ask *infinite, possibility* and *success*-questions and ponder them until you get the answer. When the answers come—and they will—don't doubt yourself; expand your power and open yourself up to new possibilities by taking consistent actions.

Asking questions is the lost art that fosters your greatest dreams. Wisdom tells us that the answer is in the questions that you ask. So, if you ask the right questions, you will get answers that will expand the field of possibilities, allowing you to create unbounded success.

Today Ask

"What is within me that can unleash my dreams and increase my initiative?"

"What are the most important dreams I am choosing to manifest?"

"What is the most important decision I can make today?"

Actions

Take some time to contemplate the unlimited realms of possibilities until you have a plan to improve your life.

Day 321

*"I acquired courage from the masterpieces of sages. I came
of age by their instructions to keep going, even in hard times.
Then I learnt not to despair, even when it seemed that my
world is falling apart. I learnt to possess fortitude."*

OGWO DAVID EMENIKE[3]

The most magnificent gift you can give to yourself is realizing that you're an infinite being. You are not a limited body and you are not your thoughts. You have a body and you have thoughts that are constantly passing through your mind.

But you are more than your thoughts and body; you are pure awareness and a high being that has unlimited power within it to generate your greatest dreams.

It is you alone who limits your success and you alone who can create whatever you choose. When you can get in touch with the infinite part of yourself and the unlimited possibilities that await your awareness, you can change quickly and dramatically.

In fact, at this moment you can choose to become the person you most admire and realize your highest visions. The choice is always yours!

Today Ask

"How can my life get even better than it is?"

"If I didn't limit my thinking, what is possible for me?"

"What can I do today that will assure a bright future?"

Actions

Determine what you will accomplish in the next twenty-four hours no matter what comes along to potentially stop you.

Day 322

"Courage, it would seem, is nothing less than the power to overcome danger, misfortune, fear, injustice, while continuing to affirm inwardly that life with all its sorrows is good."

DOROTHY THOMPSON[3]

Work with joy in your heart and peace on your mind, knowing your right efforts and actions will inevitably bring about successful results. This is good advice but sometimes it's difficult to be happy and joyful when problems arise.

It can be challenging to let go of mental worries, concerns or stress-filled thoughts. But without a sense of peace, creativity rarely flows into stressful situations. Have you ever noticed that when you walk away from a problem for a while, the answers to solving the problem show up? This is because you have calmed the mind, allowing the nature of your soul to express itself fully through you.

There is a quote that sits on my desk which was written by Paramahansa Yogananda. It says: *"I relax and cast aside all mental burdens, allowing God to express through me his perfect love, peace and wisdom."* Try using this saying this for the next seven days when you feel stressed and watch how your mind calms and your happiness returns.

Life brings challenges every day. These difficulties are not being given to crush you but to strengthen you and bring forth your greatest talents, abilities and gifts. So, remember to let go of unhealthy stressful thinking to realize success in all areas of your business and life.

Today Ask

"What can I do to calm my mind and open up my creativity?"

"How can things get better and better for my family and me?"

"What has to happen for me to let go of my stressors forever?"

Actions

Think about how you will overcome your greatest stressors permanently.

Day 323

*"It's a courageous thing to do something
that doesn't have rules or limits."*

VANESSA PARADIS[3]

To be successful, it is not enough to be rich, live in a beautiful home, be famous or have great sex all the time; lots of people have these things without a sense of lasting happiness or fulfillment. Real success is found by diving deep into the soul and realizing who is at the core of yourself and then being of service to others.

I have seen many people who are disconnected from themselves, only thinking about how they will profit from each situation they are put in. Some of these people are subtle about their self-centered ways while others are blatant but either way, these people lack real happiness.

It never ceases to amaze me how many people con themselves into believing they are givers, when in fact they look to benefit from every situation. On the other side of this, I am amazed to see how service to others creates loyal friendships, happiness and wealth.

It may not seem natural to be of service to others but the key to overcoming selfish desires and developing a successful character lies in how much service you are giving to the world. Whether the service comes in the form of business or personal giving, it tends to generate a sense of fulfillment, peace of mind and happiness.

If you want to experience more joy and happiness, follow this simple rule: Anytime you are feeling empty or upset, find someone and be of service.

Today Ask

"In what areas can I be of more service others?"

"How can I move past any fears to be of greater service to others?"

"Who do I know that I can gift some of my time, money or talents to?

Actions

Think of how big a difference you can make in the world and then take two action steps to make it happen.

Day 324

*"Brilliance comes from the willingness to be still
and the courage to take inspired actions."*

KEN D FOSTER

If you are distressed, generally it's because you have made poor choices, not understood the life-lesson or both. But you can turn this around quickly by acknowledging what is not working and committing to making the necessary changes. This sounds easy and it can be!

Have you ever been in a situation that you imagined you were buried so deep that you would never get out of it? Most people have and what it took for them to get out of the seemingly impossible situation was a shift in their thinking and a new course of action.

If you are going through trying times, it is essential to keep your mind calm and filled with the presence of peace. Because it is from a sense of calmness that you will make right choices. Remember, peace is the first signal that you have touched the soul and it is from the soul that intuition flows.

Once you have a sense of peace, I suggest you align yourself with noble goals, seeing yourself already completing them and holding a sense of certainty that your noble goals will, in fact, come to pass, no matter what the circumstances seem to be. Try doing this for a week and see what happens.

Today Ask:

"What has to happen for me to stay calm during the storms of life?"

"What is the lesson the challenges are teaching me?"

"What can I realize today that will increase my success threefold?"

Actions

Make a point to sit quietly, calm your mind with some meditation and then contemplate what direction your life is going.

Day 325

"When you are in doubt, be still and wait. When doubt no longer exists for you, then go forward in courage."

WHITE EAGLE[3]

Doubt is a sense of uncertainty which can be a very effective tool if used properly. My wife and I have a saying we use all the time: "When in doubt, don't." In other words, when we are unsure of which direction to take, we don't move forward. We wait until we have a feeling of certainty of direction.

Our feelings can tell us if we are moving in the right direction or not. They are like a barometer showing us when the pressure is high or low. When a choice must be made, tune in and read your feelings. Notice if the choice seems heavy or light. If light, then mostly likely it is a sign to proceed. If heavy or neutral, then wait.

Try not to judge your feelings or to get the mind involved, as this may blur your true insight. If you focus your mind on what is wrong, you will have a heavy feeling and if you focus on what is good, you will have pleasant feelings.

But by eliminating the mind and tuning into your feelings without judging right or wrong, you will bypass the mind and tune into your Wisdom-Self. As you do, you will start to notice quickly if your feelings are heavy or light. By practicing this, you will make better and wiser choices.

Today Ask

"What has to happen for me to consistently make better choices?"

"What are two major decisions about which I am uncertain?"

"What is the best choice in each situation?"

Actions

Practice becoming present to your intuitive feeling and making choices from here.

Day 326

*"Weakness or feeling like a victim of circumstances,
is a sign that courage and commitment are needed."*

KEN D FOSTER

Success is an "inside job" and is determined by how you use your mind, body and spirit. It can be accelerated or decelerated by your mindful habits. If you are consistently broadcasting confidence, peace, love and abundance, then your success will most likely increase.

If you broadcast doubt, uncertainty, stress, worry and anxiety then your success will most likely decrease. Think about it, don't you make better choices when you are feeling calm and have a sense that everything will work out for the best? Of course, you do!

Therefore, it is vital to think peaceful thoughts. Being in the right state of mind is key for success. Consistently staying peaceful under any circumstance is a goal you should strive to achieve.

Today Ask

"If I knew what would change my life for the better, what would it be?"

"What would I have to believe to stay calm in all circumstances?"

"If there is something that would stop my success, what would it be?"

Actions

Morning, noon and evening check-in and notice your energy. If it is low, stop and adjust your thinking before doing the next task.

Tap into your higher-self and increase your intuition with Ken D Foster's guided meditations on Business, Wealth, Expanding Possibility, Peace, and Health. Yours for free at couragetochange.us/meditation

Day 327

*"Courageous risks are life-giving, they help you grow, make you
brave and better than you think you are."*

JOAN L. CURCIO[3]

There is no shortage of money in the world; it is everywhere, just look around! But, there is a shortage of creativity, receptivity and focused efforts.

The most prominent stopper of having financial success is placing limitations on your ability to create and enjoy money. Have you heard that it takes money to make money? Not true!

What it takes is opening your receptivity and then tapping into your creative potential. If you are having money issues and are closed minded, then you will limit your supply of money. It is that simple!

However, by taking off your limitations and making a conscious choice for new possibilities to appear around receiving money, it will start to flow into your life. Also, it doesn't hurt to do what it takes to expand your presence on the planet by bringing forth your greatest gifts, talents and abilities.

Today Ask

"What if my life didn't have to be the way it is, what is possible for me?"

"What can I be, do or have in my life right now that will create more money?"

"How can I open up to receive more money in my business and life?"

Actions

Come up with three new beliefs about receiving money that you will embrace.

CHAPTER 17

BECOME FEARLESS

Day 328

"So, what is courage? It is simply acting on what we know we should do, regardless of any fear we may have. It is the choice to disregard worry. It is the choice to do right, to pursue our dreams, to be successful people, to lead the way for others."

CHRIS WIDENER[3]

The opposite attitude of fear is faith. And there is no greater way to build character, self-esteem and success than to overcome your fears by faith. It is through belief in your creator and trust in yourself that fears are overcome.

Have you ever wondered what a life without limiting fear would be like? Can you imagine what you could accomplish? In her book, "Dying to Be Me," Anita Moorjani said: "During my Near-Death Experience, it felt to me all judgment, hatred, jealousy and fear stem from people not realizing their true greatness."

Most people just live with their fears, which stops them from being all they can be. They may be afraid of starting a business or of leaving a disempowering relationship or of public speaking, just to name a few. But you don't have to live with fear; you can overcome every fearful thought you have by setting your intention to do so.

Remember, fear is the stopper of dreams. And the truth be known, you cannot live a life of excellence and be fearful. It will never happen. Your dreams are meant to be realized, not put on a shelf because of fearful thinking.

Today Ask

"What are the biggest fears that are in my life?"

"How can I increase my faith and trust in all areas of life?"

"What three actions will I take to eliminate my fears?"

Actions

Make a list of your top five fears and then pick one to overcome, starting today.

Day 329

*"The disenfranchised thinker is filled with
courageous acts none of which ever happened."*

KEN D FOSTER

"Bad moments" happen to all of us but even if you are having an off-day, you can stop it from continuing and start it over at any time. How? By increasing your awareness of what is happening.

Most people don't realize that life is an "inside job," and what you are thinking and asking is determining how you are feeling and acting. In other words, the source of what is happening to you and your business is located right between your ears.

That is why this book is a powerful force to change. With right thinking, come right motives and right actions. The propelling force to make an impact.

Are you aware that thoughts are universal and not individual? If I had a hundred people in a room and asked them about the thoughts they think about when having a "bad day," you may be astonished to know the thoughts are pretty much the same.

Thoughts have been floating around long before you came to be. So, if the thoughts you are tuning into are not yours, then why not choose thoughts that empower you.

If you want to change the effects of your thinking, you must first change what thoughts you are letting into your consciousness. The easiest way to do this is to become the observer of your thoughts and then ask powerful questions to redirect the mind.

Today Ask

"What can I focus on which will increase my courage?"

"What are three actions I can take today to propel my success?"

"What can I do to have an amazing day?"

Actions

Think about increasing your courageous thoughts by asking; "If I were courageous what would I do now." And then contemplate of how this will change your life for the better.

Day 330

"He is courageous who endures and fears the right thing, for the right motive, in the right way and at the right times."

ARISTOTLE[3]

The ordinary person becomes extraordinary when they confidently move in the direction of their greatest dreams. It's about stepping into your genius, tuning into your intuition and by being stronger with your intentions.

Let's get real! What has stopped you from generating your greatest dreams? If you are like most, it isn't lack of talent, shortage of good ideas or even lack of money; you have been stopped by taking on other people's points of view or not having the courage to move forward when things get tough. But today is the day to turn this around forever!

Remember obstacles are there for many reasons. They may be there to let you know you are on the wrong path or to strengthen your resolve and willpower to overcome. But whatever the lesson, the obstacle is there to strengthen you and teach you something important.

Today Ask

"What are three steps I can take to become extraordinary?"

"How will I generate whatever is needed to accomplish my greatest dreams?"

"What will it take for me to learn the lessons of success quickly and let go of my limitations?"

Actions

Think about this: You are endowed with greater strength than you will ever need to overcome anything in your way. Make a list of your greatest strengths and get in touch with your resolve to be the best you can be.

Day 331

"Think big and don't listen to people who tell you it can't be done. Life's too short to think small."

TIM FERRIS[3]

How courageous are you? Do you have what it takes to create your greatest dreams, or have you let your circumstances dictate how your life will be?

You have unlimited potential within you. In fact, you have the potential to tap into the wisdom of the ages and be the hero of your life. It is all within you. But you must pursue your potential, or it will lay dormant.

The only barriers standing between you and your unlimited success are the conclusions you have come to. It is your points of view that you think are real, that hold you back.

If you were to let go of your judgments and stories about what happened in the past, you would be much further along the road to success. It is your rigid adherence regarding how things were or what happened to you or someone else that keeps you stuck.

Because those patterns repeat, and they are part of your mental program, conditioning thoughts and events. When you stop judging and start asking different questions, you will bring in a wealth of new possibilities.

Today Ask

"What is possible right now for me that could change the course of my life?"

"If I could stop judging what happened in the past, how would my life improve?"

"How can I profit by thinking more of what is possible?"

Actions

Make a point to see your life from a different point of view. Imagine you have everything you need to succeed and look at your life from this point of view.

Day 332

"Hatred and fear blind us. We no longer see each other. We see only the faces of monsters and that gives us the courage to destroy each other."

THICH NHAT HANH[3]

Have you ever wondered how to get over your fears forever? Most people live a life of quiet desperation, just getting by without real hope of an amazing life. When I hear this, the first question I ask is: "If you lived fearlessly how would your life be different?"

The reason most people are stuck is because behind their choices are fears and negative emotions that are keeping them in bondage. To move past your fears, look at the results you are getting in your life and acknowledge what you are afraid of.

Try this: Make a list of your fears, then afterward choose which ones to keep and which fears to let go. The choice is yours! I suggest you elect to become fearless because if you want ongoing success, you will need to govern your mind wisely.

You are an amazing soul who and by the power of positive thought you will generate your greatest dreams. I applaud your willingness to take your life to the next level.

Today Ask

"What fears am I choosing to transform?"

"How can I master whatever I set out to do?"

"What will my business and life be like when I am fearless every day?"

Actions

Transfer your consciousness from fearful, weak thoughts to power-filled thoughts and then come up with one affirmation that you will say today.

Day 333

"Conscience is the root of all true courage; if a man would be brave, let him obey his conscience."

JAMES FREEMAN CLARKE[3]

Does your environment empower you and move you toward success or disempower you and hold you back? Many people work in places of clutter, noise and distractions but this is not the way to increase success.

It is important to put yourself in an atmosphere that inspires success; a place where you can dream big and see yourself having those dreams come true.

Whether you go to a cathedral or a mountaintop or create a home and work settings that bring you a sense of expansion and joy, your environment counts appreciably. In fact, your environment is so crucial that you will substantially diminish the chances of your success if you don't pay attention to it.

The good news is that no matter what your economic level of success, you can make your environment shine. A coat of paint, a new plant or removing clutter in your space can all make you feel good about yourself and where you are spending your time.

Today Ask

"How will I feel when my environment matches who I am?"

"What changes in my environment will put a smile on my face?"

"What is one hidden strength I can use to create an amazing environment?"

Actions

Look around your home and office and take three steps to make them reflect your highest values. Example: You value beauty, so you make sure your home and office reflect that value.

Day 334

"Staring failure in the face and not shrinking back takes courage,
but this is exactly what is needed to realize a bright future."

KEN D FOSTER

When I ask people: "What has been your biggest failure and what has been your biggest learning experience?" Most people say: "It is one and the same."

Failure is not something to be ashamed of; it is an influential teacher. In fact, most people learn their greatest lessons when they have done their best and still crashed.

I don't know any successful people who have not had many setbacks. Every time they learned from their failures, they became stronger and wiser and they thrived. As the old saying goes: "What does not crush you will strengthen you."

So, don't let anything crush your spirit! You are a fantastic being. You can change anything if you put your awareness on it. Even if you have had many setbacks, make up your mind right now that today will be the day that you turn things around for good. Why shouldn't you succeed? Someone will; it might as well be you!

Today Ask

"What is perfect about my failures?"

"What have I learned about failure that will propel me forward?"

"What am I willing to let go of thinking which will expand possibilities and increase my success?"

Actions

Think about areas of your business or life where you don't feel like a success and then resolve to make things better.

Day 335

"There are two sides to the coin of courage. On one side is faith and the other is vulnerability. Whichever you focus on will bring out your greatness."

KEN D FOSTER

The truth will set you free, just as lies will entangle you in delusion. Living a fear-based life is not something anyone starts out to do but fearful thoughts permeate many of America's families. So, let's look at fear again today.

Are you living with unacknowledged fears or are you living fearlessly? Many people would say they live fearlessly but is it true? One of the ways you can determine if you are fearful is to measure how many times you get upset or worry throughout the day.

When you are upset, you might be afraid of losing what you have or fearful of not getting what you want. This is fear-based thinking. To change this around and be fearless it takes commitment and courage. Human consciousness is usually focused on the body and its feelings. But to overcome fear permanently is to identify with the higher realms of knowledge within the Wisdom-Self.

Whenever ear comes up, ask fearless questions such as: *"How can I increase my courage? or "Knowing that I am an infinite being, what can I choose to become to overcome my fears permanently?" or "At any moment that I am afraid, what can I be aware of that will transmute my fears into courage immediately?"*.

Today Ask

"What fears am I not aware of that are running my life?"

"How can I become more conscious of my fears and let them go?"

"What will it take to live fearlessly from here on out?"

Actions

Make a list of any fears you have around money, relationships, health, religion, family or fear of heights, failing, speaking, etc. Then make up your mind to face them by asking questions that will give you the strength to overcome them.

Day 336

"Facing your fears and moving forward despite the
perceived dangers, generates courage beyond measure."

KEN D FOSTER

Fear is the greatest leveler of happiness. It zaps your energy, causes you to lose perspective and focus. It also stops the flow of brilliance and it attacks its victims like a venomous snake annihilating your dreams.

There is an acronym for FEAR: "Face Everything and Respond." But if you don't acknowledge your fears and live in denial of them, then you are doomed to repeat the fear repeatedly. Why, because you can't change what you cannot acknowledge.

Imagine one fear you have, now imagine you are eighty years old and you still have that fear, only it has become stronger and more entrenched in your thinking. How will that be for you and those you love?

There is an antidote for fear. It's simple to administer and goes down easy if you don't resist it. What is it? It is Courage. It is the courage to consider your fears and see what is driving them. What lies just behind the fear is the cause of your distress.

Maybe it is the fear of not being enough or not being loved or not being fulfilled or not having what you need or losing what you have. Whatever it is, when you know what is driving the fear you can transcend it.

Today Ask

"What is my greatest fear?"

"How can I be more courageous to help transcend my greatest fears?"

"When I am fearless, what is possible for me?"

Actions

Make a list of your fears and then decide how you will face each one of them. Once you have made your list, then set your intention and do what it takes to get rid of all your fears permanently!

Day 337

> *"There is no one more courageous than a person who has been*
> *darkened by the habit of worry but has reignited the flame of*
> *faith and now stands in the unknown, ready for anything."*

KEN D FOSTER

Most people don't think of themselves as worriers but if they look closely at the symptoms of worry, they realize that this insidious disease has a hold on them. Some of the symptoms you may want to consider are undue stress or anxiety about things you don't have control over or living in the future focused on "what might happen," or a feeling that something "bad is going to happen."

So why would anyone worry about things that will never happen and create stress and drama? It is because some people believe if they worry enough something may change for the better. Others think they are caring by worrying. Many have an unconscious habit of worry which was passed down to them.

If you have any of these symptoms or beliefs, it is time to stop and reclaim your life. Worry not only creates misery for you but it is also a contagious disease that can be transmitted and passed down from generation to generation.

But you can set a firm intention to change worry into wonder. All it takes is honesty with yourself and a strong commitment to stay on the journey of worry-free living until you are no longer a slave to this disease.

Today Ask

"What is possible for my family and me if I release the worry-habit?"

"What Can I do to deepen my faith and trust more?"

"What are three steps I can take today to get rid of worry forever?"

Actions

Keep track of the areas of your life that you worry. After you acknowledge these areas, come up a plan to let go of this habit.

Day 338

"Who could refrain that had a heart to love and in that heart courage to make love known?"

WILLIAM SHAKESPEARE[3]

Today's problems are permanently solved with evolved thinking. Remember what Einstein said, *"We can't solve problems by using the same kind of thinking we used when we created them."* In other words, your greatest thinking has got you where you are, and your greatest thinking will not get you out of your circumstances.

You must evolve your consciousness and consistently connect with the superconscious mind if you are to have a better life. One of the ways you can tap into the superconscious mind is with stillness. Become still and notice how your thoughts slow down as your breath calms. Then notice that behind your thoughts is awareness. You are aware of having your thoughts, right? Awareness is more important than rational thinking because with awareness comes all the answers to your greatest problems.

When you identify with awareness you realize the presence of awareness is within and around you. The first sign that you have tapped into greater awareness is peace. If you continue to access and expand your awareness, peace becomes your natural state.

So, practice calming yourself by taking some deep slow breaths in. Then take a breath in and tense your body, then relax. Do this a few times to release tension in the body. As you calm yourself notice how you feel. Then ask a question that you would like to have the answer to. Then be still and see what bubbles up.

Don't hurry or worry, just keep noticing what is showing up and go with the flow. If you act with poise and trust connecting with your awareness you will start to make the right decisions that will lead you to success.

Today Ask

"What can I do to calm the mind and be in the present moment?"

"What is my awareness saying to me right now?"

"How can I become more aware and make better choices from my awareness?"

Actions

Create a new habit of stopping three times a day and connect with your awareness. Then, ask a question that you would like answered.

Day 339

"Ever man of honor and courage will be faced with unjust criticism but never forget that unjust criticism has no impact whatsoever upon the truth."

ANDY ANDREWS[3]

When you realize *"who I am is enough,"* you are truly rich. But how to get to that point is a challenge for many. So many have experienced unfair criticism which can be disheartening but viewed from the right perspective it can be empowering.

Criticism is a part of life; everyone has experienced it. But how you deal with it will determine, in many cases, how successful you will be. I once watched back-to-back shows on the subject with hosts interviewing the singer Madonna and the First Lady of the United States, Hilary Clinton.

They both had similar responses when asked how they deal with unjust criticism from the media and the public. They paid no attention to it and didn't read the articles nor listen to critical commentaries. In other words, they protected their peace of mind and feelings from being hurt. They defended their happiness.

Sometimes if the criticism is spot-on, we can learn and grow from it. By changing ourselves, we can attract right circumstances into our lives. But if the criticism is not valid, the best solution is to do what real leaders do, which is focus your attention on the positive aspects of your life and not give the criticism another thought.

Today Ask

"Where have I let criticism eat away at my self-esteem?"

"What can I do to let go of thinking about past criticisms permanently?"

"What can I remember to do when criticized that will keep me calm?"

Actions

Make a list of self-criticisms and then turn those criticisms into positive statements about yourself.

Day 340

*"If you have failed in the past, so what? Increase
your enthusiasm and start taking courageous
acts today and change your destiny."*

KEN D FOSTER

When you play small and pretend you cannot attain your goals, you become part of the illusion that is holding you back from your greatness. Nothing is stopping you from generating your dreams, except your thinking, choices and actions.

You have within you the power to overcome all obstacles. What would it take for you to realize that right now? Because it is true: you have all the love, gifts, talents, skills, intelligence, courage and strength to manifest your dreams! You were born brilliant and now's the time to reclaim that brilliance. Playing small doesn't serve this purpose!

Wake up to the brilliance by cultivating enthusiasm. Having the right mindset of being enthusiastic in all you do, gives you the energy and optimism to accomplish your dreams. Try visualizing yourself as tireless, enthusiastic, energetic and optimistic right now.

Then stand up and bring all the energy you have at hand into your body and yell out three times *"Yes! Yes! Yes! I am alive, alert and ready to achieve my dreams!"* Then notice how you feel. Do this anytime you have low energy and see how much more productive you will be.

Today Ask

"What can I do to increase my enthusiasm when I start my day?"

"How can I remember to be enthusiastic during low-energy periods?"

"What can I do now to become more enthusiastic in all areas of my life?"

Actions

Think about how you could increase your enthusiasm and positivity. Then do what it takes to implement it.

Day 341

"How is it possible to banish lack and limitations, if not with a courageous heart, coupled with the determination to overcome?"

KEN D FOSTER

How much do you love your life? Are you truly living an inspired life—one that you will be able to look back on in your twilight years and say that you are proud of your accomplishments, service and how you have evolved yourself?

The most essential requirement for a happy life is the right mental attitude along with the wisdom to establish ideals, values and goals. It takes a willful mind combined with study, effort and self-discipline.

Think about this for a moment! Success comes down to some simple rules and overall those rules are basically about you having the willingness to expand yourself to be all you were meant to be. If you do this in all areas of your life (mentally, emotionally, physically and spiritually) you will be healthy, wealthy and wise.

Don't be afraid to bring all of "You" into the world. This means growing your natural gifts and developing your skills to the point you are contributing to the world by your every action. And the best way to do this is by doing what you love to do.

Today Ask

"Am I truly doing what I can to bring all my gifts into the world?"

"What has stopped me from having happiness and wealth beyond measure?"

"What has to happen for me to bring all of me into everything I do?"

Actions

Determine what you can do to bring more wisdom, discernment and compassion into your life.

Tap into your higher-self and increase your intuition with Ken D Foster's guided meditations on Business, Wealth, Expanding Possibility, Peace, and Health. Yours for free at couragetochange.us/meditation

Day 342

*"If you are lucky enough to find a way of life you love,
you have to find the courage to live it."*

JOHN IRVING[3]

To bring all of you into the world, you will need to follow your inner calling and set yourself apart from the pack. No one is made up like you, so never be limited by anything others have done before your time.

Sometimes we look at what others have accomplished and think, "I could never do that." But the truth is: what one person has accomplished has "set the bar" so that others can follow and do even greater things their way.

If you have not achieved what you desire yet and are not happy about it, normally it is because you have not visualized strongly enough the great things you want to accomplish.

Always keep your mind as a garden of creative thoughts. Don't let it become a muddy pond filled with thoughts of what you can't do. Remember, if you think you can't accomplish something, then you are right and if you believe you can, then you are right also. Either way, your thinking will make it so.

Today Ask

"What negative thoughts have I planted in the garden of my mind that are stopping my success?"

"What has to happen to focus my mind on my dreams until I accomplish them?"

"What can I do to fire up my brilliance with determination to accomplish my dreams?"

Actions

Give yourself some compassion and the time you need to feel connected to your dreams.

Day 343

"The strongest, most generous and proudest of all
virtues is true courage."

MICHAEL DE MONTAIGNE[3]

One of the greatest ways to increase your success is to let go of fault-finding. This means letting go of fault-finding with yourself and others. It is a matter of shifting your focus from looking at the dark to looking at the light.

Don't dwell on negative thoughts. If you do, your subconscious mind records this in the library of your consciousness. Repeated negative thinking drives these thoughts deeper and deeper until you have created a mind rut which becomes difficult to overcome.

It is important to outgrow disempowering thinking if you want to increase success. Why not dwell upon thoughts that empower you and make you feel successful as opposed to anything else? You must think and act with confidence and use the power of your will to overcome negative thoughts or any obstacles in the way of your success.

Remember, success-thinking is a habit. It is formed by daily awareness of the thoughts you are choosing to let into your consciousness. If you choose to be responsible for your mental states, you will only allow positive thoughts to enter. With an affirmative state of consciousness, you will think rationally, be wisely decisive and create or attract success in your business and life.

Today Ask

"How can the perfume of success-thoughts blow through me consistently?"

"What can I do to let go of fault-finding permanently?"

"What is a new success-habit I can put in place that will increase my positivity?"

Actions

Meditate a few minutes and feel the success thoughts of God flowing through your life.

Day 344

"There is nothing that can stand in the way of
your dreams when you are connected to Courage."

KEN D FOSTER

Within you is a great light that is trying to be born into this world. It is the light of your authentic self, which ever shines within your soul. This great light only shines when you free it from the confines of your human consciousness.

See yourself as what you can be, not what you have been in the past. The past does not equal your future unless you remain a victim of it. Why don't you use the camera of your mind to take beautiful pictures of where your life is today and where you are going? Don't use your intention to focus on the dark side of your life. Focus on the garden of plenty that has been given to you.

No one has your gifts, talents, abilities. No one has your face, hands, hair or smile like yours. You are a unique expression of the divine. The expression of the infinite that is in you is found in no one else. Your greatness is needed in the world; otherwise, you wouldn't be here.

You can transcend every limitation you have set in motion by uncovering the secret power that lies just behind your flesh, your sensations and your mind. When you can penetrate the deepest reaches of this power, then you are free. To do this, go deeper and deeper into the silence within.

Today Ask

"What are the three steps I can take today to let my soul shine through?"

"What is the great light within me that is trying to be born into the world?"

"What is amazing about myself and the journey that I am on?"

Actions

Determine what new product or service that you would like to bring into the world.

Day 345

"Enlightenment starts with the courage to realize you can't lift yourself by yourself. It takes the wisdom of those who have gone before, to wakeus out of our delusion and realize our divinity."

KEN D FOSTER

This world is designed around cause and effect. You are the cause and the effects show up. As Jesus said: "What you sow you will reap." If you focus your mind negative or good seeds of thought, you will out-picture these thoughts.

In this world, everyone is seeking health, happiness, riches and success. These seem to be the highest goals to achieve, but are they? Today you are happy, tomorrow you are sad. Today you have health, tomorrow you have a disease. Today you have riches, tomorrow you have poverty. Could there be something greater to pursue?

What if you could develop the consciousness within yourself of peace? What if you could realize that no matter what you are experiencing you can be even-minded? Your thoughts and emotions are controlled, neither too high when good comes along, nor too low when the negative challenges come.

The way to do this is to let go of the attachment to things. Realize that you are not your car, house, relationship, business, etc. You are an infinite spirit with unlimited capacity. There is no lack anywhere in this world unless you create it. When you can let go of possessiveness and realize your Wisdom-Self you have come a long way to being even-minded.

Today Ask

"What would I have to conceive in thought and then believe to live a greater life?"

"What are some steps I can take to be even-minded in all circumstances?"

"What do I need to affirm to remind me to stay even- mindedness?"

Actions

Today tune into your soul in the morning and stay connected to peace throughout the day.

CHAPTER 18

READY AIM PERSIST

411

Day 346

"Courage is defined by listening to the soul and following through with your commitments."

KEN D FOSTER

An infinite being (that is you) must remain true to their commitments; no matter how difficult those commitments may be or how many times they must start over until those commitments are fulfilled.

In other words, it is through making and keeping commitments to yourself that you create the foundation for lasting success. It is with perseverance that an unshakable power to overcome any obstacles is often acquired. Without it there is a wavering of direction, lack of clear intent and absence of energy to accomplish the task.

If you have not succeeded in the past, you will need to make a greater effort. Don't dwell in the past, nor live in the future; make the effort today to make the changes that are necessary to assure a successful life. Your fate is not predestined but determined by every thought you think, choice you make and action you take.

If you are ready to take your life to a completely new level, then think of one commitment that you will keep no matter what. Visualize what your life would be like with this new commitment in place and then take daily action steps every day to cement the commitment in your life.

Today Ask

"In what areas of life will I put new commitments in place?"

"How can I escalate the success by keeping my commitments?"

"What is the most important commitment I can make and keep in my life?"

Actions

When blocks to keeping commitments show up, increase your resolve to be more powerful than the obstacles blocking your success.

Day 347

"Life is mostly froth and bubble; two things stand like stone—
kindness in another's trouble, courage in your own."

ADAM L. GORDON[3]

It has been scientifically proven that matter is concentrated energy. Our bodies are little more than frozen dream-matter made up of atoms, electrons, protons, molecules and according to the Yogis, the soon-to-be-revealed, lifetrons and thoughtrons.

So, behind our bodies is much more than flesh. What is waiting to be realized by you is your soulful power that can light up the world and move the mountains of obstacles in your path.

By just focusing your awareness in the direction of what is possible for you and taking persistent inspired action, nothing can stand in your way of success.

Today Ask

"If I expand my awareness and open to receive the unlimited supply of wealth that is waiting for me, what is possible for my life?"

"By allowing myself to receive wealth how much good will I bring into the world?"

"How can I enjoy more wealth in all areas of my life?"

Actions

Your wealth is awaiting you to claim it, so what are you waiting for? What is holding you back? What goal will you accomplish today that will increase your supply of wealth?

Day 348

*"Freedom lies in taking daily courageous acts
as you face your fears with growing wisdom."*

KEN D FOSTER

Efficiency that leads to success is developed through concentrated effort. Within you is power, the universal creative principle, for facing every challenge. It is not just in some of us but in everyone. You have the power to create the business and life of your dreams.

But, if you use your creative power to move from one project to the next without completion, you will suffer because without completion you will not reap the rewards of success. I have seen many people get caught up in creating for the sake of creating.

In other words, instead of focusing on one project, they spread their efforts on many projects. They don't complete most of what they start and eventually lose confidence and self-esteem. This is not the way to create success.

If you have this pattern, then choose to change it right here and now. Make a list of all your projects, prioritize, and concentrate on one project until you complete it. If this doesn't work, then increase your daily meditation until you learn to focus adequately.

Today Ask

"Why is it important for me to complete what I start?"

"With my indomitable willpower, what can I complete today?"

"How much time will I set aside daily to complete my projects?"

Actions

Determine the most important projects to complete this month and committee to completing them no matter what.

Day 349

"Courageous people do not fear forgiving, for the sake of peace."

NELSON MANDELA[3]

When you can release shame, blame, guilt and regret through forgiveness, you will change how you perceive life. Sure, life is tough, and people have hurt you in many ways but that is no excuse to play small or worse: give up on having an amazing life.

An easy life isn't necessarily a successful life. In fact, I have realized that Gods way is not the easy way but ultimately the way to building strength and character.

We are all here to learn and evolve our consciousness and that rarely happens when things are going smoothly. If you want to be successful, you must learn to take the good with the bad and be even-minded in all situations.

The reason this is so important is that when you are calm under fire, you make better choices and better choices lead to more success.

Today Ask

"What has to happen for me to stay calm under stressful situations? "

"What can I do to let go of any past challenges that have hurt me?"

"What has to happen for me to consistently make better choices?"

Actions

Write about the qualities and values of your greatest heroes and decide which qualities you would like to model.

Day 350

"Courage is fueled by the motivation to take the first step into the unknown."

CHERYL NIELSEN[108]

Social scientists tell us that it takes about ten thousand hours of practice to become a master at what you do. Becoming a master is a sound target because anything you master will take you on a journey of growth, evolution, change, progression to be your very best.

What it truly takes to become a master at anything is getting to a level where you not only know how to perform your skill, but you are able to anticipate what is coming next through the power of your intuition. This is a soulful skill that combines reason with wisdom resulting in immediate knowing of which actions to take.

Large accomplishments such as becoming a master are not done with a weak mind; they are completed with dynamic will, commitment and sustained actions. It takes daily training of the mind to master large tasks.

The weak mind says: "This is too large a task," or "I don't really have what it takes" or "I will do it tomorrow." The person who has mastered their mind asks unstoppable questions (questions that expand possibilities), make good choices and take consistent actions.

Today Ask

"What will I become a master at?"

"What will it take for me to become the master I long to be?"

"What steps will I take in the next fifteen days to move my mastery forward?"

Actions

Decide what you must know to be the master of your fate. As the answers come, step into courage and get out of your comfort zone so you can move forward toward mastery.

Day 351

*"It doesn't matter what happens, if you're only
strong and have great courage."*

LOIS LENSKI[3]

So many people start projects and then stop. They are inspired at first; then things don't go their way, or they get distracted and quit. Can you recall times this has happened to you? It happens to most of us but there is a way to increase your persistence four-fold and realize your dreams.

How is this possible? It is quite simple! First, you must relinquish the notion that you are separate from the all-knowing mind of your Wisdom-Self. The idea that you are separated from your Self is a complete illusion and will stop you from being persistent.

Second, you must correct your mind and realize that no matter how you showed up in the past; the past does not exist at this moment. The truth of this will set you free from recreating the past.

Right now, embrace the fact that you are persistence itself. Persistence was born in you. It dwells in you. This is a part of who you are. And third, let nothing weaken your conviction that you will persist and accomplish whatever you set out to do.

You have so much more that is coming to you. You will persist and overcome all obstacles to your success. Realize this and allow the spirit of persistence to become as much a part of you as you are a part of this force.

Today Ask

"What is possible for me when I am persistent beyond measure?"

"How can I consistently connect with the persistent power of my spirit?"

"What steps can I take to increase my persistence and overcome all obstacles to my success?"

Actions

Contemplate on how persistence and success go hand in hand. If you think you already know the answer, then journal about this until you have a breakthrough.

Day 352

"Courage isn't increased with schooling, seminars,
spiritual phenomena or anything outside of yourself;
it is discovered by listening to your Wisdom-Self."

KEN D FOSTER

A determination is fired up within you when you make up your mind to accomplish your dreams. It works hand in hand with an enduring commitment to do whatever it takes until you succeed. There is only one thing that can obstruct your success. It is the misunderstanding of who you are and why you are here.

You were born to bring forth the greatness that is within you. Correct your mind and realize that you are an infinite spirit with the power to move any obstacles in the way of your success.

Fate is an illusion; you choose your destiny. The Highest of the high lives in your being and works through you. You are always evolving and getting better and better. Think about this and make it real for yourself.

Get yourself to a point where you are unstoppable and accomplish what you set out to do. When you can do this, you will stop telling yourself disempowering stories of why you can't be successful, because that would be impossible for a wise Soul like yourself to believe.

Today Ask

"What has to happen to increase my determination threefold?"

"What is the biggest lie I tell myself that limits my success?"

"What steps will I take to increase my determination and realize my full potential?"

Actions

Come up with three action steps that will give you a sense of accomplishment at the end of the day.

Day 353

"When God gives us courage and inspires our dreams; some sit and listen, some question, and some take bold actions that leads to greatness."

KEN D FOSTER

Obstacles come your way for two reasons: to help you realize who you are and to strengthen your inner resolve and overcome them. It's all about growing and becoming the best version of yourself. So, don't let your mental blocks or feelings of inadequacy stop you from achieving your dreams. If you haven't accomplished what you want, then increase your resolve!

As you increase your resolve, you will start to think differently. Most likely you will look at any obstacle as an opportunity to strengthen your "resolve to solve." What this will do is increase your success.

Say to yourself repeatedly; "I am doing it and I am doing it no matter what comes my way." These powerful words coupled with a strong commitment can move mountains of challenges.

Also, check in and notice if any fears may be blocking your success. If there are fears, acknowledge them and then affirm: *"I am fearless and more powerful than fear itself,"* and *"I will overcome, and I will conquer my challenges now and forever more."*

When you are repeating these affirmative words, don't make it a mental exercise; stand up and feel them penetrating every cell in your body. Say them over and over until you are inspired to achieve your dream. Then see yourself succeeding, feel yourself being victorious and celebrate your success repeatedly in your mind until your dreams are fulfilled).

Today Ask

"What am I committed to overcoming this week?"

"If I had the courage to realize my dreams, what would I be doing?"

"What will it feel like to overcome and succeed in my greatest dreams?"

Actions

Reignite your dreams by connecting with your life purpose. Figure out why it is essential for you to generate your greatest dreams no matter what stands in your way.

Day 354

*"Does anyone care about how many complaints
you have, or will they remember your courage
when the storms of life are battering you?"*

KEN D FOSTER

You probably realize that the way you communicate with yourself will determine how much joy, happiness and success you will have. But what you may not be aware of is how much your internal communication is impacting who you are attracting in your business and life.

If you are hard on yourself, more than likely your communication with others will be strained. Just the same, if you are easy going and joyful in your conversations to yourself, you will most likely portray this to others.

If you consistently have the perfume of happiness-thoughts blowing through your mind, I guarantee you will attract other happy and prosperous people to you.

Persistence in overcoming negative thoughts is the key to healthy inner communication. It's not so much which thoughts cross your mind; it is about which thoughts you choose to dwell upon.

By dwelling on thoughts, you make them real for you; therefore, it is important to dwell upon what you want to have in your life rather than upsets with people, places or things you have little control over.

Today Ask

"What are the happiest thoughts I can dwell upon today?"

"How can I increase my happiness?"

"When I face challenges, how can I remain happy?"

Actions

As you wake up, be determined to focus on only happy thoughts that bring a sense of happiness or joy. It this is a new habit, practice waking up with happy thoughts for the next fourteen days.

Day 355

"Success is not final; failure is not fatal. It is the courage to continue that counts."

SIR WINSTON CHURCHILL[3]

Unless you succeed beyond what you have already mastered, your potential will become stagnant and your life will be unfulfilled.

Have you ever met someone who was telling you a story of how great they were in the past, but you noticed their life wasn't anything to brag about in the present? Complacency is not something to brag about; it's a warning sign that things need to change. Life is about getting outstanding results in areas that matter to you the most.

If making money, family, relationships, health, career—or even spiritual evolution is important to you; then getting excellent results in these areas should matter to you also. It is easy to stay busy and over-committed but that won't get you the results you want.

Staying focused is the key. What would it take for you to focus on learning and evolving continually? And what must happen for you to commit to eliminating all barriers and limitations standing in the way of your success?

Today Ask

"What area of my life is important for me to get outstanding results?"

"What can I do today to generate outstanding results?"

"As I get outstanding results, what happens to the rest of my life?"

Actions

Take some time to set up one goal which will propel your life forward. Note: (Mastery of anything is said to take approximately ten thousand hours, so be patient with yourself and enjoy the journey).

Day 356

*"You can enroll the world in your dreams if you have
the courage to envision, plan. and act upon them."*

KEN D FOSTER

As the old quote goes: *"Many lives are filled with terrible misfortune, most of which never happened."* I am not talking about real misfortunes. I am talking about the challenges people roll around in their minds repeatedly, telling themselves stories about how difficult things are or how worried they are about things that have never happened.

Dwelling on worries or problems is not the proper way to use the mind. If you dwell on the negative, you will not only become negative yourself. Real success comes once you have become victorious over your mind and consistently connect with your Wisdom-Self.

Remember, whatever you focus your mind and energies on will come to pass because the mind is the generator of everything.

If you want to change what is showing up in your life, the place to start is by putting your full attention on what your future creation will look like. In other words, start with the assumption that what you would like to have is already there and then hold your attention on it with faith, until you generate it.

Today Ask

"What is possible for an infinite being like me now?"

"What can I assume is true that will generate more success in my life?"

"How can I increase my awareness of what must happen for me to succeed?"

Actions

Come up with a written success plan and do it within fifteen minutes.

Day 357

Procrastination is a symptom of a soul that is out picturing low self-worth and often experiencing overwhelm. If you are putting off what needs to be done, you are most likely playing a failure game with yourself that will hurt you in many ways.

Did you know the subconscious mind keeps track of everything you do or don't do? It also keeps track of every article in your environment from scraps of paper to clutter in all forms. If you rationalize you will take care of business tomorrow, guess what - tomorrow never comes.

The opposite of procrastination is a completion. It is when you make a firm commitment to accomplishing your goals and then take consistent actions until they are completed, that you form new success-habits in your brain.

This is how things will change permanently.

Today Ask

"What has to happen for me to complete everything I start?"

"What will I complete today that will change my life for the better?"

"What will expand in my life as I release every thought, belief or action from the past that has kept me procrastinating or identified me as a procrastinator?"

Actions

Focus your awareness on being proactive and accomplishing what you set out to do. Note: (You can be, do and have just about anything you want when you become aware of just how powerful you are).

Day 358

"Bravery is the capacity to perform properly even when scared half to death."

GENERAL OMAR BRADLEY[3]

Willpower combined with an unstoppable attitude will open doors uncommon to most men. I encourage you never to let life's challenges get you down for more than fifteen minutes. Sure, you have problems—everyone does—but it is how fast you can recover from these upsets that impacts how much success you will have.

Use your willpower to change your attitude. Why is this important; because thoughts have a vibration to them! When you vibrate lack, limitations, upsets, anger or any other harmful thoughts, at the least you create chaos and most likely you will stop your success.

The reverse is also true when you vibrate calmness, happiness and abundance you increase your success because you attract more of the same to you. The more you open up to receive and vibrate these states of consciousness consistently, the more you become a magnet for health, wealth, joy and abundance.

Today Ask

"What is the attitude I would most like to vibrate today?"

"How can I increase my resolve to stay in high states of consciousness all day?"

"If I have an upset, what can I immediately remember, to overcome the upset within fifteen minutes?"

Actions

Choose a high energetic attitude that you will hold the entire day; such as joy, bliss, abundance, prosperity, happiness, etc. Then measure your attitude four times during the day. If at any time your attitude has changed, just reset your thinking and vibrate a higher thought such as: "I am an infinite being who has the power to be calm while overcoming challenges." Note: (The power to hold the right attitude resides only with you alone and no outside circumstance or force can take you off course if you are determined to succeed).

Day 359

*"You get from this life what you have the
courage to ask for."*

OPRAH WINFREY[3]

Have you thought about what it means to live a great life? A life filled with contribution and service, where you have brought the magnificence of you into everything you do and have left a legacy for others to follow?

Greatness is a quality that springs forth from the soul. It requires truth and courage. I know of no one that was born great. The great saints, sages, kings, queens and great industrialists all had challenges which stepped them into greatness.

It is not your circumstances that define you; it is what you do with your circumstances that define you. No one on the planet is considered great unless they have gone through significant challenges which brought forth and forged their greatness.

Greatness is attainable for you. It can be developed over time by the daily thoughts you think and actions you take. Greatness is linked to the mind that is calm and can make wise choices.

To live a great life, therefore, you must be the master of your mind, because whenever your mind is agitated, you will not be making the highest or best choices. A disturbed mind never solves anything—anything! In fact, it prevents you from solving problems, because it disconnects you with your inner wisdom.

Today Ask

"What can I do today which will help me calm my mind and make wise choices?"

"What challenges am I facing that is forging greatness in me?"

"What great dream do I have which will bring forth my greatness into the world?"

Actions

Decide what it means to you to live a great life. Then, take two action steps toward it today.

Day 360

*"Real courage is when you know you're licked before you begin
but you begin anyway and see it through, no matter what."*

HARPER LEE[3]

Have you ever seen a dog try to catch three rabbits at one time? He ends up with no rabbits, frustrated and running from one rabbit to the next. It is the same tactic that many people use to sabotage themselves in business or life, never catching their dreams.

Here is how this destructive habit works. You start creating one goal and then the going gets tough, so you stop and start working on something else. You go from one dream to the next never really focusing on completing one. This cycle will never end, as long as you are unfocused.

One-pointed concentration is the key to changing this pattern permanently. Start with a small project and complete it no matter what. Then, try to accomplish something bigger and finish it.

To move out of this circle of defeat, commit to focusing on one dream and then set up daily action plans to consistently meet your goals. Also, the most significant way to increase concentration is through scientific meditation techniques. You can get my The Science of Meditation Guide for free at http://kendfoster.com/resources/

Today Ask

"What is one project I will complete before moving to another?"

"What 'incompletes' do I have to prioritize and focus on, one at a time?"

"How can I stay consistently completing one project at a time?"

Actions

Make a list of projects you are working on, then prioritize them and set completion dates for each one.

Day 361

*"In the world you will have trouble but take courage
for I have conquered the world."*

JESUS CHRIST[3]

Today is a day of celebration for many around the world. But what are we truly celebrating? At the core is Freedom. It is freedom from our past mistakes, freedom from past darkness of all kinds and the joy of knowing we can transcend our human limitations and conquer the world just as Jesus Christ did. We can be free once and for all in this lifetime. Isn't that good news!

Take some time and tune into just how deeply God loves you—unconditionally. I believe if God were sitting across from us right now, he would say something like: *"This is just a passing phase, you will get through it, so just do your best. You can do it! I am always there with you and you are always loved—unconditionally."*

As Paramahansa Yogananda said: *"A saint is a sinner who never gave up."* So, don't give up on yourself! And make the effort to free yourself from past wrong thinking and actions.

This may sound like a big subject, but you can do it! I would like to help you with this process and give you an exercise called: Release—Renew—Evolve. It will support you in letting go, forgiving, and releasing permanently any past mental or emotional baggage. To get the book: KenDFoster.com/our-products.

Remember we may be imperfect humans, but at or core we are perfect. We are not our bodies, minds, emotions, senses or egos. We are the Soul, ever filled with power and light to move the mountains of difficulties placed before us and be victorious in life.

Today Ask

"What is the spiritual effort I will commit to making today?"

"What has to happen for everything to improve in the future?"

"How can I remember daily that I am the invincible Soul?"

Actions

Come up with one action that will convince yourself that you are the infinite soul.

Day 362

*"Everyone has failures and setbacks. The courageous speak
not of past troubles but the blessings that are on the way."*

KEN D FOSTER

I have a saying that has helped my Coaching clients become aware of how to create success. It goes like this: *"Environment is stronger than will but faith coupled with resolve will conquer all."*

Let's face it; when you are in a negative environment surrounded by people who are fearful, complaining and worried about their future, it is difficult to stay upbeat and confident. But, when you surround yourself with positive people who are encouraging you to create your dreams and be the best you can be, it is much easier to stay upbeat.

This doesn't mean you cannot overcome environmental factors to succeed; it means you must tap into the essence of yourself—your actual power and nature—to realize your dreams. So, what do you value in life and what is your true nature? Make a list of these. It will help you become more aware of who you are and what you stand for.

Once you have done this, combine it with the power of faith to overcome stressful situations. You may ask: *"Faith in what?"* I say; faith in realizing that the infinite power that resides within you will increase your will power and guide you to overcome all challenges.

Today Ask

"What can I do to increase my faith?"

"What challenges do I have that increased faith and resolve will overcome?"

"Why is my life getting better every day in every way?"

Actions

Make some time to journal how magnificent you indeed are. Then resolve to apply what you learn to create success beyond measure.

Day 363

"Serenity comes from the ability to say "Yes" to existence. Courage comes from the ability to say "No" to the wrong choices made by others.

AYN RAND[3]

Most people are looking for answers outside of themselves. They are looking for the next thing that will make them money or make them happy in some way. The problem with this formula is that it is a never-ending treadmill of unending desires.

This path is filled with many poor choices and frustrations. As the great sage, Sri Yukteswar said: "Forget the past. Human conduct is ever unreliable until man is anchored in the Divine. Everything in the future will improve if you are making a spiritual effort now."

Success is not something to be found; it is something to be discovered within you. The inner game of business and life is where success starts. Take time for meditation and release the past. Live only in the moment and include introspection, contemplation and willful actions daily. This will increase your success.

Remember, there is no one blocking your success but yourself. You are free to discover how to generate ongoing success. But will you do the work? Success will not magically happen; you will have to become an explorer and find out what has stopped your progress in the past.

You will also have to find out the way for you to generate ongoing success with your greatest gifts, talents and abilities while serving the betterment of humankind.

Today Ask

"Why am I choosing to be unstoppable?"

"Which of my greatest talents will I use to serve in a greater way?"

"What am I committed to doing to increase my connection with the divine?"

Actions

Make a list of five reasons why you are unstoppable.

Day 364

*"The world is not perishing for the want of clever
or talented or well-meaning men. It is perishing for
the want of men of courage and resolution."*

ROBERT J. MCCRACKEN[3]

Magnificence is your birthright. But your birthright cannot come into fruition without the inner battle to overcome limited thinking. Most people are not born as virtuosos or masters of their lives. They must evolve their mind and personal power to bring forth their greatest talents.

Many try to become enlightened by reading books or attending workshops by unenlightened fakers. (This applies to business, relationships, career, spiritual and just about any other area of life.) But the wise seek Masters of their crafts. These are teachers who have not only immersed themselves in wisdom principles but applied them to their businesses and lives until they realized the principles of success.

It is important to find master teachers because otherwise you will one day wake up and find that you have been subject to "the blind leading the blind."

Today Ask

"What three steps will I can take today to find the right teacher for me?"

"What limiting beliefs can I release to have master teacher show up for me?"

"What beliefs must I embrace to evolve myself?"

Actions

Make a list of possible teachers who will empower you mentally, emotionally, physically and spiritually.

Tap into your higher-self and increase your intuition with Ken D Foster's guided meditations on Business, Wealth, Expanding Possibility, Peace, and Health. Yours for free at couragetochange.us/meditation

Day 365

"The most heroic conquerors within their spiritual life are those who have conquered their fears and have persevered until they were victorious over their weaker self."

PARAMAHANSA YOGANANDA[3]

You made it! This is the last day. I encourage you to celebrate your life and all your accomplishments. Think about the courage it took to do, be and accomplish what you did. It seems that amazing grace has touched your life in so many ways. Thank you for being you and blessing this world with your gifts, talents and service.

I hope you have realized that you are the dreamer in the dream of God. And your dreams are the gifts from the heart of creation to your soul. It is only you who can permit yourself to pursue them! It is only you who can release the past ways of being and embrace a brilliant future. It is only you who change what you need to change. It is only you who can say YES to living in an attitude of gratitude, abundance and happiness.

It is all an inside job. So, don't let yourself remain restless. Be still, meditate and realize that inside of you is a blueprint of brilliance. You and your Creator are one. There is no separation! Feel His Presence and pray from God to God.

Pray with deep concentration. Then raise your frequency by affirming several times: "I am one with my Creator." "I am filled with courage." I am filled with abundance." I am filled with power and light." Then, as you feel a sense peace or inspiration, ask; "Spirit, will you grant me health?" or "Will you fill me with courage?" or "Will you bring me prosperity?" Realize what you have asked for is coming to you and freeing you from all limitations.

Today Ask

"Who is behind my body, thoughts and senses, leading me to greatness?"

"Why is there nothing preventing me from having my dreams come true?"

"How much courage, joy and prosperity will I allow into my new year?"

Actions

Be still and know that the force that lights up this world is lighting you up. Take some time to reflect on the past year. Look at what worked, what didn't and where you can improve next year. Then, just relax and celebrate your amazing life.

Final Thoughts

On October 11, 2011, there was a memorial service for the most successful entrepreneur of our time, Steven Jobs, the founder of Apple Computer. Steven had planned every detail of his memorial service, including the giving of a brown box that each attendee received as a farewell gift.

Many in the audience who knew Steve and realized the gift was going to be something to remember. It was going to be the last thing that Steve Jobs wanted the world to think about. Inside the brown box was a surprise to many, it was a book, Autobiography of a Yogi by Paramahansa Yogananda. Many wondered why Steven Jobs would give this book out, after all, there are millions of books he could have chosen. I believe the last message Steven Jobs wanted to send to the world was; "find your own path to Self-Actualization." Because that is what the book is all about.

This is the same book, that I saw on a bookshelf in Anthony Robbins office in 1998. I was working for him at that time and was called into his office for a meeting. I had a few minutes prior to Tony arriving, so I browsed through his bookcase and noticed several books by Paramahansa Yogananda, which intrigued me. Shortly thereafter I purchased Autobiography of a Yogi and I can honestly say, "it changed my destiny", because it gave me what I had been searching for my entire life. It showed me how to find wisdom, peace, power and love on the way to Self-Realization.

If you have an interest in finding out where many of the principles to write this book came from and what Steven Jobs wanted you to know, then visit: Yogananda-SRF.org and also visit KenDFoster.com to find out more about my Programs and free Resources.

Thank you for taking the time to read the book. I hope you are well on your way to Self-Realizing your greatness and bringing forth your gifts, talents and abilities to make the world a better place for everyone.

Annotated Bibliography

1. Corra Mae Harris, was an American writer and journalist.

2. Clive Staples Lewis was a British novelist, poet, academic, medievalist, literary critic, essayist, lay theologian, broadcaster, lecturer and Christian apologist.

3. Jim Butcher is a *New York Times* bestselling author is best known for his contemporary fantasy book series The Dresden Files. He also wrote the Codex Alera series.

4. Robert Fanney was born on November 4, 1972, in Southeastern Virginia. He is the author of "Dreams of the Ringed Vale."

5. Joan L Curcio is a published author.

6. Mignon McLaughlin was an American journalist and author. In the 1950s, she began publishing aphorisms that were later collected in three books, entitled, The Neurotic's Notebook, The Second Neurotic's Notebook and The Complete Neurotic's Notebook.

7. John Lancaster Spalding was an American author, poet, advocate for higher education, the first bishop of the Roman Catholic Diocese of Peoria from 1877 to 1908 and a co-founder of The Catholic University of America.

8. John Fitzgerald "Jack" Kennedy, commonly referred to by his initials JFK, was an American politician who served as the 35th President of the United States from January 1961 until his assassination in November 1963.

9. Grace Lichtenstein is an author, book critic and former *New York Times* reporter.

10. Robert J. McCracken was a Scottish-born professor of systematic theology. He preached that racism was a sin and said of atheists, "we can learn from radical doubters ... It is the heretics who have forced the church to clear its mind, opened up to it new insights, spurred it on to deeper thinking about God and Christ and man ... Their concern is a challenge to our complacency

11. Maya Angelou was an American author, poet and civil rights activist. She published seven autobiographies, three books of essays and several books of poetry and was credited with a list of plays.

12. John Irving is an American novelist and screenwriter.Irving achieved critical and popular acclaim after the international success of The World According to Garp.

13. Edward Estlin Cummings, known as E. E. Cummings, with the abbreviated form of his name often written by others in lowercase letters as e e cummings, was an American poet, painter, essayist, author and playwright.

14. Herbert Kaufman (March 6, 1878—September 6, 1947) was an American writer and newspaperman

15. Delmore Schwartz was an American poet and short story writer.

16. Vincent van Gogh was a Dutch Post-Impressionist painter who is among the most famous and influential figures in the history of Western art.

17. Charles Augustus Lindbergh, nicknamed Slim, Lucky Lindy and The Lone Eagle, was an American aviator, author, inventor, military officer, explorer and social activist.

18. Marcus Tullius Cicero was a Roman philosopher, politician, lawyer orator, political theorist, consul and constitutionalist.

19. Aristotle was a Greek philosopher and scientist born in the Macedonian city of Stagira, Chalkidice, on the northern periphery of Classical Greece.

20. Confucius was a Chinese teacher, editor, politician and philosopher of the Spring and Autumn period of Chinese history.

21. Henri-Émile-Benoît Matisse was a French artist, known for both his use of color and his fluid and original draughtsmanship. He was a draughtsman, printmaker and sculptor.

22. Gail Blanke is an executive and life coach and bestselling author.

23. Athenaeus of Naucratis was a Greek rhetorician and grammarian, flourishing about the end of the 2nd and beginning of the 3rd century AD.

24. Robert Harold Schuller was an American televangelist, pastor, motivational speaker and author.

25. Aleksandr Isayevich Solzhenitsyn was a Russian novelist, historian and outspoken critic of the Soviet Union, especially its totalitarianism, who helped to raise global awareness of its gulag forced labor camp system.

26. Coventry Kersey Dighton Patmore was an English poet and critic best known for The Angel in the House, his narrative poem about an ideally happy marriage.

27. Ernest Miller Hemingway was an American novelist, short story writer and journalist. His economical and understated style had a strong influence on 20th-century fiction, while his life of adventure and his public image influenced later generations.

28. Paramahansa Yogananda (1893–1952) is considered one of the preeminent spiritual figures of modern times. Author of the best-selling spiritual classic Autobiography of a Yogi, this beloved world teacher came to America in 1920 from his native India and was the first grand master of yoga to live and teach in the West.

29. David Herbert Richards Lawrence was an English novelist, poet, playwright, essayist, literary critic and painter who published as D. H. Lawrence.

30. Albert Einstein was a German-born theoretical physicist. He developed the general theory of relativity, one of the two pillars of modern physics.

31. Don Juan is a legendary, fictional libertine.

32. Nora Roberts is an American bestselling author of more than 209 romance novels.

33. Nelson Rolihlahla Mandela was a South African anti-apartheid revolutionary, politician and philanthropist who served as President of South Africa.

34. William Salter was an American Congregational minister, public orator, social activist and historian.

35. Blaine Lee Pardoe is an award-winning, *New York Times* Bestselling author, known primarily for writing the Battletech and MechWarrior.

36. Louise Penny is a Canadian author of mystery novels set in the Canadian province of Quebec centered on the work of Chief Inspector Armand Gamache of the Sûreté du Québec.

37. Nelle Harper Lee is a novelist widely known for her novel To Kill a Mockingbird, published in 1960.

38. Carrie Jones is an American author, known for her work in young-adult fiction. She has written both fantasy and non-fantasy novels, including the paranormal series

39. Marian Anderson was an American contralto and one of the most celebrated singers of the twentieth century. Music critic Alan Blyth said: "Her voice was a rich, vibrant contralto of intrinsic beauty."

40. Francis Ford Coppola is an American film director, producer and screenwriter. He was part of the New Hollywood wave of filmmaking.

41. Erica Jong is an American author and teacher best known for her fiction and poetry and particularly for her 1973 novel Fear of Flying.

42. Justin Cronin is an American author. He has written four novels: Mary and O'Neil and The Summer Guest, as well as two of three books of a vampire trilogy: The Passage and The Twelve.

43. Nelson Rolihlahla Mandela was a South African anti-apartheid revolutionary, politician and philanthropist who served as President of South Africa.

44. Bettina R. Flores Arthur of Chiquita's Cocoon: The Latina Woman's Guide to Greater Power, Love, Money, Status and Happiness.

45. Steven Jobs was an American entrepreneur, business magnate, inventor and industrial designer.

46. Thucydides was a Greek historian who was born in Alimos between the years 460 and 455 B.C and died between 411 and 400 B.C. He is known for his book The History of the Peloponnesian War which details the war between Sparta and Athens in the 5th Century.

47. Alexander George "Alex" Karras, nicknamed "The Mad Duck", was an American football player, professional wrestler and actor. He played football with the Detroit Lions in the National Football League.

48. Wai Lan Yuen is the author of The Legend of Sir Francis Windermere.

49. Paulo Coelho is a Brazilian lyricist and novelist. He is the recipient of numerous international awards, amongst them the Crystal Award by the World Economic Forum. The Alchemist, his most famous novel.

50. Albert Camus was a French Nobel Prize–winning author, journalist and philosopher. His views contributed to the rise of the philosophy known as absurdism.

51. Walt Disney was an American entrepreneur, animator, voice actor and film producer. A pioneer of the American animation industry, he introduced several developments in the production of cartoons.

52. Martin Luther King, Jr. was an American Baptist minister, activist, humanitarian and leader in the African-American Civil Rights Movement.

53. Patrick Henry was an American attorney, planter and politician who became known as an orator during the movement for independence in Virginia in the 1770s.

54. Maxwell Maltz was an American cosmetic surgeon and author of Psycho-Cybernetics, which was a system of ideas that he claimed could improve one's self-image. In turn, the person would lead a more successful and fulfilling life.

55. Charles Rozell "Chuck" Swindoll is an evangelical Christian pastor, author, educator and radio preacher.

56. Baltasar Gracián y Morales, SJ, formerly Anglicized as Baltazar Gracian, was a Spanish Jesuit and baroque prose writer and philosopher. He was born in Belmonte, near Calatayud. His writings were lauded by Nietzsche and Schopenhauer.

57. Robert Harold Schuller was an American televangelist, pastor, motivational speaker and author.

58. Samuel Langhorne Clemens, better known by his pen name Mark Twain, was an American author and humorist.

59. Vincent Gallagher has spent over 30 years researching and reporting on dangerous work environments. He is an author and consultant to the World Bank, USAID and the UN as well as corporations and labor unions; he currently directs the Romero Centre at St Joseph Pro-Cathedral Parish in New Jersey.

60. Victor Marie Hugo was a French poet, novelist and dramatist of the Romantic Movement. He is considered one of the greatest and best-known French writers.

61. Maxwell Maltz was an American cosmetic surgeon and author of Psycho-Cybernetics, which was a system of ideas that he claimed could improve one's self-image. In turn, the person would lead a more prosperous and fulfilling life.

62. Dejan Stojanović is a Serbian poet, writer, essayist, philosopher, businessman and former journalist.

63. John Wayne who was born Marion Mitchell Morrison and nicknamed Duke, was an American actor and filmmaker. An Academy Award-winner for True Grit (1969), Wayne was among the top box office draws for three decades.

64. John Quincy Adams was an American statesman who served as the sixth President of the United States from 1825 to 1829.

65. James Allen was a British philosophical writer known for his inspirational books and poetry and as a pioneer of the self-help movement. His best-known work, As a Man Thinketh.

66. Barbara Barksdale Clowse holds a Ph.D. in History from the UNC, Chapel Hill and is an author.

67. Muhammad Ali is an American former professional boxer, generally considered among the greatest heavyweights in the history of the sport

68. James Neil Hollingworth was a beatnik, hippie, writer and former manager of the psychedelic folk rock bands Quicksilver Messenger Service and Ace of Cups. He wrote under the pseudonym Ambrose Hollingworth Redmoon.

69. Ayn Rand was a Russian-born American novelist, philosopher, playwright and screenwriter. She is known for her two best-selling novels, The Fountainhead and Atlas Shrugged and for developing a philosophical system she called Objectivism.

70. Chris Bradford is an author, professional musician and black belt martial artist, best known for his children's fictional series, Young Samurai. The first Young Samurai book, The Way of the Warrior.

71. Maxwell Maltz was an American cosmetic surgeon and author of Psycho-Cybernetics (1960), which was a system of ideas that he claimed could improve one's self-image.

72. Mary Tyler Moore was an American actress, known for her roles in the television sitcoms.

73. Friedrich Nietzsche Friedrich Nietzsche was a German philosopher, poet, Latin and Greek scholar whose work has had a profound effecy on Western philosophy and history.

74. Shannon L. Alder is the author of 300 Questions LDS Couples Should Ask Before Marriage.

75. Michael McKee is a radio host and the economics editor for Bloomberg Television, covering market and political developments, economic trends and central banks in the United States and around the globe.

76. Robert Louis Balfour Stevenson was a Scottish novelist, poet, essayist and travel writer. His most famous works are Treasure Island, Kidnapped and Strange Case of Dr. Jekyll and Mr. Hyde.

77. Richard Russell "Rick" Riordan, Jr. is an American author known for writing the Percy Jackson & the Olympians series, which is about a twelve-year-old who discovers he is the son of Poseidon.

78. Laozi was a philosopher and poet of ancient China. He is known as the reputed author of the Tao Te Ching and the founder of philosophical Taoism and as a deity in religious Taoism and traditional Chinese religion.

79. Honoré de Balzac was a French novelist and playwright.

80. Jarod Kintz is an American author.

81. Paula Giddings is a writer and an African-American historian. She is the author of When and Where I Enter: The Impact of Black Women on Race and Sex in America and In Search of Sisterhood.

82. Dorothy Bernard was an actress of the silent era. She appeared in 87 films between 1908 and 1956.

83. Keshavan Nair was born in Patalia, India. He was a corporate executive and author.

84. Robert Lee Frost was an American poet. His work was initially published in England before it was published in America. He is highly regarded for his realistic depictions of rural life and his command of American colloquial speech.

85. Michael Josephson is a former law professor and attorney who founded the nonprofit Joseph and Edna Josephson Institute of Ethics located in Los Angeles, California.

86. Adam Gidwitz is the author of the bestselling children's books A Tale Dark and Grimm, In a Glass Grimmly and The Grimm Conclusion.

87. Napoleon Bonaparte was a French statesman and military leader who rose to prominence during the French Revolution and led several successful campaigns during the French Revolutionary Wars.

88. Neal Ash Maxwell was an apostle and a member of the Quorum of the Twelve Apostles of The Church of Jesus Christ of Latter-day Saints from 1981 until his death.

89. August Wilson was an American playwright whose work included a series of ten plays, The Pittsburgh Cycle, for which he received two Pulitzer Prizes for Drama.

90. Clive Staples Lewis was a British novelist, poet, academic, medievalist, literary critic, essayist, lay theologian, broadcaster, lecturer and Christian apologist.

91. George Smith Patton, Jr. was a United States Army general, who commanded the Seventh U.S. Army in the Mediterranean and European Theaters of World War II.

92. Catherine Anderson, is an American best-selling writer of historical and contemporary romance novels since 1988.

93. R.J. Palacio is a #1 *New York Times* bestselling author of children's literature.

94. Freeman John Dyson FRS is an English-born American theoretical physicist and mathematician, known for his work in quantum electrodynamics, solid-state physics, astronomy and nuclear engineering.

95. Anne Spencer Lindbergh was an American author, aviator and the wife of aviator Charles Lindbergh. She was an acclaimed author whose books and articles spanned the genres of poetry to non-fiction.

96. Dr. Amit Ray is an Indian author and spiritual master. He is best known for his Om meditation and vipassana meditation techniques. He is an author of several books on meditation and other spiritual topics.

97. John F. Kennedy commonly referred to by his initials JFK, was an American statesman who served as the 35th President of the United States from January 1961 until his assassination on November 1963.

98. Edward Estlin Cummings, known as E. E. Cummings, with the abbreviated form of his name often written by others in lowercase letters as e e cummings, was an American poet, painter, essayist, author and playwright.

99. Sir Winston Leonard Spencer-Churchill, KG, OM, CH, TD, DL, FRS, RA was a British statesman who was the Prime Minister of the United Kingdom from 1940 to 1945 and again from 1951 to 1955.

100. John Fitzgerald "Jack" Kennedy, commonly referred to by his initials JFK, was an American politician who served as the 35th President of the United States from January 1961 until his assassination in November 1963.

101. Albert Einstein was a German-born theoretical physicist. He developed the general theory of relativity, one of the two pillars of modern physics. Einstein's work is also known for its influence on the philosophy of science.

102. André Paul Guillaume Gide was a French author and winner of the Nobel Prize in Literature in 1947 "for his comprehensive and artistically significant writings".

103. Paulo Coelho, is a Brazilian lyricist and novelist. He is the recipient of numerous international awards, amongst them the Crystal Award by the World Economic Forum. The Alchemist, his most famous novel.

104. Ruth Gordon was an American film, stage and television actress, as well as a screenwriter and playwright.

105. Winston Churchill

106. Christopher James Paolini is an American author. He is best known as the author of the Inheritance Cycle, which consists of the books Eragon, Eldest, Brisingr and Inheritance.

107. Alice M. Swaim is an American political scientist, former professor of political science and law at Vanderbilt University and former television host.

108. Martin Luther King, Jr. was an American Baptist minister, activist, humanitarian and leader in the African-American Civil Rights Movement.

109. Sarah E. Anderson is the associate online editor of First Looks.

110. John Elliot Bradshaw is an American educator, counselor, motivational speaker and author who has hosted some PBS television programs on topics such as addiction, recovery, codependency and spirituality.

111. Ernest Miller Hemingway was an American novelist, short story writer and journalist.

112. Gail Blanke is a motivational speaker, renowned executive and life coach and bestselling author.

113. Aristotle was a Greek philosopher and scientist.

114. Dr. Steve Maraboli is a life-changing Speaker, Bestselling Author and Behavioral Science Academic.

115. Cornell West is a prominent Professor of Philosophy and Christian Practice at Union Theological Seminary and Professor Emeritus at Princton University. He has also taught at Yale, Harvard and the University of Paris.

116. John Ronald Reuel Tolkien CBE FRSL was an English writer, poet, philologist and university professor who is best known as the author of the classic high-fantasy works The Hobbit, The Lord of the Rings and The Silmarillion.

117. Dave Weinbaum author.

118. Annie Besant was a prominent British socialist, theosophist, women's rights activist, writer and orator and supporter of Irish and Indian self-rule.

119. Gail Brook Burket, 91, an Evanston poet, was an author of six books of poems and a volume on how to write poetry.

120. Catherine Britton is an actress known for the movie Bookies 2003)

121. Diane Conway is a popular speaker, author and occasional comedian.

122. Karen Cushman is an American writer of historical fiction.

123. Mary Anne Radmacher author, artist, apronary, trainer, shares original writings.

124. Sharon Rainey is president and founder of myNeighborsNetwork, an online community network in the Washington DC Metro area. She also created a local non-profit foundation Neighbors Foundation.

125. Henri-Émile-Benoît Matisse was a French artist, known for both his use of color and his fluid and original draughtsmanship. He was a draughtsman, printmaker and sculptor but is known primarily as a painter.

126. Joan L. Curcio author.

127. David Michael Letterman is an American former television host, comedian, writer, producer and actor.

128. Laozi was a philosopher and poet of ancient China. He is known as the reputed author of the Tao Te Ching and the founder of philosophical Taoism and as a deity in religious Taoism and traditional Chinese religions.

129. Howard D. Schultz is an American businessman. He is best known as the chairman and CEO of Starbucks and a former owner of the Seattle SuperSonics. He was a member of the Board of Directors at Square, Inc.

130. Paramahansa Yogananda was an Indian yogi and guru who introduced millions of westerners to the teachings of meditation and Kriya Yoga through his book.

131. August Wilson was an American playwright whose work included a series of ten plays, The Pittsburgh Cycle, for which he received two Pulitzer Prizes for Drama.

132. Dale Turner is an American trumpet player, best known for being a member of the American new wave band Oingo Boingo. Turner was born in Minnesota.

133. Napoléon Bonaparte was a French military and political leader who rose to prominence during the French Revolution and led several successful campaigns during the Revolutionary Wars.

134. Laozi was a philosopher and poet of ancient China. He is known as the reputed author of the Tao Te Ching and the founder of philosophical Taoism and as a deity in religious Taoism and traditional Chinese religion.

135. Lisa Tawn Bergren is the best-selling, award-winning author of over 40 books, with more than 2.5 million copies sold.

136. Winston Churchill was a British statesman, army officer and writer. He served as Prime Minister of the United Kingdom from 1940 to 1945 and again 1951 to 1955.

137. Toni Sorenson is the author of several bestselling books for both the national and LDS markets. In 2006, her Covenant novel, Redemption Road, won the prestigious Association of Mormon Letters honor for novel of the year.

138. Maya Angelou was an American author, poet, dancer, actress and singer. She published seven autobiographies, three books of essays and several books of poetry and was credited with a list of plays.

139. Pablo Casals, was a Spanish cellist and conductor from Catalonia.

140. Reverend Christian Sorensen is an acclaimed author and the spiritual leader of Seaside Center for Spiritual Living in San Diego, CA.

141. Madeleine L'Engle was an American writer best known for young-adult fiction, particularly the Newbery Medal-winning A Wrinkle in Time and its sequels: A Wind in the Door.

142. Mark Twain was born Samuel Langhorne Clemens was an American writer, humorist, entrepreneur, publisher and lecturer.

143. John Patrick Shanley is a Pulitzer Prize and Tony Award-winning American playwright, an Oscar-winning screenwriter and a theatre and film director.

144. Marianne Deborah Williamson is an American spiritual teacher, author and lecturer. She has published ten books, including four New York Times number one bestsellers.

145. Plato was a philosopher in Classical Greece and the founder of the Academy in Athens, the first institution of higher learning in the Western world.

146. Erma Louise Bombeck was an American humorist who achieved great popularity for her newspaper column that described suburban home life from the mid-1960s until the late 1990s. Bombeck also published 15 books, most of which became bestsellers.

147. Dr. Roopleen is a motivational counselor, speaker and author of the books 'Principles of Success made easy- 14 easy steps to climb the ladder of Success' and 'Words To Inspire The Winner In YOU.'

148. Thucydides was an Athenian historian, political philosopher and general. His History of the Peloponnesian War recounts the 5th century BC war between Sparta and Athens to the year 411 BC.

149. Mother Teresa was the founder of the Order of the Missionaries of Charity, a Roman Catholic congregation of women dedicated to helping the poor.

150. Albert Einstein was a German-born theoretical physicist. He developed the general theory of relativity, one of the two pillars of modern physics.

151. John Lancaster Spalding was an American author, poet, advocate for higher education, the first bishop of the Roman Catholic Diocese of Peoria from 1877 to 1908 and a co-founder of The Catholic University of America.

152. Ralph Waldo Emerson was an American essayist, lecturer and poet who led the Transcendentalist movement of the mid-19th century.

153. George Horace Lorimer was an American journalist and author. He is best known as the editor of The Saturday Evening Post.

154. Corra Mae Harris, was an American writer and journalist.

155. Ogwo David Emenike is an author, sage, motivator, poet, positive change facilitator, life coach, inspirational writer and speaker and visionary leader.

156. Dorothy Thompson was an American journalist and radio broadcaster, who in 1939 was recognized by Time magazine as the second most influential woman in America next to Eleanor Roosevelt.

157. Vanessa Chantal Paradis is a French singer, model and actress. She became a child star at 14 with the worldwide success of her single "Joe le taxi." Since 1991, Paradis has been a spokesmodel for Chanel.

158. White Eagle was born a PohTikaWah which essentially means A Spirit Walker or one that can easily walk through the veil as it is called between the physical and Spiritual realms.

159. Dr. Curio was the first female professor in Educational Administration at Virginia Tech and a leader in mentoring and enhancing the professionalism of women in education. Joan was also a co-founder and editor of the Journal for a Just and Caring Education.

160. Chris Widener is an American author and motivational speaker. Widener has written several books on motivation and business. Widener first entered the public speaking industry in 1988.

161. Aristotle was an ancient Greek philosopher, logician and scientist (482-322 BCE) student of Plato and teacher of Alexander the Great.

162. Tim Ferris is an American author, entrepreneur, self-proclaimed "human guinea pig" and public speaker

163. Thích Nh t H nh is a Vietnamese Buddhist monk, teacher, author, poet and peace activist. He lives in Plum Village in the Dordogne region of France, traveling internationally to give retreats and talks.

164. James Freeman Clarke was an American theologian and author.

165. William Shakespeare was an English poet, playwright and actor. He was widely regarded as the greatest English writer and the world's pre-eminent dramatist.

166. Andy Andrews is an American author known for his 2002 bestselling book The Travelers's Guide. He has written over 20 books and sold more than 3.5 million copies around the world.

167. John Irving John Irving is an American novelist and Academy Award winner as a screenwriter.

168. Michael de Montaigne was one of the most significant philosophers of the French Renaissance. His work called Essais contains some of the most influential essays ever written.

169. Adam L. Gordon an Australian poet and politician.

170. Nelson Mandela was a South African anti-apartheid revolutionary, political leader and philanthropist who served as President of South Africa.

171. Lois Lenski was a popular and prolific writer of children's and young adult fiction.

172. Sir Winston Leonard Spencer-Churchill was a British statesman who was the Prime Minister of the United Kingdom from 1940 to 1945 and again from 1951 to 1955.

173. Richelle E. Goodrich is an author.

174. General Omar Bradley was a highly distinguished U.S. Army Officer who saw service in North Africa and Western Europe during World War 2. He later became General of the Army.

175. Oprah Winfrey is an American talk show host, actress and producer. She has given millions to various charities. She is best known for her show, The Oprah Winfrey Show.

176. Harper Lee is an American novelist widely known for bestselling book To Kill a Mockingbird, published in 1960. The book was Immediately successful and won her a Pulitzer Prize in 1961.

177. Jesus Christ Jesus Christ is a religious leader who became the central figure of Christianity. He is considered by Christians to be the Son of God and Messiah.

178. Ayn Rand was an author, philosopher, playwright and screenwriter. She is known for her two best-selling books, The Fountainhead and Atlas Shrugged. She is also the inspiration behind the philosophical system she called Objectivism.

179. Robert J. McCracken was a Scottish-born professor of systematic theology. He preached that racism was a sin and said of atheists, "we can learn from radical doubters ... It is the heretics who have forced the church to clear its mind, opened up to it new insights, spurred it on to deeper thinking about God and Christ and man ... Their concern is a challenge to our complacency

180. Paramahansa Yogananda is an Indian yogi and satguru. He has introduced millions to the teachings of Kriya yoga meditation and self-realization. His book Autobiography of a Yogi changed this authors life.